ROUTLEDGE LIBRARY EDITIONS: ALCOHOL AND ALCOHOLISM

Volume 11

ECONOMICS AND ALCOHOL

ECONOMICS AND ALCOHOL

Consumption and Controls

Edited by
MARCUS GRANT,
MARTIN PLANT
AND
ALAN WILLIAMS

LONDON AND NEW YORK

First published in 1983 by Croom Helm Ltd
This edition first published in 2024
by Routledge
4 Park Square, Milton Park, Abingdon, Oxon OX14 4RN

and by Routledge
605 Third Avenue, New York, NY 10158

Routledge is an imprint of the Taylor & Francis Group, an informa business

© 1983 Marcus Grant, Martin Plant and Alan Williams

All rights reserved. No part of this book may be reprinted or reproduced or utilised in any form or by any electronic, mechanical, or other means, now known or hereafter invented, including photocopying and recording, or in any information storage or retrieval system, without permission in writing from the publishers.

Trademark notice: Product or corporate names may be trademarks or registered trademarks, and are used only for identification and explanation without intent to infringe.

British Library Cataloguing in Publication Data
A catalogue record for this book is available from the British Library

ISBN: 978-1-032-59082-0 (Set)
ISBN: 978-1-032-60574-6 (Volume 11) (hbk)
ISBN: 978-1-032-60583-8 (Volume 11) (pbk)
ISBN: 978-1-003-45974-3 (Volume 11) (ebk)

DOI: 10.4324/9781003459743

Publisher's Note
The publisher has gone to great lengths to ensure the quality of this reprint but points out that some imperfections in the original copies may be apparent.

Disclaimer
The publisher has made every effort to trace copyright holders and would welcome correspondence from those they have been unable to trace.

Economics and Alcohol
CONSUMPTION AND CONTROLS

Edited by
Marcus Grant, Martin Plant
and Alan Williams

CROOM HELM
London & Canberra

GARDNER PRESS, INC.
New York

©1983 Marcus Grant, Martin Plant and Alan Williams
Croom Helm Ltd, Provident House, Burrell Row,
Beckenham, Kent BR3 1AT

British Library Cataloguing in Publication Data

Economics and alcohol.
    1. Drinking customs   2. Alcoholic beverages
    I. Grant, Marcus   II. Plant, Martin A.
    III. Williams, Alan
    306'.48   GT2884
    ISBN 0-7099-1132-7

ISBN 0-89876-089-5 (Gardner Press)

GARDNER PRESS, INC.
19 Union Square West
New York 10003

Typeset by Leaper & Gard Ltd, Bristol
Printed and bound in Great Britain

CONTENTS

List of Tables
List of Figures
Acknowledgements
Introduction *Marcus Grant, Martin A. Plant and Alan Williams*   9

1. What can Economists Contribute? *Robert E. Leu*   13
2. Alcohol Studies from an Economic Perspective *Robert Weeden*   34
3. Programmes, Interests and Alcohol *Dean R. Gerstein*   43
4. Societal Costs of Alcohol Abuse in the United States: An Updating *Leonard G. Schifrin*   62
5. Calculating the Costs of Alcohol: The Scandinavian Experience *Esa Österberg*   82
6. The Costs and Benefits of Alcohol in Ontario: A Critical Review of the Evidence *Eric W. Single*   97
7. Alcoholism: An Econometric Model of its Causes, its Effects and its Control *Stuart O. Schweitzer, Michael D. Intriligator and Hossein Salehi*   107
8. Modelling Alcohol Consumption and Abuse: The Powers and Pitfalls of Economic Techniques *Alan Maynard*   128
9. The Relationship Between Taxation, Price and Alcohol Consumption in the Countries of Europe *Phil Davies*   140
10. An Evaluation of the Control of Consumption Policy *David J. Pittman*   159
11. The Economics of Alcohol Taxation *Brendan M. Walsh*   173
12. Alcohol Taxes as a Public Health Measure *Philip J. Cook*   190
13. Government Policies Concerning Alcohol Taxation: Beyond the Excise Tax Debate *James F. Mosher*   197
14. Advertising Exposure, Alcohol Consumption and Misuse of Alcohol *Donald E. Strickland*   201
15. Advertising, Alcohol Consumption and Policy Alternatives *M.J. van Iwaarden*   223
16. The Demand for Beer, Spirits and Wine in the UK, 1956-79 *Tony McGuinness*   238
17. Alcohol Advertising Reassessed: The Public Health Perspective *Larry Wallack*   243
18. The Structure and Role of the British Alcoholic Drinks Industry *C.W. Thurman*   249

19. Paternalism, Rationality and the Special Status of Alcohol *Robin Room*	262
20. Alcohol and Health Economics: The Policy Perspective *David Taylor*	267
References	277
Notes on Contributors	293
Name Index	295
Subject Index	300

TABLES

2.1	Range of Values for Price and Income Elasticities	36
3.1	Estimated Deaths Related to Alcohol in the United States, 1975	55
3.2	Percentage of Excess Deaths in a Clinical Alcoholic Population in Canada	56
3.3	Economic Costs of Alcohol Misuse and Alcoholism in the United States, 1975	58
3.4	Rates of Problem Drinking Among US Drinkers, by Drinking Population, 1973-5	60
4.1	Health Research Dollars in Relation to Economic Cost	63
4.2	Estimated Excess Deaths for Males and Females Due to Alcohol Abuse, 1975	70
4.3	Estimated Net Percentage of Crashes Attributable to Alcohol Abuse, By Type of Crash	74
4.4	Tentative Estimates of the Economic Cost of Fire in 1975 That Might Be Attributable to Alcohol Abuse	75
4.5	Societal Costs Related to Alcohol Abuse, 1975, Berry and Revised Estimates ($ millions)	78
4.6	Estimated Societal Costs Related to Alcohol Abuse, 1979 ($ millions)	79
5.1	Finnish State Alcohol Costs by Administrative Sectors in 1975 as seen by Johannes Virolainen, million Marks	92
5.2	Public Economy Costs arising from Alcohol Problems in Finland in 1975 as seen by Klaus Halla, million Marks	92
5.3	Cost of Damage Caused by the Use of Alcohol in 1978 as seen by Veikko Kasurinen, million Marks	93
7.1	Price and Income Elasticities of Demand for Alcoholic Beverages	110
7.2	Estimates of Cross-price Elasticities	112
7.3	Statistics Relating to Variables of the Model	114
7.4	Estimation of the Reduced Form	117
7.5	Estimates of the Structural Form	118
7.6	Simulations of Policy Initiatives Affecting States Differently	122
7.7	Simulations of Policy Initiatives Affecting States Uniformly	124
9.1	Special Taxes on Alcoholic Beverages in Canadian Dollars, per litre of 100% Alcohol, 1977	143

9.2	Percentage Change in Taxation on Alcoholic Beverages in the Countries of the EEC 1972-7	144
9.3	Price of Spirits and Taxes Levied on Spirits in the Countries of the EEC, 1973	144
9.4	Percentage of Taxation in the Price of Beer, the Countries of the EEC, 1973	145
9.5	Alcohol Consumption per Person Aged 15 Years and above, and Deaths from Liver Cirrhosis, the Countries of the EEC, 1976	146
9.6	Per Capita Consumption of Pure Alcohol in Litres per Person Aged 15 Years and over in the Countries of the EEC	147
11.1	Reported Expenditure on Alcoholic Beverages as Percentage of Total Household Expenditure (Urban Areas), 1977	183
11.2	Share of Taxes in Retail Prices of Beer and Spirits in Ireland (%)	185
12.1	Effect of State Liquor Tax Increases, 1960-74, on Cirrhosis Mortality Rates	194
14.1	Means, Standard Deviations, and Correlations: Focal Variables, Control Variables and Alternate Social Learning Variables (Drinkers Only) (N = 772)	210
14.2	Effects of Advertising Exposure on Alcohol Use/Abuse: Total Effect and Decomposition of Direct and Indirect Causal Effects	214
14.3	Effects of Differential Peer Association on Alcohol Use/Abuse: Total Effect and Decomposition of Direct and Indirect Causal Effects	217
14.4	Comparison of Advertising Exposure and Differential Peer Association on Alcohol Use/Abuse: Total Effects and Decomposition of Direct and Indirect Causal Effects	219
15.1	Alcohol Consumption (per Drinker) and Advertising Expenditures on Alcoholic Beverages in the Netherlands (1968-80)	230
16.1	OLS Estimates of the Volume of Alcohol Consumed per Adult, 1956-79 Variables Measured in First-Difference Form	240
16.2	Estimated % Change in Volume following a 1% Increase in the Real Prices of all Types of Alcohol (% based on 1979 levels)	241
18.1	Beer, Wines and Spirits: Background Data, 1979	250
18.2	Usage of Glass Bottles (Millions of Bottles)	254

18.3 Employment Statistics, GB (000) 255
18.4 Location of Breweries Analysed by Size of Town, 1980 256
18.5 Importance of Brewers as Employers 257
18.6 Imports and Exports of Alcoholic Drinks, 1980, £ million 258
18.7 Revenue from Alcoholic Drink in the Fiscal Year 1980, £ million 259

FIGURES

1.1	The Basic Cost Estimation Model	19
1.2	Cost Concepts	22
9.1	The Relationship Between the Price of Alcoholic Beverages and Alcohol Consumption in the Netherlands and in West Germany	148
9.2	The Relationship Between the Price of Alcoholic Beverages and Alcohol Consumption in the United Kingdom and in Denmark	149
9.3	The Relationship Between the Price of Alcoholic Beverages and Alcohol Consumption in Belgium and in Italy	150
9.4	The Relationship Between the Price of Alcoholic Beverages and Alcohol Consumption in Ireland and in France	152
9.5	Trends in Per Capita Alcohol Consumption and the Real Price of Alcoholic Beverages in the Republic of Ireland, 1970-9	154
9.6	Trends in Per Capita Alcohol Consumption and the Price of Alcoholic Beverages in the United Kingdom, 1970-79	155
10.1	The 'Ledermann Curve'	162

ACKNOWLEDGEMENTS

Thanks are due to the Scotch Whisky Association (SWA) for financing the 1981 Wyvenhoe Conference upon which this book is based. In particular, the editors acknowledge the encouragement and help provided by Mr Richard F.W. Grindal of the SWA in arranging and facilitating that enjoyable and fruitful meeting.
The final form of the book owes much to the comments and advice of the participants of the Wyvenhoe meeting. These were:

Mr E. Bennett, Employment and Social Affairs, Commission of the European Communities, Luxembourg
Mr J. Cavanagh, World Health Organisation, Geneva
Dr C. Davis, Centrally Planned Economics Service, Wharton EFA, London
Mr J. Duffy, MRC Unit for Epidemiological Studies in Psychiatry, University Department of Psychiatry, Edinburgh
Dr N. Giesbrecht, Social Policy Research Department, Addiction Research Foundation, Toronto
Mr J. Henderson, Health Economics Research Unit, University of Aberdeen
Dr N. Kreitman, MRC Unit for Epidemiological Studies in Psychiatry, University Department of Psychiatry, Edinburgh
Dr P. Mosse, LEST/CNRS, Laboratorie D'Economie et de Sociologie du Travail, Cedex, France
Mr K. Pedersen, Institute of Social Sciences, Odense University, Denmark
Mr C. Ralph, Department of Health and Social Security, London
Dr D. Robinson, Institute for Health Studies, University of Hull, North Humberside
Ms G. Stevenson, Scotch Whisky Association, London
Mr P.M. Tiesema, Koninklikje Algemena Vereniging, Volksbond Tegen Drankmisbruik, S-Gravenhage, Holland
Dr L.H. Towle, Department of Health and Human Services, National Institute of Alcohol Abuse and Alcoholism, Maryland, USA
Ms J. Townsend, Epidemiology and Medical Care Unit, Northwick Park Hospital, Middlesex
Mr M.J. Waterson, The Advertising Association, London

Acknowledgements

Dr R. Wawman, Department of Health and Social Security, London
Dr B. Wickstrom, Department of Business Administration, University of Goteborg, Sweden
Mr G. Winstanley, The Brewers' Society, London
Mr G.B. Wright, Research and Education Department, Association of Canadian Distillers, Ontario

The typing and much other work was carried out speedily and efficiently by Mrs Elma Macdonald of the Alcohol Research Group, University of Edinburgh.

INTRODUCTION

Marcus Grant, Martin A. Plant and Alan Williams

The tendency to seek insights from other areas of science and scholarship is a mark of both the strength and the weakness of alcohol studies. The strength lies in the recognition that alcohol studies represent, at best, an ill-assorted kind of academic specialism in which contributions from quite disparate disciplines are equally likely to have relevance. Such eclecticism has led in the past to many brave links being forged. Its weakness lies most obviously in the rather embarrassing eagerness which those involved in alcohol studies display when confronted by interest from previously unexpected areas of scholarship. During the late 1970s and early 1980s, increasing attention has been paid to the possibility that economics might provide useful insights into the nature of alcohol problems. This connection has become the subject of an acrimonious and frequently uninformed debate. Economists, cautious in the face of unreasonable optimism, have now begun to respond. This book, and the meeting on which it is based, provides the first serious attempt in recent years to open what may, indeed, prove to be a rich vein of understanding.

It is hoped, therefore, that the contents of this book will provide information about the relationship between the discipline of economics and the use and misuse of beverage alcohol. The primary purpose of this book is to assemble a selection of contributions, each of which explores the nature and strength of the inter-relationship between economics and alcohol use and abuse. Some of these contributions deal with general conceptual and theoretical issues, while others present empirical information which, ultimately, must be the testbed of any reasoned analysis. Neither the editors nor the contributors, individually or as a whole, attempt to come to an overall conclusion. On the contrary, the material presented, although wide-ranging, is by no means either exhaustive or definitive. Many different perspectives are presented and several areas of disagreement are highlighted.

It is worth noting here the origins of the meeting on which this volume is based. It took the form of a small international gathering in November 1981 at the University of Essex and was remarkable for the extent to which its structure really did facilitate an interchange of ideas and experience between economists and those involved in alcohol studies. Three of the principal architects of that meeting have edited this book. The fourth, the Scotch Whisky Association (and in particular Richard Grindal, whose personal contribution through the planning stages proved invaluable) provided the funding without which it would have been impossible to bring together so much excellence from so many countries. All the chapters in this book are based upon papers presented at that meeting. They have, however, all been revised, some very substantially, in the light of the discussions which took place in Essex. Not every contribution to that meeting has been included and this is, perhaps, an appropriate place to record again our thanks to those other participants who, though not represented as authors of particular chapters in this book, did nevertheless have a very substantial impact upon the way the meeting developed and the way this book has been written.

During the past 30 years, general levels of alcohol consumption have risen considerably, not only in Western and industrialised countries, but also in the Third World. In association with the upsurge in alcohol use there has been a proliferation of 'alcohol-related' problems. These include liver cirrhosis deaths, alcohol dependence (addiction), drunkenness offences, accidents and a constellation of other forms of damage, such as marital disharmony and employment difficulties. The increasing popularity, and diversity in form, of beverage alcohol, together with the increase in its misuse, have led to heightened efforts to seek explanations for, and solutions to, excessive or harmful drinking.

Alcohol misuse clearly is only one aspect, even if extensive and tragic, of alcohol consumption. Most drinking is moderate, harmless and much benefit is derived from it. Even so, a major dilemma exists since there is abundant evidence that the general extent of harm somehow associated with or attributed to alcohol appears to ebb and flow hand in hand with the overall level of alcohol use. Countries such as France, Spain and Italy, whose per capita alcohol consumption is particularly high, have correspondingly high rates of liver cirrhosis mortality and other forms of alcohol-related problems. Conversely, countries such as Norway, Sweden and Israel, where alcohol consumption is much lower, also have lower rates of liver cirrhosis and associated problems. Considerable differences exist in relation to the patterns of harm stemming from varying local or national styles of drinking. It is not suggested that any given level of per capita alcohol consumption inevitably involves a precise level of problems. On the contrary, some social groups appear far more likely than others to suffer harm or to act in a problematic manner at specific levels of alcohol consumption. Many factors appear to influence not only drinking habits, but also the likelihood that an individual will experience alcohol-related problems. These factors include age, sex, race, religion, hereditary disposition, nationality, income, occupation and the general availability of alcohol.

The recognition of the importance of this diversity of influences has led to the view that anybody may develop alcohol problems if that person drinks enough or in an inappropriate manner. This conclusion is far removed from the 'disease concept of alcoholism', whereby problems were regarded as attributable to the personal characteristics of some drinkers, and not to the interactions between the drinker and the world around him or her.

Considerable controversy exists in relation to the role of economic factors in influencing alcohol use and misuse. Interest has focused on several topics, each of which is relevant to the more general debate about the need for a choice of policies to curb alcohol misuse. These topics include cost-benefit analysis of alcohol production, consumption and misuse; the effects of advertising; and the role of price and taxation in determining the volume and pattern of alcohol use and misuse.

More discursively, this book explores such issues as what there is upon the economist's workbench that can be of relevance to alcohol studies. Expectations may in the past have run high amongst those in alcohol studies regarding what exactly economists do have on offer. If nothing else, therefore, this book should help to dispel the notion that economists will, in some magical and previously undisclosed way, provide all the answers. It should provide a useful corrective by demonstrating the supreme importance to economists of discrete theoretical models. It is clear, for example, that economists are far more influenced by theoretical structures than are many of those engaged in alcohol research. The latter often indulge in theorising, but tend to do so only as a secondary activity, their primary aim being a descriptive one. Classic economic assumptions of rationality and perfect knowledge have only dubious and slight relevance to the debate about alcohol misuse. In addition, economic criteria such as 'efficiency' may have only limited explanatory power concerning whether or not government intervention of any type is justified since the criteria are often equally influential. Nevertheless, economists do possess an analytic machinery for evaluating the effectiveness and efficiency of policies and programmes to minimise alcohol misuse which can

12 *Introduction*

provide valuable insights. Even so it appears that this machinery has a great appetite for data of a kind that are not always acceptable at present, and it is up to epidemiologists and others to provide them if the full potential of the economist's models is to be realised.

It is easy to get depressed working in the alcohol problems field. Neither 'treatment' nor 'education' have been convincingly demonstrated to work. Policy-makers appear to pay only minimal regard to research findings and alcohol problems proliferate. Even so, it is clear that economists have several major roles to play in the future response to the problems caused by alcohol misuse. One of these roles should be advising other researchers about what information to seek and to collect. It is hoped that, at the very least, economists will in future be involved in the design of some alcohol research. Such participation appears crucial if economists are ever to be in a position to fulfil the two primary aims hereafter identified by Dr Robert Leu, namely to 'provide a normative framework for government' and to provide 'specific analytic instruments for evaluating effectiveness and efficiency, that is, the social desirability of government programmes and policies aimed at reducing alcohol-related damage'.

Another major function that economists are clearly well able to perform is to bring the often emotive debates on issues such as the effects of alcohol advertising or of banning such advertising, or of manipulating the price of alcohol, back into a rational and objective mould.

Economists do not have a magic solution to offer, but they are in a unique position to remind other scientists (and policy-makers) of the resource implications and constraints which research (and policy-making) must face up to if action in this field is to be realistically based. Economics can and should be used to identify and eradicate, in a rational and practical manner, policy options and priorities for research, service development and government intervention, in order that we can better reduce the costs of alcohol consumption without sacrificing unduly its undoubted benefits.

1 WHAT CAN ECONOMISTS CONTRIBUTE?

Robert E. Leu

The purpose of this chapter is to outline the contribution of economics to the evaluation of alcohol-related problems and policies. It is argued that economists can contribute in two basic ways: first, in providing a normative framework for dealing with alcohol use and misuse and for establishing the proper role of government in this area. Second, in providing specific analytical instruments for evaluating effectiveness and efficiency, that is, the social desirability of government programmes and policies aimed at reducing alcohol-related damage.

The chapter is organised in five sections. Section one reviews briefly some basic economic concepts which will serve as a normative framework in later stages of the chapter. Specifically, the role of efficiency is stressed as a criterion in economic policy evaluation. In section two, it is shown that several market failures are associated with alcohol consumption. To establish the quantitative significance of these market failures, costs and benefits of alcohol consumption must be considered. This is done in section three. A necessary condition for government intervention, on economic grounds, is that government policies are efficient in the sense that they do not make a bad situation worse. This is the subject of sections four and five. In section four, different approaches to taxing alcohol are discussed. Section five stresses the potential of two analytical techniques, econometric methods and cost-benefit analysis, in evaluating effectiveness and efficiency of government programmes and policies regarding alcohol.

Where We Come From: A Rapid Review

In this section are briefly reviewed a few concepts of welfare economics which will serve as a normative framework for evaluating policy alternatives in later stages of this chapter.

The Theory of Consumer Behaviour

This theory assumes that every consumer has a set of tastes or preferences for the goods and services (commodities) that he or she can buy in the market. Contrary to the approach of other social sciences, these tastes are taken as 'given', that is, they are treated as exogenous. Tastes and preferences are reflected by consumption decisions. Consuming goods and services provides satisfaction or utility to the consumer. This is revealed by the fact that he *does* consume these commodities, since consuming one commodity always means forgone consumption of another. The rational consumer will arrange consumption to maximise satisfaction, given his income. In the equilibrium position of maximum utility, he will consume so many units of each commodity that he cannot increase his utility by rearranging consumption, say, by consuming more of one commodity and less of another. Following this deductive theory, we can infer that consumers derive satisfaction or utility from drinking alcohol simply because they do it.[1]

Two assumptions which underlie consumer theory are relevant in the present context. The first is that the consumer knows the alternatives among which he chooses (perfect information). The second is that the consumer acts in a rational way. This means that he always chooses that bundle of commodities which maximises his utility, given his tastes and income.

Economic Efficiency

A second basic concept is economic efficiency, a criterion widely used by economists in policy evaluation. Roughly speaking, an efficient programme, policy or economic system is one that makes people as well off as possible, e.g. one that maximises people's well-being or welfare. The term welfare is used in a very broad sense, including, for example, life expectancy and life quality. Contrary to what non-economists often believe, economic efficiency is in no way restricted to narrow materialistic issues like cost minimising, profit maximising, and so on. The underlying value judgement is that it is individual consumer preferences which count (consumer sovereignty).

A more formal definition of efficiency is as follows:[2] an efficient allocation of resources is one in which it is impossible, through any change in resource allocation, to make some person or persons better off without making anyone else worse off. By contrast, an inefficient allocation of resources is one in which some person or persons can be made better off without making anyone else worse off. Inefficiency (*market failure*) implies waste in the sense that the economy is not catering to the wants of people as well as it could.

The Price System

A third basic concept is the price system. 'Price system' refers to an economic system that relies on prices determined in open markets to co-ordinate economic activities. These market-determined prices are signals guiding resource allocation. One of the major conclusions of modern economics is that a competitive price system tends, under certain conditions, to produce an efficient allocation of resources. Business firms in competition with one another for the patronage of consumers have incentives to provide commodities in the quantities and qualities that are most preferred by consumers. The incentives provided encourage resource owners to employ their resources in ways that are valued most highly by consumers.

Reality is admittedly rather different from the ideal price system outlined above. Nevertheless, the competitive price system is widely used in economic theory and in policy evaluation as a reference system. It is used thus later in this chapter.

What Role for Government?

Most economists believe that the price (market) system, with all its imperfections, is more efficient in maximising social welfare than government policies. In order to convince an economist that there is a case for public intervention, *on efficiency grounds*, three conditions usually have to be met:

1. There is a market failure.
2. The market failure is quantitatively significant.
3. Government intervention is efficient in that it does not make a bad situation worse. In other words, the benefits of intervention must outweigh its welfare costs.

Of course, efficiency is not the only criterion by which an economic system may be judged. In addition, governments intervene in the interest of equity or for paternalistic reasons, when individuals are judged incompetent to make wise choices. However, efficiency, in the sense defined earlier, is the main economic criterion for government intervention in the case of alcohol. Equity considerations enter mainly as a constraint on certain taxation policies and paternalistic arguments are rarely used by economists qua economists. Therefore, the three criteria set out above are employed to evaluate, on efficiency grounds, the case for government intervention concerning alcohol consumption.

Alcohol Consumption and Market Failures

In this section, it is argued that there are four market failures associated with alcohol consumption: (i) externalities (costs or benefits to others); (ii) lack of risk awareness (imperfect information); (iii) chronic alcoholism (non-rational behaviour); (iv) inefficient level of prevention (public good).

Externalities

In the production, distribution or consumption of certain commodities, there are sometimes harmful or beneficial side effects that are borne by people who are not directly involved in the market exchanges. These side-effects are called externalities: external benefits when the effects are beneficial and external costs when they are harmful. Externalities lead to an inefficient allocation of resources, or market failure. Market demands and supplies will reflect only the benefits and costs of the participants in the market; the benefits and costs that fall on others will not be taken into account. Put more formally, externalities lead to a divergence between private and social costs or benefits, where private refers to the costs and benefits to those participating in the market transactions and social refers to the costs and benefits to all members of society.

Drinking alcohol by one individual may have external *benefits* for others who are in his or her company, because drinking alcohol can be relaxing, cheering, etc. However, the benefits of drinking seem to stay mainly with the consumer (Chafetz, 1976) and there appear to be no significant beneficial side effects.

Two types of external *costs* are associated with the acute and chronic effects of alcohol: Type I external costs include direct physical, psychical or emotional harm to identifiable others. Examples are injuries through accidents or physical and emotional distress to family members of alcoholics (Chafetz *et al.*, 1971). Type II external costs involve financial burdens to subgroups of the population, for example, to taxpayers who cannot be identified individually. These external costs are imposed on others through an institutional framework. As an example, consider medical treatment costs. Without health insurance, or a tax-financed national health system, every patient would have to cover all treatment costs out of his pocket; there could be no divergence between private and social costs. However, financing treatment costs through taxes or health insurance inevitably implies such a divergence, since not everybody uses the health services according to his financial contribution. Heavy alcohol users as a group are thought commonly to have higher health care costs, creating external costs for moderate drinkers and abstainers.

To the extent that external costs are *not* included in the price of alcoholic beverages before tax, the price is too low and alcohol consumption too high, assuming that demand is not completely inelastic (insensitive to price changes).

Lack of Risk Awareness

Heavy alcohol use is associated with morbidity, disability, premature mortality and chronic alcoholism (dependency) and may thus be interpreted as risk-taking behaviour. Such behaviour can be perfectly rational, and many activities in daily life involve risks, for example, driving a car or crossing a street. Rational risk-taking behaviour implies, however, that the individual has an appropriate idea of what risks are involved and how likely they are to occur. Studies in several countries suggest that this may not be so with alcohol consumption.[3]

How significant this lack of risk-awareness is as a determinant of alcohol-related damage is not clear. However, a case can be made that the market does not provide sufficient information about the risks involved in heavy drinking: the prices are distorted because of externalities, and explicit information as a commodity is not produced in efficient quantity because of its public good character.

Chronic Alcoholism and Rational Behaviour

There is no unambiguous and uniformly applicable definition of chronic 'alcoholism'.[4] For the present purpose of discussing the relationship between alcoholism and rational behaviour the following definition by Lundquist (1972) is used: 'Chronic alcoholism is that stage of disease or degree of dependency which is manifested mainly in a loss of ability to give up alcohol despite the fact that drinking has led to distress, difficulties or problems.' One interpretation of this definition would be that chronic alcoholism interferes with the basic rationality postulate of consumer theory, in that an alcoholic is not free to choose whether or how much he will drink. If one accepts this interpretation, then alcoholism constitutes a market failure. It should be noted, however, that advocates of a strictly economic approach seem to reject entirely the concept of dependency or addiction (Mishan, 1971).

18 *What can Economists Contribute?*

Prevention as a Public Good

The term 'prevention', is employed here to describe the whole range of activities (preventive commodities) which may help people to avoid the harmful effects of alcohol consumption. 'Public good' refers to commodities which are not provided, or not in efficient quantities, by the market because of two characteristics: non-rival consumption and non-exclusion. Non-rival consumption means that a number of people may consume simultaneously the same good without impairing each other's utility (national defence is the usual textbook example). Non-exclusion means that it is impossible, or too costly, to confine the benefits of the commodity to those who buy it. In other words, non-buyers cannot be excluded from the benefits by a price. Therefore, markets will fail to provide these goods adequately.

Preventive commodities in relation to heavy alcohol use typically have the characteristics of public goods (Leu, 1978). Consider the following example: In a community there are a number of alcoholics causing costs to taxpayers. Alcoholism treatment programmes might reduce these costs and hence benefit every taxpayer. However, no taxpayer would be willing, on purely economic grounds, to finánce such programmes since he would have to bear fully the implementation costs while the benefits would spread among all taxpayers (e.g. he would get only a marginal part of total benefits). For this reason, there will be no private demand for such programmes and the market does not provide them, unless government steps in and forces every taxpayer to contribute to the programme costs.

Costs and Benefits of Alcohol Consumption

In the last section, it has been shown that there are market failures associated with alcohol consumption. According to the criteria set out above, a second necessary condition for government intervention, on efficiency grounds, is that these market failures be quantitatively significant. To establish their magnitude, costs and benefits of alcohol consumption must be considered.

Cost Estimation: the Basic Model

Estimating the costs of alcohol consumption always involves comparison of two states: one with and one without heavy alcohol use. In other words, we have to choose a counterfactual (a hypothetical situation without heavy alcohol use) and compare this counterfactual

Figure 1.1: The Basic Cost Estimation Model

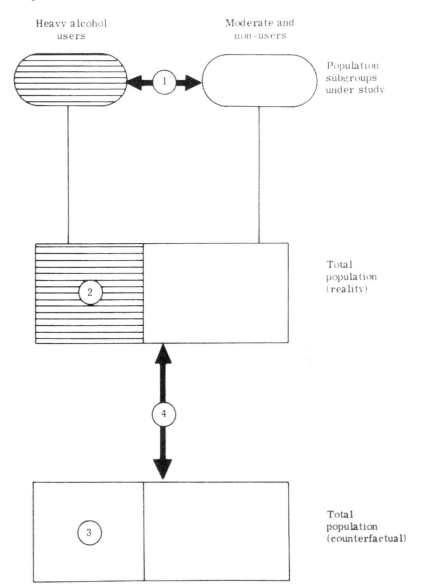

20 What can Economists Contribute?

with reality. Differences between these two states reflect costs or benefits of alcohol consumption.

The process of cost estimation can be split into four different parts or research areas (see Figure 1.1): step one involves investigating the causes and effects of alcohol consumption. Specifically, the role of alcohol in inducing harmful behaviours and health consequences must be determined. In step two, the prevalence of alcohol use, particularly heavy alcohol use, must be established. Step three involves choosing a set of counterfactual parameters for heavy alcohol users and modelling a hypothetical world without alcohol abuse. Finally, in step four, the two states (with and without alcohol abuse) are compared, based on an appropriate theoretical framework, to derive a policy-relevant cost estimate.[5]

Causes and Effects of Alcohol Consumption (Step One)

There is an impressive literature from many disciplines dealing with the causes, behaviours and health effects of alcohol consumption. Although major problem areas can be delineated, the research within these areas does not, in general, succeed in isolating the social behaviours or specific health consequences that might be attributed to alcohol alone. Many studies do not adequately account for socio-economic factors, other health risk factors and possible interaction (synergistic effects) multiple drug use or other health behaviours. They frequently fail to use adequate control groups and usually do not provide nationwide generalisable results. As a consequence, empirical cost estimates have two major shortcomings: first, they are frequently based on what the above-mentioned studies suggest as a conservative estimate of the role of alcohol in inducing cost relevant behaviour or health consequences. Second, they often rely on studies done at different times and in different places, which are hardly comparable.

The Prevalence of Heavy Alcohol Use (Step Two)

Prevalence of alcohol use is extremely difficult to establish, because consumers, particularly heavy users, tend to under-report their consumption. Interview studies appear usually to reveal only about two thirds of total consumption, as suggested by sales statistics (Wüthrich, 1976). However, accurate information on the prevalence of heavy alcohol use is essential for assessing its impact on the population and for empirical cost estimates.

Choosing a Counterfactual (Step Three)

The difficulties of choosing appropriate counterfactual parameters are closely related to the difficulties of determining the causal role of alcohol in inducing certain harmful effects (step one). The crucial question is whether heavy alcohol users differ from moderate or non-users *only* in the amount of alcohol consumed; since smoking and other forms of drug use are highly reliable correlates to drinking (USDHEW, 1979), this seems unlikely. Therefore, the pertinent question is what behavioural parameters, survival probabilities and patterns of health services use should be assigned to heavy alcohol users in the counterfactual.[6] Existing empirical studies all assume that heavy users are equal to moderate and non-users in the counterfactual and therefore tend to overestimate the costs of alcohol consumption.

Another shortcoming of existing empirical cost estimates due to an inappropriate counterfactual is that they do not consider competing risks. The quantitative significance of this pitfall has been documented recently with respect to the effect of smoking on health care costs. Smokers use health services more often than non-smokers. Eliminating smoking eliminates part of these excess costs, but simultaneously increases longevity. This, in turn, increases health care costs because health services use is highest among the elderly (Frey and Leu, 1981). It has been shown that these two cost effects may about compensate each other (Atkinson and Townsend, 1977; Leu, 1982a) and that there may be even a net increase in health care costs if smoking were eliminated (Leu, 1982b). Heavy alcohol use reduces life expectancy by ten to twelve years (USDHEW, 1972, 1974, 1978; Comité OMS, 1975). If competing risks were adequately accounted for, we would expect similar compensating effects in the case of heavy alcohol use, instead of the high health care costs estimated in existing studies.

The Relevant Costs: in Search of a Theory (Step Four)

The last step of the basic cost estimation model involves comparison between reality and the counterfactual, based on an appropriate theoretical framework. The question is what costs are relevant when discussing the case for government intervention and subsequent intervention policies. After a brief review of some basic cost concepts, three perspectives on this issue will be presented.

In evaluating alcohol-related costs, the following relevant concepts should be distinguished (see Figure 1.2): a first category is *production costs*, that is, the value of the resources employed in producing alcoholic beverages. The price of alcoholic beverages consists of

Figure 1.2: Cost Concepts

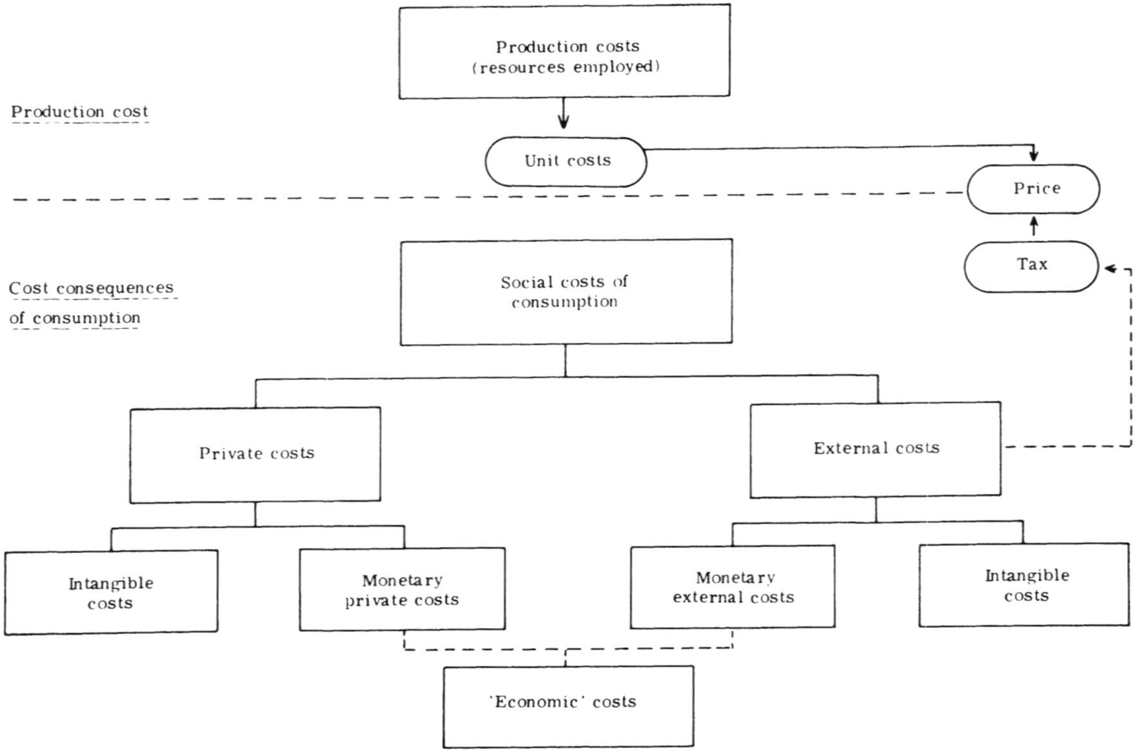

Production cost

Cost consequences
of consumption
---

production costs plus tax per unit of alcohol. A second category is the *social costs of alcohol consumption*, that is, costs arising as a consequence of consuming alcohol. Social costs are made up of *private* and *external* costs. Both private and external costs can be subdivided further into *intangible* and *monetary* costs. Intangibles are costs that cannot be measured in monetary terms. The distinction between intangibles and monetary costs is determined by the state of the art in measuring and valuing cost components which do not have a market price. The so-called 'economic costs' are the sum of monetary private and monetary external costs. Inverted commas are used because the concept, contrary to its label, appears to portray costs in a way which is rather different from mainstream economic thinking.

Three different perspectives on relevant costs for government intervention are outlined below: the economic model, a modified economic model and the 'vaccination' (disease-costing) model.

The Economic Model

The economic model posits that consumers have full information and act rationally in the sense defined earlier. Under certain conditions, the price system produces an efficient allocation of resources, in which case there is no efficiency-based reason for government intervention. One of the conditions ensuring efficiency is the absence of external costs. Such costs distort the price mechanism and lead to an inefficient allocation of resources which can, in principle, be corrected by levying an appropriate tax (see below). Hence, there may be a case for government intervention.

Clearly, heavy alcohol use involves external costs. The natural economic approach, therefore, would be based on these external costs, treating alcohol consumption like any other activity in which individuals voluntarily assume risks, such as skiing. A case for intervention could be made, if the external costs of alcohol consumption were significant and if there were an efficient government policy to improve the situation.

In this model, government intervention is justified entirely on the costs imposed on others, that is on external costs. Private costs (and hence economic costs) are not relevant as a reason for government intervention, since the consumers rationally take these costs into account when making their decisions.

For example, if skiers ski despite the accident risk involved, this is because the consumption benefits outweigh the expected private costs. Nobody would suggest that government ignore skiers' consumption benefits and intervene to protect skiers against private costs.

A Modified Economic Model

In the case of alcohol, the traditional economic approach, assuming full information and rational behaviour on the part of consumers, may not be appropriate; alcohol consumption may be associated with lack of risk-awareness and dependency and, hence, is different from skiing. If consumers really are not aware of the risks involved in drinking, it cannot be argued that they have taken into account rationally the private costs of disability and premature death (Atkinson and Meade, 1974). In this case, private costs should also be considered as a reason for intervention.

The argument is more complicated in the case of alcohol dependency, because it is not clear how dependency should be interpreted in the framework of consumer theory. To indicate the span of possibilities, an extreme case is cited which is polar to that of the fully informed and rational consumer. Assume that alcoholics derive no utility at all from drinking and consider a consumer who is both dependent and unaware of any risk. In this case, proper evaluation would include both the social costs of consumption (private plus external costs), and the real costs of production, that is, expenditures on alcohol minus tax (compare Atkinson and Meade, 1974, for the case of smoking).

The argument goes as follows: if the alcoholic derives no benefit at all from drinking, then his consumption choices are distorted, e.g. he overvalues his alcohol consumption by an amount equal to what he spends on alcohol. If he could be convinced to spend this money on another commodity instead of on alcohol, he could increase his consumption (utility) by that amount without giving up anything. His expenditures on alcohol equal production costs plus tax. The latter represents a transfer and must not be included. Hence, the real costs of the alcoholic's distorted consumption choice are production costs for producing the quantity he drinks plus any subsequent social costs of consumption.

The view of dependency set out above is clearly extreme. The discussion should have made clear, however, that there is no unambiguous concept of what constitutes the costs of alcohol consumption. Depending on how one interprets possible lack of risk-awareness and alcohol dependency, the relevant costs include, at one extreme, only external costs and at the other, private and external costs of consumption *plus* production costs. The quantitative significance of these conceptual differences is indicated by one study which estimates separately private and external costs of consumption (Leu and Lutz, 1977). These results indicate that private and external costs are of about equal magnitude (approximately 600 million Swiss francs in 1972). By contrast, in the case of smoking, external costs have been shown recently to be only about one third of private costs, e.g. the economic costs of smoking consist of 25 per cent external and 75 per cent private costs (Leu, 1982a).

The 'Vaccination' (Disease-costing) Model

Existing empirical studies have been concerned mainly with estimating the *economic costs* of alcohol consumption (Berry, 1976; Berry and Boland, 1977; Luce and Schweitzer, 1978). A few studies have additionally provided estimates of intangible costs such as life years lost, years with impaired health, etc. (Leu and Lutz, 1977). In all these studies, heavy alcohol use is treated like a disease which can be eradicated completely by, say, vaccination (Atkinson, 1974). The disease (heavy alcohol use) causes costs to the consumer and to society, such as health care costs, production loss through work absence and premature death, etc., without providing any benefits. 'Vaccination' therefore could eliminate these costs without causing a welfare loss in terms of forgone benefits. Hence all private and external costs resulting from alcohol consumption are considered relevant in this framework.

How appropriate this approach is, again depends on how one interprets heavy alcohol use in terms of consumer theory. Heavy alcohol use is a much broader concept than chronic alcoholism, and the assumption that there is no benefit from heavy drinking is probably not very realistic. Clearly, the analogy to vaccination is not valid, if consumers derive satisfaction from heavy alcohol use which has no parallel in the case of disease.

Benefits of Alcohol Consumption

In political debates, two kinds of 'benefits' are attributed frequently to alcohol consumption which appear to be rather different from the concept of benefits as used by economists. The first is that alcohol consumption creates jobs and hence income (wages and profits) for those who produce and distribute alcoholic beverages. Reducing alcohol consumption through preventive policies would lead to an income loss for the producers, and this loss should be taken into account as a cost of such policies, so the argument goes. Two objections should be made. First, in an efficient economic system, it is the allocation of resources which adapts to consumers' preferences rather than vice versa. Second, there seems to be confusion between structural change and changes in the level of aggregate demand. It is unlikely that consumers who reduce their alcohol consumption save the money previously spent on alcohol. It is more likely that they simply buy other commodities. Whether this results in a net increase or decrease in the overall number of jobs cannot be determined *a priori* and depends on the labour intensity of production and the import share of the different commodities affected.

The second misperception is that tax revenues should be viewed as 'benefits' of alcohol consumption. Taxes are transfers which merely redistribute purchasing power and do not increase the consumption possibilities of society as a whole. A case can be made that other forms of taxation (for example, a VAT on all commodities) are more efficient in raising tax revenues than a special excise tax on a single commodity such as the tax on alcoholic beverages. However, as pointed out earlier, the tax on alcohol can be used to offset the external costs of alcohol consumption (see below).

For economists, the benefits of alcohol consumption are the satisfaction or utility which the consumers derive from drinking. Total expenditures on alcoholic beverages, reflecting consumers' aggregate willingness to pay, have been interpreted as indicating the size of these benefits. Clearly, this indicator is not valid. It ignores possible lack of risk-awareness and dependency and does not account for consumers' surplus.[7]

Taxing Alcohol

The previous discussion has shown that alcohol consumption is associated with significant market failures. Another necessary condition for government intervention according to the criteria set out previously is that government policies will improve the situation. The classic economic tool for dealing with market failures, such as the ones related to alcohol, is taxation. Four forms of alcohol taxation will be discussed below: an efficiency (Pigou) tax, an insurance approach to taxing externalities, a sumptuary tax, and a fiscal tax (for a formal treatment of these four approaches see Leu and Lutz, 1977).

Taxing for Efficiency

Economists have long recognised that price distortions caused by external costs can be corrected, in principle, by an appropriate tax (Pigou tax). The principle is simple: the price per unit of alcohol is too low in that it does not include the external costs that may be associated with the consumption of this unit. If we knew the marginal external costs per unit, we would simply tax each unit accordingly. In other words, tax would be set equal to marginal external costs. The price would then reflect the full social costs of production *and* consumption. Neglecting the specific characteristics of alcohol as a drug for the moment, this would restore the efficiency of the price mechanism. This approach is, in general, preferred by economists because it is based entirely on efficiency as a criterion.

Unfortunately, such a tax is impossible in the case of alcohol, because marginal external costs associated with consumption of each unit cannot be determined in advance. These costs depend on who drinks the unit (a heavy or a moderate user, a smoker or a non-smoker, etc.), under what circumstances it is drunk (social setting, state of mind, stage of drinking, etc.), and what subsequent actions are taken (driving a car or going to bed). In other words, imposition of a Pigou tax is impossible because information costs are prohibitive.

An Insurance Approach to Externalities

A second best solution for economists is an insurance approach to taxing external costs of alcohol consumption. The principle involved can be explained best by analogy to compulsory motorcycle insurance. Insurance companies calculate premiums based on expected average costs per motorcycle per year. Similarly, each unit of alcohol could be taxed according to the expected average external costs associated with its consumption. Expected average external costs can be approximated by estimating total external costs for a previous year and dividing by that year's total alcohol consumption.

Two major problems are associated with this approach. First, such a tax falls short of restoring efficient alcohol prices. For the moderate drinker who is unlikely to cause external costs, the tax is too high, imposing a welfare cost. For the heavy drinker who is likely to cause external costs, the tax is too low. Assuming that demand of both moderate and heavy drinkers is not completely inelastic, consumption of the former is too low, and of the latter, too high.

Second, it is not clear what costs should be taken into account when there is lack of risk-awareness and alcohol dependency. One view is that

external costs should be modified to account for these specific
characteristics of alcohol as a drug (Atkinson, 1974). An opposing
view is that, for tax purposes, only external costs should be taken into
consideration (Leu and Lutz, 1977; Leu, 1982a).[8]

The Alcohol Tax as a Sumptuary Tax

Sumptuary taxes are designed to reduce harmful behaviours and health
effects related to heavy alcohol use by deterring overall consumption.
This approach is based on ethical or paternalistic considerations and is
favoured by social groups opposed to alcohol consumption and by
many medical doctors involved in prevention. Economic efficiency
considerations are not implied.

This tax can take two forms. In the first, the tax is set as high as
possible to minimise consumption. A high tax policy is limited by
political constraints, for example, equity considerations, and by the
possibility that a black market or heavy smuggling activities will
develop. In the second form, a desired level of alcohol consumption is
chosen politically, and the tax is set so that consumption descends to
that level. This is known as 'standards and pricing' approach and has
been proposed for environmental protection (Baumol and Oates,
1971, 1975, 1979).

The social desirability of a sumptuary tax may be judged by its costs
and benefits. Although it is often regarded as a cheap preventive tool
involving only small administrative costs, a sumptuary tax may impose
heavy welfare costs on alcohol consumers (excess burden). The benefits
of this tax are defined by its preventive success. There is disagreement,
however, on whether a reduction in the overall consumption level
simultaneously will reduce alcohol-related damage. For example,
consider alcoholism prevalence. One rather over-simple hypothesis
posits that rates of alcohol damage in a society and, specifically,
prevalence of alcoholism as indicated by rates of alcohol-related
cirrhosis, are determined by overall per capita consumption of alcohol
(Ledermann, 1956, 1964; De Lint and Schmidt, 1971). An opposing
view is that alcohol is not the issue. Problems which arise with alcohol
lie with people's misuse of the substance, not with the substance itself
(Chafetz, 1965). It is clear that the benefits of a sumptuary tax would
be larger in the first case than in the second.

The Alcohol Tax as a Fiscal Tax

An old principle of public finance recommends taxing the inelastic
factor. Alcohol consumption in most countries is rather inelastic and

has been exploited extensively for fiscal reasons. Implicitly or explicitly, the fiscal motive still dominates most alcohol taxation policies. Economic efficiency considerations are not implied. Modern economics does not favour such a tax because of the welfare costs to consumers.

Techniques for Evaluating Preventive Programmes and Policies

A single instrument, such as taxation, clearly cannot solve all problems associated with alcohol consumption. A basic rule of thumb in economic policy evaluation is that one tool should be used for each goal. By analogy, it appears that in the case of alcohol, there should be one instrument for each problem area. For example, external costs might be dealt with by taxation, lack of risk-awareness by health education and publicity campaigns, alcoholism by early detection and treatment programmes, harmful behaviour in specific areas by stricter controls such as police control in the interest of traffic safety. Rather than evaluate specific programmes, two analytical instruments are briefly outlined, which may be used for this purpose: econometric methods and cost-benefit analysis.

Econometric Methods

Econometric methods are the backbone of empirical research in economics and are employed for hypothesis testing and forecasting. One major application of econometrics is in consumer demand analysis where it can be used for investigating two questions: (a) what factors determine the demand for a specific commodity; and (b) how demand can be influenced by government policy if this seems desirable. Contrary to the normative economic framework discussed in sections one to four, demand analysis is an exercise in positive economics requiring no specific value judgements.

Application of this type of analysis to the demand for alcoholic beverages is straightforward. It implies estimating demand equations (or systems of equations) for either cross-sectional or time-series data of the following general form:

$$x = \alpha + \beta_1 p + \beta_2 y + \beta_3 z + \epsilon, \tag{1}$$

where x = quantity of alcohol consumed, p = price of alcoholic beverages, y = disposable income per capita or per household, z = a vector of all other relevant variables such as advertising, health publicity or characteristics of individual consumers in cross-section analyses, and ϵ = a disturbance term.

Estimating demand equations provides information about the *effectiveness* of key policy variables such as taxation (price), regulations (restrictions on advertising or on the availability of alcohol), and health education (publicity, health scares) as deterrents of alcohol consumption. Existing empirical studies have concentrated mainly on price elasticity of the demand for alcohol and, in general, have found that alcohol consumption is rather inelastic (summaries of the literature are provided by Leu and Lutz, 1977 and by Schweitzer, Intrilligator and Salehi, below). However, demand studies, focusing entirely on consumption, do not provide information on the relationship between policy variables and alcohol-related damage. Yet the relationship between consumption and alcohol-related damage is far from clear (Pittman, 1980a). Recent studies, therefore, have expanded the narrow scope of demand analysis and have focused directly on the relationship between policy changes and changes in alcohol-related damage such as traffic fatalities or liver cirrhosis death rates (see Cook, below; see also Schweitzer, Intrilligator and Salehi, below).

It should be emphasised, however, that econometric studies can provide information only about the *effectiveness* of government programmes or policies, but do not allow any inference about the *efficiency* and, hence, the social desirability of such policies. In a second step, therefore, these policies should be evaluated by cost-benefit analysis, using econometric estimation results as an input. The following section provides a brief discussion of cost-benefit analysis and its application in the field of alcohol research.

Cost-benefit Analysis: a Way of Thinking

Cost-benefit analysis (CBA) merely formalises the common-sense concept of rationality described in section one; rational behaviour implies that individuals weigh up the advantages and disadvantages of a particular action. There are two major differences between CBA and individual utility maximising, however. First, CBA relates to social rather than individual decisions. Second, CBA is not confined to costs and benefits of the decision-maker, but accounts for all costs and benefits of all those affected. Rather than providing rigid prescriptions for social evaluation of projects, CBA is a way of thinking which involves adapting certain basic procedures to the specific nature of a problem. A project or programme is deemed desirable if 'the benefits to whomsoever they may accrue, are in excess of the estimated costs' (United States Flood Control Act, 1936).

CBA consists of two steps. The first is to assess the effectiveness of a programme or policy, for example, to reduce alcohol-related damage. This clearly calls for a multidisciplinary approach. The second is to enumerate all costs and benefits of the programme, transform them into comparable, preferably monetary, units, and compare them according to specific investment criteria.

Harmful behaviours and health effects associated with alcohol consumption cause costs to the consumer and to society as a whole. Preventive programmes, if effective, reduce these harmful effects and hence costs. Thus, the *benefits* of such programmes are the alcohol-related costs that subsequently can be avoided. The programme *costs* equal the value of the resources employed.

CBA in the field of alcohol has been applied mainly to alcoholism treatment programmes (Holtmann, 1972; Schramm, 1977; Swint and Nelson, 1977; Leu, 1978). Two major problems are involved in these studies. The first is that they all evaluate *ex post* the efficiency of existing programmes. *Ex ante* evaluation, tackling the question 'should an additional programme be implemented?', is much more difficult because one can usually identify only average rather than marginal benefits. For example, it is clear that the average success rate of previously treated alcoholics cannot simply be extrapolated on all untreated alcoholics because of selection bias. The second problem concerns, once more, the relevant costs that should be included as benefits in the case of alcohol. Reducing alcohol consumption is one thing, preventing harmful behaviours and health effects, another. In the first case, the traditional economic interpretation of external costs seems more appropriate for identifying benefits. In the second case, total social costs of alcohol consumption should be considered, since nobody derives utility from, say, having an accident or being addicted to alcohol.

Concluding Remarks

In conclusion, three points are emphasised. First, the evaluation of alcohol-related problems and subsequent government policies invariably demands a multidisciplinary approach. Second, economists can contribute in two basic ways: (i) by providing a normative framework for dealing with alcohol use and misuse and for establishing the

32 What can Economists Contribute?

appropriate role of government in this area; (ii) by providing specific tools, particularly econometric methods and cost-benefit analysis, for evaluating effectiveness and efficiency of government programmes and policies aimed at reducing alcohol-related damage. Third, in economics, as well as in other disciplines, many questions have been raised that have not been answered satisfactorily. Both more research and improved research methods are called for in areas such as: the causes and effects of heavy drinking; the prevalence of heavy alcohol use; the effectiveness of preventive and treatment programmes; and last, but not least, their efficiency. Evaluating the latter requires further development of the economic framework so as to deal more adequately with the very specific characteristics of alcohol as a drug.

Notes

1. It is interesting to contrast this deductive approach with a similar basic statement from a sociological perspective: 'Man does not ordinarily continue to do something that does not fulfil some real or imagined need. To persist, behaviour must be reinforced. To the extent that this does fulfil a need, it will recur, often at some risk, unless it interferes with some more important need. The need for a drug may be closely related to its real or imagined effects or it may be grounded in social rather than chemical elements. Use of specific substances may determine group membership or status within a group, or among groups. It may function as either a symbol of rebellion, alienation, independence or sophistication' (Shafer, 1973).
2. The outline of basic concepts advanced in this section closely follows Browning and Browning (1979).
3. A recent interview study in the US, for example, concludes that 'The public suffers from much ignorance concerning alcohol . . . Heavier drinkers know less about alcohol than the lighter drinkers or abstainers' (USDHEW, 1974). Similar conclusions are reported in a representative study in West Germany. The authors state that 'most people do not seem to have sufficient knowledge to interpret properly the character of alcoholism as a disease, or at least as a progressive process with comparable harmful consequences' (Wieser, 1973); translated by the author.
4. As one critic has put it: 'In the case of alcoholism it is modest to say that the criteria for inclusion are mostly themselves so fuddled that they are as opaque as the condition itself' (Seeley, 1959). Jellinek (1960) speaks of a chaos of definitions.
5. Economists are only minimally involved in steps one and two. Step three, setting up a counterfactual, is a familiar exercise in economics since much applied research involves this (for example cost-benefit analysis). The main contribution of economists is found in step four, both on a theoretical and empirical level.
6. The issue is discussed by Shepard and Zeckhauser (1980) and Zeckhauser and Shepard (1980) under the heading of mixed or homogeneous v. heterogeneous populations.
7. Roughly speaking, consumers' surplus is the difference between the maximal price which the consumer would be willing to pay and the actual price

for a certain commodity.
8. The Atkinson (1974) model assumes an efficient tax and lump sum redistribution. Both assumptions are not met in reality. Hence it appears that for policy purposes, only external costs should be taken into account.

2 ALCOHOL STUDIES FROM AN ECONOMIC PERSPECTIVE

Robert Weeden

Economics has a clear and important role to play in the field of alcohol studies. This role relates to disentangling key variables such as price, income, availability and advertising. In addition, a wider contribution exists in the form of cost-benefit studies.

This chapter reviews some of the general economic issues related to alcohol. In addition, a new and possibly fruitful theoretical orientation towards this important topic is mentioned.

Econometrics

One of the great difficulties with modern econometrics, particularly for those with a limited knowledge of mathematics, is that the models and the estimation methods have become more and more complex. This has occurred partly because more and more brilliant minds are studying the subject and partly because of the advent of more and more powerful computers and the rapid decline in the real cost of performing complex calculations. The estimates of price and income elasticities for alcoholic drink and other commodities that Professor Stone published in his 1945 paper (Stone, 1945) were, apparently, computed by hand, so that each multiple regression took several hours, if not days, to calculate. Such calculations now take a matter of seconds.

There is great danger, because of the complexity of modern econometrics, that economists may confuse their non-economist colleagues by concentrating on rather technical issues and failing to emphasise the general features of the results they are obtaining.

There are a large number of economic studies which provide estimates of price and income elasticities[1] and Table 7.2 in Chapter 7 which is taken from Ornstein (1980) reviews some of these. Other chapters in this book provide yet more estimates. This chapter presents some further estimates for the United Kingdom. The price and income elasticities for the main alcohol drinks used by the UK government to calculate the effects of tax changes (HM Treasury, 1980) are as follows:

Alcohol Studies from an Economic Perspective 35

	Price elasticity	Income elasticity
Beer	−0.2	0.7
Spirits	−1.6	2.2
Wine	−1.1	2.5

These figures are subject to a considerable margin of error and may change in the future. McGuinness, in Chapter 16, estimates a similar price elasticity for beer, but obtains rather lower figures for the price elasticity of spirits and wine. It is perhaps worth drawing a contrast with the pre-war picture for the UK. Stone (1945) quotes estimates of price and income elasticities based on data for the period 1920-38. The figures are as follows:

	Price elasticity	Income elasticity
Beer	−0.7/0.8	0.1
Spirits	−0.7	0.5

In the pre-war period, the price of beer and spirits remained fairly constant over the whole period in money terms, but the general price level fell, so that the relative price of drink rose and consumption declined. In contrast to the post-war period, it seems that income was not a major influence on consumption but, as income levels changed very little in this period, the estimate of the income elasticity may not be entirely reliable.

Are there any useful generalisations that might be drawn from these studies that would be of use to those interested in alcohol studies? In order to answer this, a summary is presented of the estimates given in the Ornstein table by country, distinguishing broadly between the predominantly beer, wine and spirit-drinking countries and adding the UK estimates referred to above. One problem with this summary is that even for a given beverage in a given country there are quite large variations in the estimates. These variations may result from differences in the specification of the model, type of data used (time-series or cross-section), choice of time period and the quality of the studies concerned. Another problem is that we seem to have a lot of gaps in terms of the availability of estimates for the non-English-speaking countries – presumably because Ornstein did not survey the non-English literature.

Despite these problems, one can draw some useful generalisations.

Table 2.1: Range of Values for Price and Income Elasticities

	Price			Income		
	Beer	Wine	Distilled spirits	Beer	Wine	Distilled spirits
Beer-drinking Countries						
UK	0.2-0.8	0.4-1.1	0.5-1.6	0.1-0.7	1.0-2.5	0.5-2.2
Ireland	0.2	n.a.	0.6	0.8	n.a.	2.0
USA	0-0.9	0.4-1.6	0.2-2.0	0-0.4*	0.4-2.4	0.2-1.8
Canada	0-0.3	0.5-1.7	0.9-1.5	0-0.2	0-1.4*	0.1-0.7
Belgium		1.1			1.8	
W Germany		0.4			0.5	
Spirit-drinking Countries						
Finland	0-0.5	0.8-1.0	0.1-1.1**	0.2	0.4-1.0	0.3-1.3**
Sweden		0.9	0.4-3.2**			0.3**
Wine-drinking Countries						
France		0			*	
Italy		1.0			1.3	
Portugal		0.7			0	
Spain		0.4			0.1	

Notes: Long-run elasticities are excluded from this table.
    * negative values also observed
    ** estimates for vodka are lower than for other spirits
    n.a. not available

Source: Ornstein (1980), HM Treasury (1980).

Alcohol Studies from an Economic Perspective 37

These are indicated by Table 2.1. The first of these conclusions is that price elasticities are often quite low, so that increases in price would often need to be very large in order to reduce consumption by a given amount. As income elasticities tend to be higher than price elasticities, even larger price increases may be necessary to restrain consumption if real incomes are increasing. The Table also suggests that for a given type of drink, both the price and the income elasticities tend to be lower the more important that drink is in terms of its share of total consumption. Thus in beer-drinking countries beer has low price and income elasticities, in wine-drinking countries wine has low elasticities (except for Italy curiously enough) and in Finland and Sweden and probably the USSR[2] vodka has low price and income elasticities.

Other Variables

Ideally, one wants to go beyond price and income and look at the effect of other variables on consumption. There are difficulties of course. Some are technical, for example the new variable added may be correlated with other variables already present in the model so that the estimate of its effect is subject to a wide margin of error. Alternatively, there may be difficulties in identifying the direction of causality. This is particularly the case with variables that attempt to measure the effects of advertising and availability, both of which may follow demand rather than lead it. It is possible to estimate models that allow for two-way causal relationships, but there may be greater difficulty in obtaining a reliable specification of the model which indicates what the precise relationship between the variables actually is.

Perhaps the main problem is one of data rather than one of technique. Unfortunately economists have to contend with non-experimental data. Frequently it may be impossible to obtain precise estimates of elasticities using time-series information. For example, until recent years beer consumption in the UK followed a steady upwards time trend with very little variation about the trend. As a consequence it is extremely difficult to obtain a statistically significant value for the price elasticity of beer for the UK. One possibility, if time-series data are inadequate, is to resort to the use of cross-sectional data for individuals or regions of a country. Outside North America such data are often scarce.

In referring to other variables that might be added to an econometric model, particular emphasis could usefully be accorded to the inclusion of one variable in particular in consumption equations. This variable, which is used only occasionally in econometric studies, is air temperature which may serve as a measure of the effect of the weather on alcohol consumption. It is well known that beer consumption in the UK tends to rise in the summer months and fall in the winter months. In an unpublished study carried out by the author five years ago, it emerged that the 'temperature elasticity' for beer was about 0.3 holding other factors constant. In other words, a 10 per cent rise in temperature led to a 3 per cent rise in the consumption of beer. It is emphasised, however, that this variable is likely to have a threshold effect on drinking. It is only when temperature rises above a certain level that consumption is likely to rise.

Welfare Issues

Econometric issues are important but many economists feel that they have more to offer than expertise in econometrics, which, after all, any good mathematical statistician should be able to supply as well. Their training in welfare economics[3] gives them an advantage in analysing general policy issues concerning alcohol.

There are now quite a large number of estimates of what are often called the economic costs or the societal costs of alcohol abuse to the nation for various countries. The list of studies includes Berry and Boland (1977) updated by Schifrin (see below) for the USA and Holtermann and Burchell (1981) for the UK. Such estimates tend to be quoted frequently in the medical literature and elsewhere. Without going into detailed aspects of the calculations it is suggested that they have limited usefulness. Their role is to demonstrate that an economic dimension to the alcohol problem exists and they should be considered as a starting-point for economic research rather than as the final output.

Welfare economics starts from the idea of maximising social welfare defined as total benefits less total costs. Total benefits may be approximated by the whole area under the demand curve, i.e. benefits may be represented by expenditure on the commodity in question plus 'consumers' surplus.[4] In the case of alcohol, the costs include not only the resources used in producing the various types of drink but also the 'social' costs of the various kinds of harm associated with alcohol consumption. The objective of maximising social welfare leads to the proposition that the tax on a commodity that is potentially harmful should be equal to the marginal social cost per unit of consumption.

The marginal social cost is the increase in costs to society (extra harm) that would result if consumption increases by a small amount from its present level. It is, however, difficult to link the various empirical estimates of economic or societal costs with the concept of marginal social cost. For example, one part of an estimate of economic costs is the increased morbidity or mortality experienced by alcohol consumers. But it could be argued that if one is dealing with a rational individual who is fully informed of all the risks involved then the fact that he is willing to continue consuming alcohol is evidence that he is willing to accept the risk. This will be more likely if the harmful effects are delayed and individuals have a high subjective rate of discount, i.e. a pronounced preference for benefits now as opposed to benefits later. In this instance, therefore, the costs associated with loss of life, etc., fall on the individual who willingly accepts the risks and it is useful to distinguish them from costs which fall on others, e.g. third parties in road accidents.

In contrast, the issue whether extra health care or sickness absence costs should be counted as social costs depends in this analysis on how the health care or social security system is financed. In tax-financed systems as in the UK, health care is provided free or at a low cost to the patient and the extra health care costs are borne by the general taxpayer and ultimately society. But where health care is financed by private insurance, insurers have the incentive to assess the risks of consuming alcohol or cigarettes or any similar activity and charge different premiums to different individuals. In such a system the excess costs would be borne by the individuals and not by society. Of course, in private insurance systems careful risk assessment may not actually take place or may be deliberately suppressed so that premiums may not fully reflect social costs but the incentive is there for insurers to do so.

Marginal Social Costs

Even if we manage to find an acceptable definition of social costs, we still have to estimate marginal rather than average social costs per unit of consumption in order to implement the rule (tax = marginal social cost). Marginal social cost could be greater or less than average social cost depending on the nature of the relationship between the total consumption of alcohol and the various indicators of 'harm', e.g. liver cirrhosis rates, driving/drunkenness offences, sickness absence rates. The crucial question to ask is whether or not these indicators rise or fall in line with rising or falling levels of consumption. In other words, the key question to ask is whether the 'consumption/harm' elasticity is unity. If it is unity then marginal social cost will be equal to average social cost. If not, then we have to look much more carefully at the precise relationship between consumption and harm.

This point is emphasised not just because it is important in conceptual terms but also because there is a very limited empirical literature on the precise relationship between consumption and harm. Many studies simply attempt to establish that there is a positive correlation between (for example) liver cirrhosis and consumption. There are very few studies that attempt to estimate precisely what the link is, taking full account of time lags, etc. This issue is discussed further in the chapter by Schweitzer, Intriligator and Salehi and in that by Cook. To illustrate this point, reference is made to a different paper (Skog, 1980a) that attempts to explain why, during the 1930s in the UK, the liver cirrhosis rate was dropping while consumption was rising. By looking at a long time series for the UK over the period of 1920-75, Skog finds that the male cirrhosis rate is correlated with a weighted average of the lagged values of consumption using a Koyck distributed lag model. The average lag implied by the model is of the order of 9-13 years,[5] so, to oversimplify drastically, liver cirrhosis rates now are a function of consumption levels 9-13 years ago.

Unfortunately, no estimate is given in Skog (1980a) of the value of the 'consumption/harm' elasticity, but rough calculations based on his graphs suggest the value is about 2, which is substantially larger than the critical value of unity. In other words, the marginal social cost for at least one indicator of harm is well above average social cost. In contrast, the data on spirits consumption and cirrhosis mortality given in Cook (1981) for the USA suggest a 'consumption/harm' elasticity less than one (about 0.4), although of course spirits consumption grew faster than total ethanol consumption over the period considered (1962-77).

Another piece of evidence that is relevant here is Table 9.5 in the chapter by Davies. This table indicates that per capita consumption in France or Italy is about double that in the UK or Ireland, but cirrhosis death rates in France or Italy are about eight times the corresponding levels in the UK. One has to be careful about drawing conclusions from international comparisons, but this table again suggests that marginal social costs exceed average social cost.

An Alternative Theoretical Approach

The theoretical apparatus that most economists were taught at an early age is based on the proposition that individuals derive utility from the consumption of goods and services. If one makes certain assumptions about behaviour, for example, that individuals rank in order of preference alternative bundles (combinations) of goods and services, that individuals prefer more to less and that marginal utility diminishes as more and more of a given commodity is consumed, then one can derive demand curves of conventional downward-sloping shape.

It has to be admitted that economists tend to be rather cautious about extending this theoretical approach to addictive substances because the underlying assumptions of the model may be violated. For example, the desired level of consumption of an addictive substance depends on how much you have previously consumed and marginal utility may increase over time in an unplanned way. Nevertheless, economists do tend to work in terms of this framework.

However, an alternative approach (associated with the name of Kelvin Lancaster) has recently been developed which emphasises that consumers derive utility not from the goods or services themselves, but from the *characteristics* of those goods. The advantage of thinking in these terms is that greater emphasis is laid on whether the characteristics of a particular good are similar to those of other goods and services. For example, in the case of alcohol the characteristics offered may be similar to those offered by other psychotropic drugs and the clear implication is that we should not study alcohol in total isolation but examine the extent to which the demand for, let us call it, the 'relief of stress' characteristic may be met by the consumption of different mind-altering substances (alcohol, tobacco, cannabis, barbiturates, tranquillisers, etc.).

All this is probably blindingly obvious to alcohol researchers and clinicians. Indeed, they probably all think in these terms already. This commentary has set out to state that economists have developed this new approach which might have fruitful applications, not just to alcohol research but to the whole field of the use and misuse of psychotropic drugs.

Notes

1. An elasticity is the percentage change in the dependent variable (in this case per capita consumption of an alcoholic beverage) resulting from the percentage change in an independent variable (for example price or income). An income elasticity of +1.5 implies that a 1 per cent change in income leads to a 1.5 per cent increase in consumption.
2. In the case of the USSR Treml (1975) quotes low price elasticities for alcoholic beverages as a whole.
3. Welfare economics is the study of normative aspects of economics.
4. Consumers' surplus is the difference between what consumers are willing to pay and what they actually pay.
5. This estimate is derived from the estimates of the lag parameter (x) quoted by Skog using the formula for the average lag $x/(1 - x)$.

3 PROGRAMMES, INTERESTS AND ALCOHOL

Dean R. Gerstein

Introduction

The principal aim of this chapter is to cast some useful light on the purposes that cost and benefit analyses of alcohol use and misuse may serve. First, the chapter reviews the logical principles that govern the reckoning of cost and benefit deriving from alcohol use and misuse. This review recalls the origins of such principles. Its main argument is to distinguish a type of analysis here called programme comparison from the rather different set of analyses that are here called interest-demand calculations, and to distinguish their respective uses. The chapter then surveys some issues in measurement, that is methods of counting or figuring particular sums of alcohol use and misuse. The chapter opens some perspectives on estimates that have been widely circulated regarding the rate and effects of alcohol misuse in the US, discussing some problems in attributing significance to these figures, and commenting on their purposes.

The Logic of Cost and Benefit Analysis

Two main types of analyses can be used to assess the economic and epidemiologic effects of alcohol use. One of these two types approximates to what economists sometimes call cost-benefit analysis. But this is not the type that is ordinarily cited in public policy debates about alcohol. The other, more commonly cited type of analysis does not have a distinct name, although instances of it carry titles suggestive of cost-benefit analysis, such as 'the economic cost of alcohol abuse', 'the economic contributions of the alcoholic beverage industry', 'the prevalence of problem drinking', 'deaths related to alcohol', and the like.

I wish to draw a sharp distinction between the two types of analyses. To emphasise the distinction, the more particular name *programme comparisons* is assigned to CBA. The other type is called *interest-demand calculation*. Since the introduction of jargon by an author always puts an unwelcome burden on the reader, I will try

44 Programmes, Interests and Alcohol

immediately to lighten this, as best I can, with a reasonable if slightly roundabout explanation.

Both types of analyses derive from the view that society is an appropriate object for rational scientific study, a view that arose in the late eighteenth and early nineteenth centuries. The thinkers who first put quantitative teeth into the study of society were, principally, the utilitarians David Ricardo and Jeremy Bentham (Halevy, 1955). Ricardo, a highly successful stockbroker, Member of Parliament, and distinguished theorist of enterprise, taxation and trade, viewed the study of political economy as a particular means by which the expansion of wealth could be facilitated. Bentham, the universal philosopher of his time in England felt that scientific analysis of human behaviour would prove essential for achieving the great object of all economic, political and ethical inquiry, namely, achievement of the greatest happiness of the greatest number. The optimism of early nineteenth-century utilitarianism has been fulfilled, in the sense that social-scientific and especially economic analysis has indeed moved into the role of informing and guiding decisions that bear on the wealth and happiness of society (cf. Aaron, 1978).

But the sciences of society have never resolved an essential division between Ricardo's interest in the expansion of wealth and Bentham's concern for the mass distribution of happiness. This division spans a number of dimensions, but I am interested here in one consequence especially, the division of modern economics into two relatively autonomous zones of inquiry, usually called microeconomics and macroeconomics. This type of distinction is familiar to epidemiology and to the other behavioural and social sciences; but in economics as in the other fields, the particular way in which the distinction is drawn varies from analyst to analyst. For my purposes here, I would like to think of it as a contrast in the level and character of decision-making. A micro-decision is one made by an individual or a relatively small social unit, trying to evaluate alternative programmes of action across a large field, the overall nature of which it does not hope to affect, but through which it can hope to navigate in an optimally self-improving or self-preserving way. A macro decision is one made collectively by a large group, or its leadership, that is designed to modify its whole field of action in the interest of a common good, thus altering the incentives, opportunities, penalties, and to some degree the motivations that generally shape the actions of its constituent micro decision units.

Of course, there is no more assurance that macro decisions will have the desired effect than that micro ones will achieve optimal results

(National Research Council, 1980). But I am interested here less in the results of decisions than in the analytic and informational needs of decision-makers.

For micro units, what matters is the cost and benefit of possible courses of action for the units themselves and for their immediate clients or dependants. Cost and benefit that fall external to the decision-making unit and its coterie are, if not disregarded, at least heavily discounted. For macro actors, there is no such discount for 'external' cost or benefit. These are calculated in relation to the whole, for all of the parties affected. Instead of externalities there are internal transfers of cost or benefit, which may be deemed good, bad or relatively indifferent on some other grounds of calculation or principle.

In gathering data and calculating prospects, a micro analysis is oriented to the projected results of action. Its method is first to postulate a series of alternative programmes of action over a defined period of time (in the simplest case, the alternatives of continuing the *status quo ante* v. changing it in some detail). Then the assorted elements of cost and benefit that would accumulate for the immediate company under each alternative programme are forecast. Next, the net balance of projected cost and benefit for each programme is calculated. Finally, the programmes are rank ordered, or less ideally, sorted roughly, according to the direction and quantity of their overall result. This is cost-benefit analysis; comparing alternative programmes by forecasting in each case the net balance of cost and benefit for the company of immediate interest, in order to determine and select the most favourable alternative. Hence such analyses are called *programme comparisons*.

Two important notes should be interjected here, before introducing the other type of analysis. First, the most obvious scale for an economist to use in analysing cost and benefit is a monetary one. The cost of a programme may be treated as the monetary-equivalent sums of all its expenses, or, in other words, as the total cost of its factors of production. For example, time and effort can be represented as a total wage bill, land as a rental or depletion value, capital consumed as an amortised payment; even entrepreneurial costs (e.g. 'good will' that is drawn on, or secured by propaganda or other means) can be converted to a cash equivalent. The benefit of the programme can be treated in parallel as an aggregate of produced commodities valued at their market prices. For example, employment days, property gains or losses, lives, or increments to education or skills (human capital) may each be converted by formula to a present cash value. With all cost and benefit transformed into such values, the net profit or loss associated with each programme may be calculated in monetary terms, and these 'bottom lines' easily compared.

To be sure, economists are by no means hobbled by an inflexible obeisance to monetary metrics. The mathematical tools of microeconometric analysis can accommodate a variety of units. It should be kept in mind, however, that whenever programme cost and benefit can not all be reduced to a single dimension, the result will have a degree of indeterminacy. Which leads to the second note.

The worth of programme comparisons varies quite directly with the precision with which one can delineate the alternative programmes, forecast their results, and compare the net balances of these respective forecasts against each other. Each of these operations can be troublesome. The relation between a programme as envisioned and as actually implemented – hence the precision with which one can define it – is precarious, especially so the more innovative the programme. The forecasting of results generally hinges on vagaries in the environment or field of action, which often can only be presumed to 'remain equal' or to 'follow straight-line projections', presumptions that are frequently dashed by events. And finally, as indicated, results can not always be reduced to a single scale or dimension, or purged of very wide confidence intervals. Thus, the conclusion of a programme comparison may well have the following character:

Programme A would cost somewhat less than the current programme but would be the most troublesome to co-ordinate; it is not likely to yield less benefit than the present operation, but is also quite unlikely to improve on it.

Programme B would cost about twice as much as the present programme, it would be relatively easy to administer, and it would definitely deliver more. But how much more is uncertain: somewhere between one and a half and three times the current result.

Programme C would be very cheap, but it may or may not last for long in the present climate; if it does stick, its result will be much better even than Programme B; but if it does not, the result will be nil, and restarting one of the other alternatives will be difficult and expensive.

A programme comparison may thus leave plenty of room for the exercise of judgement, including the expression of risk preferences, bowing to overall fiscal winds, hedging with multiple programmes and the like.

When comparing programmes, a goal or policy direction is already given, and the aim is to analyse the efficiency of alternative means or policy instruments, taking into account mainly – if not exclusively – the direct cost and benefit accruing to the acting decision unit and its clientele. The second type of analysis to be reviewed here *does not begin with specific programmes* for which forecasting and subsequent weighing of bottom lines is the business at hand. Instead, this type tries to gauge cost and benefit as total opportunities for gain or loss, independent of any specifically-formulated programme proposal. For this type of analysis, the goal or policy is not to be taken as settled; indeed, the aim of these analyses is to provide macro decision-making units with information that will aid in the formulation of goals or policies, by identifying and indicating the scope or size of relevant social interests. The sense of interests that I intend here is drawn from political systems theory, particularly as developed by Easton (1957) and elaborated by Parsons (1969; Gould, 1981; Warner and Cartwright, 1976). This view conceives of the government as, in part, an arbiter of claims submitted by different parties in the societal community, claims for which formulation of government policy is the appropriate response. These claims are called 'interest-demands'; hence this type of analysis is called *interest-demand calculation*.

There are four important aspects to such demands. First, while they may be privately motivated by any number of needs or wishes, the advancement of such claims in a modern democratic state requires that the demands be formulated in terms appropriate to broadly-held conceptions of the 'public interest'. Present-day conceptions of public health, national and domestic security, opportunities for employment and entrepreneurial activity, and a variety of other rights and entitlements comprise the language of public interest, and thus provide the categories in which interest-demands have to be conveyed.

The second, following point is that the sum of interest-demands that could be expressed always far outstrips the capacities of government to respond effectively. To be sure, a government may choose to announce new policies to settle each and every claim, but the result of such promiscuous policy-making is the inflation of policy into empty rhetoric, and the dilution of authority into posture. To retain the effectiveness of their decisions and the legitimacy of their commitments, governments must pick and choose sparingly among interest-demands. These demands therefore need to be compared or balanced against one another. This balancing or comparison may take several forms. One possibility is that a series of interest-demands may be ordered in terms of priority within a class; for example, there may be designated a number one public health problem, a number two public health problem, and so forth. This ordering could become a guide for deciding the relative quantity of government resources allocated to each problem within the class, a decision that may be made without comparing specific programmes that might be undertaken within the proposed allocations. This type of priority-setting requires the analyst first to identify the members of the class, e.g. public health problems, and then to arrange estimates of their respective sizes in terms of whatever metric is most acceptable, e.g. morbidity, mortality, service delivered, etc.

In a larger context, each class of problems (e.g. health, crime, defence, unemployment, underinvestment, etc.) may need to compete with the other classes, and thus common metrics need to be found for quite diverse interests, in order to help decide allocations. The most attractive course for the claimants representing given interests may well be to calculate the scope of their claims to public consideration as generously, and on as many dimensions, as possible.

The third point is that interest-demands may be in conflict, not only in the sense that a limited capacity for government action is available, but also in that policies providing benefit to one interest may impose or transfer costs to another interest. Whatever the size (and whether or not it is possible to estimate the size) of such transfers, it is of considerable interest to macro decision-makers to take some measure of the size of the interests that array themselves on the different sides of a policy debate, even though such a calculus of conflicting interests will seem crude if laid against the greater apparent precision of virtually any programme comparison.

If one can crudely judge, for example, that the industrial activity associated with alcohol use is roughly on a par with the medical activity associated with its misuse, on some measure which makes it possible to compare these two, then one can expect (or demand) that macro decision-makers pay roughly equal attention to the interest-demands addressed to alcohol policy from each of these two sectors, in contrast to what the case would be if the industrial interest exceeded the medical by an order of magnitude – or vice versa. This judgement of scope is independent of the cost and benefit of any particular programme proposal; in fact, the possibility that programme proposals may be considered at all is heavily predicated on the interest-demand calculations employed by macro decision-makers.

The final point is that governments, and in particular, governmental agencies in a competitive, pluralistic state, do not necessarily await with equanimity the free presentation of interest-demands, choosing passively among those accumulated. State agencies may actively encourage or discourage, attract or avoid, shape or amplify interest-demands, a process that is sometimes called 'constituency-building'. The modern bureaucratic state may thereby reflect, reproduce and recombine within itself the conflicts and factions of the society that it governs. When this constituency-building process is well developed, the distinction between programme comparisons and interest-demand calculations becomes somewhat muted, as the requirements of efficient programme selection and management on the one hand, and of maintaining continuity in the alignment of supportive interests on the other, become inseparable or interchangeable criteria for decision-makers in government agencies. This is most especially true when the time horizon across which programme pay-offs are to be calculated is a long period, and when the programmes under review have effects that ramify into a number of areas of public interest, such as fiscal policy, public health and industrial regulation.

To sum up the argument: two distinct sorts of accounting procedures tend to be thought of as types of cost-benefit analysis. The first type involves explicit comparison of the net local cost and/or benefit of alternative programmes for achieving a given goal or objective. This type of approach is called programme comparison. The second type of analysis involves the estimation and (often implicit) contrasting of the global scope of interests that advance public claims relevant to determining government policies or resource allocations, claims that typically derive from interests (or their representatives) that expect to register benefit or cost as a result of political decision-making. This type of analysis is referred to as interest-demand calculation.

For the most part, policy discussions of alcohol use and misuse have drawn most heavily on calculations of interest-demand rather than on programme comparisons (for some early and valuable exceptions, see Warburton, 1932; Shadwell, 1923). The latter section of this chapter discusses the significance of the several most prominent of such calculations in the US. Before entering into particular calculations, however, it is necessary to survey some general issues bearing on the measurement of alcohol use and misuse.

Measuring Alcohol Use and Alcohol Misuse

Before one can speak of measurement, definitions must be put in order and in context. Ethyl alcohol is a volatile, universal solvent with many applications in research and manufacture. Certain common micro-organisms can, without much ado, produce large amounts of this alcohol while digesting (more precisely, fermenting) nearly any kind of fruit or grain. Alcohol so produced mixes freely with water, and it can thus be concentrated (by distillation) or diluted in virtually any beverage. In nearly every known society, many people like to drink such beverages. All of these properties help to explain why alcohol products have become cheap mass commodities with quite important roles in the economies of many societies.

But as a rule, when people speak of alcohol use, what they mean is more specific: drinking as such. This common-sense meaning of alcohol use is too narrow to serve our purposes, but it is worth spelling out. Sulkunen (1976, 1978) has conveniently identified three kinds of *use values* for alcohol. Beyond these use values, and of central importance for modern economic analysis, the concepts of exchange value and utility will be introduced.

The use values of alcohol are as a foodstuff, as a symbol of society and as an intoxicant. As a food, alcohol itself is a carbohydrate; most alcoholic beverages contain additional nutrients and flavours; these beverages are generally quite resistant to spoilage or infestation, and they are free of most waterborne diseases. Thus, fermented beverages have long been agricultural staples that people use to satisfy hunger, thirst and cuisinary tastes (Gastineau *et al.*, 1979).

Secondly, alcohol carries symbolic values that are independent of its nutritive effects, for example, the religious symbolism of communion and sabbath wines, the celebratory moments that are marked by champagne, the slave-trade heritage of 'demon rum', and the laughter in numberless jokes about drunkenness. More commonly, the offer and acceptance of alcoholic drinks conventionally signifies a range of social bonds from casual affection to serious intent.

Lastly, alcohol is an intoxicant, with multiple effects on mood, alertness and dexterity. It is a stimulant and depressant, euphorigen and soporific, irritant and anxiety reducer — the mixture depending in particular instances on a myriad of factors such as dose and schedule of use, individual metabolism, personality factors and situation. Alcohol, like most other intoxicants, can produce such chronic dependency phenomena as persistent search behaviour, withdrawal, relapse and loss of control (Jaffe, 1980).

The idea of use value has a counterpart economic notion of *exchange value*: that is, aside from the use that someone with a stock of alcohol might personally make of it, he (or she) can trade part or all of this stock for something else, some other goods or services. Of course, in a commoditised economy, such trades or exchange of goods are not arranged by simple barter, but are transferred indirectly through the medium of money. Where this intermediary is broadly used, alcohol and other commodities acquire a set of standardised values in the form of market prices; and where such prices are established for most goods and services in a society, alcohol acquires a calculable cash value relative to (almost) everything and anything else. Given appropriate conditions in the producer and consumer markets — such as scale economies, imperfect competition and continuity in custom — the production and trade in alcohol products can generate steady surplus exchange value, which may be retained as regular profits. Moreover, any unit of alcohol, from a single drink to the entire annual production, can be measured in money.

However, the principal interest here is not the exchange or cash value of alcohol *per se*, but the measurement of alcohol use and misuse. The cash equivalent of the value of alcohol use (its utility) is not simply the market price of the alcohol used. Where alcohol is priced cheaply and widely used, the total value of its use (its total utility) can safely be assumed to be much greater than what people actually pay for it. However, totting up this cash value of total utility is not easy, and economists have little interest in the exercise, in part because this figure would only make sense in relation to the total utility of all goods and services produced in society — as distinct from their total market prices, which when added up are the gross domestic product — or in relation to a dramatic overall societal decision about whether alcohol should or should not be produced, a decision that in most societies today is clearly moot.

In contrast to thinking about the total utility of alcohol use, one can think about the marginal utility, that is, what value could be placed on a small increase or decrease in the amount that people currently drink. This kind of inquiry is the bread and butter of economic analysis. By observing the effect of small changes in price on the quantity of alcohol that people purchase (or the effect of small changes in available quantities on the market price), economists are able to infer how much people value its use, or at least how much they value being able to purchase one more drink.

To this point nothing has been said about the concept of alcohol misuse. The introduction of this concept subtly alters the grounds of discussion, for it widens the focus from drinking, or voluntary consumption decisions *per se*, to the effects or consequences, intended and unintended, of drinking. To study this broader field entails a series of problems in measurement that have their roots in the difference between counting objects, on the one hand, and attributing causes, on the other. A brief mathematical digression may help clarify the problem.

Counting is a process of establishing correspondence between the mental system of cardinal numbers (1, 2, 3, and so on) and some set of visible objects or events in the concrete world. In everyday life, our notion of counting is most firmly grounded in the availability of fingers, which we can easily use to measure and record (within obvious limits) the plurality of objects around us. The most primitive counting procedure is the one-to-one association of consecutive fingers with distinct objects — traditionally apples and oranges. Whatever complex form may be imposed on it, the link between numbers and objects is always forged in the notion of one-to-one correspondence: we imagine that a basket or collection of discrete objects (fruit or bottles, deaths or sickbeds, coins or bills, consecutive marks on a dial or stick) may be reliably associated with one specific number along the fixed sequence of cardinal (counting) numbers, where this association consists of pairing, one at a time, objects in the basket with consecutive numbers in the sequence, until every last object is paired. That this correspondence is so natural to us and easily visualised lies at the heart of our interpretation of all measures.

Yet most of the operational measures used in economics, epidemiology and all other sciences are actually estimated figures rather than counts, and are derived from collections of data by sophisticated interpolative procedures far removed from the simplicity of one-to-one correspondence. This interpolation from available data to numerical estimate always depends on some concept of a causal relation, that is, a (partially or wholly proven) theory about cause and effect. But for virtually every effect of alcohol use that is of economic or epidemiologic interest, alcohol is neither a necessary nor an always-sufficient cause, but is rather one in a series of factors that combine in various ways to yield the effect. These effects are what we characterise on some normative scale as good or bad. *The presence of bad effects, theoretically interpreted to be caused by drinking, is what we mean by alcohol misuse.*

The problem is that in measuring what we can agree are bad effects, such as fatal, injurious or damaging accidents, bodily illness, decreased or inefficient work, and strife or violence at home or in public places, we find that such effects do not divide neatly into those that are caused by alcohol and those that are not. For example, sustained heavy alcohol use can be clearly and demonstrably proven to cause, under appropriate conditions, the pathological and potentially fatal liver deterioration called cirrhosis. The data on this connection are stronger than those linking heavy cigarette smoking with lung cancer. But the mechanism by which alcohol use causes this gradual breakdown of liver cells into scar tissue is still speculative. Cirrhosis can also occur in people who have never drunk alcohol. Various nutritional deficiencies or imbalances can not only cause cirrhosis directly, but can markedly change the vulnerability of liver tissue to alcohol-induced cirrhosis. (Good nutrition almost certainly cannot prevent alcoholic cirrhosis; but bad nutrition can certainly hasten it along.)

Another example is road accidents. Drunken driving is notoriously a precursor to accidental fatalities. But no more than one in 500 to 2,000 drunken driving episodes (as legally defined) results in arrest in the US, and there are far more arrests than fatalities. The vast majority of road accidents, and the bulk of road fatalities, occur without benefit of alcohol. A series of expensive quasi-experimental studies and subsequent Bayesian analysis have been required to make defensible quantitative estimates of alcohol's causal contribution to accidental death and disability (Reed, 1981).

These two examples involve negative effects on physical well-being. Similar issues arise in looking at psychological and social well-being. A number of studies have found some common properties among the personalities of diagnosed alcoholics: depression, anxiety, low frustration tolerance, feelings of powerlessness, etc. These can be interpreted as effects of the disease, alcoholism. But virtually the same properties have been deemed by some researchers to *cause* alcoholism (MacAndrew, 1981). If depression is both a cause and effect of pathologically heavy drinking, how can one decide what proportion of an alcoholic's depression, or of suicides that occur in depressive episodes, is due to drinking?

Similarly, attempting to pinpoint the exact part played by drinking in problematic social behaviour is exceedingly difficult, compounded as it is by interaction with others during numerous situations over time. Statistical methods to separate alcohol consumption from other causes do offer some help in disentangling multiple causes, but since the problems are generally long-term ones, in which both the drinker and significant others build up a history of cumulative perceptions and judgements, such attempts to isolate and assign weight to one factor may have little relationship to reality.

To conclude this discussion: alcohol use and misuse are not really parallel terms. Alcohol use is generally taken to mean 'drinking' as such, while alcohol misuse refers to a set of negatively valued (bad) events that are interpreted to have been caused by drinking, that is, in the absence of drinking they would presumably have not occurred at all or occurred with lower frequency. It is easier (though by no means free of difficulties; cf. Gerstein, 1981) to measure drinking *per se* than its effects, especially to evaluate these effects in terms of benefit and cost, utility and disutility. Rather than make an abstract survey of the problems, a review is presented of sets of calculations that have been circulated in the US in recent years, each attempting to portray an aggregate measure of alcohol misuse.

Aggregate Alcohol Misuse: Three Approaches

The accounts of alcohol misuse to be discussed here were prepared for the National Institute on Alcohol Abuse and Alcoholism (NIAAA), and were prominently featured in the *Third Special Report to the US Congress on Alcohol and Health* (NIAAA, 1978a). Each examines a different dimension of effects: mortality; economic costs; and psycho-behavioural problems.

Mortality

Table 3.1, compiled by Day (1977), and reproduced in the 1978 report to Congress (NIAAA, 1978a), estimates that the number of cause-specific deaths related to alcohol use in the US in 1975 was between 61,000 and 95,000. The basis of this estimate was an exhaustive review of the epidemiological evidence. It seems to be as accurate an estimate as the state of the art permitted at the time. But the associated text in the NIAAA report notes that other mortality studies have respectively estimated 140,000; 185,690; and 'as high as 205,000 deaths per year', which the report points out 'was 11 per cent of the total 1.9 million deaths [in the US] in 1975'. The largest figure has consequently received the widest publicity.

Although the report cites no source for the largest figure, these estimates in excess of Day's range are not fanciful. A comprehensive

Table 3.1: Estimated Deaths Related to Alcohol in the United States, 1975

Cause of death	Number of deaths 1975	Percent related to alcohol	Estimated number related to alcohol
Alcohol as a direct cause			
Alcoholism	4,897	100	4,897
Alcoholic psychosis	356	100	356
Cirrhosis	31,623	41-95	12,965-30,042
Total	36,876		18,218-35,295
Alcohol as an indirect cause			
Accidents			
Motor vehicle	45,853	30-50	13,756-22,926
Falls	14,896	44.4	6,614
Fires	6,071	25.9	1,572
Other*	33,026	11.1	3,666
Homicides	21,310	49-70	10,442-14,917
Suicides	27,063	25-37	6,766-10,013
Total	148,219	29-40	42,816-59,708
Overall Total	185,095		61,034-95,003

* Includes all accidents not listed above, but excludes accidents incurred in medical and surgical procedures.
Source: NIAAA (1978a, p. 13; data from Day, 1977, and National Center for Health Statistics, 1975).

study of deaths among clinical alcoholics (Schmidt and Popham, 1980b; also see Polich, Armor and Braiker, 1980) suggests how the totals in Table 3.1 might plausibly be increased. In 12,000 alcoholism patients in Ontario, Canada, followed up for an average of 8½ years, over 1,000 *excess* deaths (compared to age-standardised population norms) were attributed to the causes given in Table 3.2. Forty per cent of the deaths in Table 3.2 were from causes not directly considered in Table 3.1; hence, a figure in the range of 150,000 for annual deaths 'related to alcohol' in the US (which is quite comparable to Ontario in the relevant respects) might be plausible, presuming mainly that untreated alcoholics have run the same death risks as clinical patients.

But what does this mean? The authors of this Canadian study caution that alcoholics smoke cigarettes at considerably higher rates than comparison populations, and hence that the excesses of heart disease and cancer deaths are associated to some degree with tobacco rather than alcohol exposure. They also warn that nutritional and other life-style factors intervene in the relation between drinking alcohol and

56 *Programmes, Interests and Alcohol*

Table 3.2: Percentage of Excess Deaths in a Clinical Alcoholic Population in Canada

Heart disease	20% *
Accidents	20
Cirrhosis	16
Suicide	12
Alcoholism	9
Cancers of the mouth, throat, esophagus, windpipe	9 *
Pneumonia/bronchitis	6 *
Alimentary ailments	5 *
Other causes	3
Total	100%

* Not counted in Table 3.1.
Source: Adapted from Schmidt and Popham (1980b).

alcoholics dying. In addition, if we wished to determine how alcohol affects the overall death rate in the US, that is, to discover its net causal impact, then we would have to estimate both deaths resulting from and deaths prevented by alcohol use. There is some evidence, for example, that moderate patterns of drinking may be correlated with decreased risk of death, particularly death due to ischemic heart disease; but this effect may be confuted by collinear variations in nutrition or other behaviour (cf. Schmidt and Popham, 1981). Being 'related to' or 'correlated with' are not as such causal analyses, and especially are not net causal results.

The 150,000 figure is, in effect, simply a pool within which whatever deaths that might be caused by alcohol — and thus possibly prevented by minimising its misuse — are to be found. One can think of this pool as deaths for which alcohol was a probable contributing risk factor. But many of these deaths were sufficiently strongly determined by the concatenation of other risk factors that they would have occurred during the year even if no alcohol were involved. Thus, the actual number of deaths that the radical elimination of alcohol use or misuse might prevent, all other things being equal, would be substantially less than the pool figure. How much less is not certain; 50,000 deaths theoretically preventable each year seems a reasonable guess.

The main point here is that all of these mortality figures amount to a demand for public attention by the medical interest in public health. Any of these figures argues persuasively that alcohol misuse is a major public health concern. It makes little difference, in gaining the attention of policy-makers, whether 50,000, 95,000 or 200,000 deaths are mentioned; anywhere in this range of figures, the message of public health concern is loud and clear. Only further scientific study or a specific programme comparison would require a greater degree of precision.

Of course, none of these figures sets out a specific programme, or suggests what would be the results of programmes intended to prevent or further reduce deaths due to alcohol misuse. Since a complete quantitative estimate has not been attempted, one can only speculate what conclusions a policy analysis, drawing on the full range of current scientific knowledge and mobilising all of the relevant institutional resources, would draw concerning the actual number of lives that a major new commitment on the part of relevant US governmental units could realistically hope to save. One may speculate 20,000 lives a year, after a few years of effort, at a cost to be determined. This is not 200,000+, nor is it 50,000 — but it is not negligible.

Economic Costs

Table 3.3 is a tabulation of how much 'alcohol abuse and alcoholism cost the US in 1975'. This $42.75 billion figure is not a net cost estimate; that is, it is not intended to represent the net reduction in gross domestic product resulting from alcohol use. It is a conglomeration of several distinct dollar values: the discounted value of life-time earnings attributable to 69,000 people whose deaths in 1975 were estimated to have been alcohol-related (25 per cent of the $42.75 billion); lessened production by the civilian workforce, as estimated by certain household wage differentials (35 per cent); assignment of health care resources to alcohol-related problems (21 per cent); and assorted other estimates. This collection of dollar values is held by its authors (Berry *et al.*, 1977; Berry and Boland, 1977) to be the 'external cost' of alcohol abuse — paid not by the alcohol abuser, but by the rest of society. These values have been updated by Schifrin in Chapter 4.

It is very difficult to assign a precise significance to this precise-looking figure of $42.75 billion. For one thing, a large fraction of the costs tabulated here — from 25 per cent to 50 per cent of the total amount — do appear to be borne by the alcohol abuser, casting the 'external costs' interpretation into doubt. The transposition of 'associated with alcohol' into 'due to alcohol abuse', which is to say transformation of a correlational estimate into a causal claim, occurs in the discussion of this table although the authors supply instructions to

Table 3.3: Economic Costs of Alcohol Misuse and Alcoholism in the United States, 1975

Item	Cost (billions $)
Lost production	19.64
Health and medical	12.74
Motor vehicle accidents	5.14
Violent crime	2.86
Social responses	1.94
Fire losses	0.43
Total	42.75

Source: NIAAA (1978a, p. 17; from Berry et al., 1977).

the contrary. The lost production estimate makes implicit assumptions about the labour supply in 1975 — basically that it was short — that do not seem consistent with then-prevailing economic indicators (unemployment at 8.5 per cent): if labour is in over-supply, then alcohol misuse probably acts as a selection factor in labour-force participation, costing alcohol misusers their access to jobs, but not costing the society very much in net production. Along the same lines: the productivity of labour generally is considered to be a joint function of quantities of labour-power, human and material capital committed to production, and other factors; the lesser productivity of alcoholised workers may therefore result from their being shunted into undercapitalised or otherwise intrinsically less productive sectors of the economy.

It appears that this $42.75 billion dollar figure, like the large mortality numbers, is a pool within which lie whatever economic costs are incurred by alcohol misuse in the US annually. Many analysts believe the pool figure should be expanded, and no doubt it can be, although this operation usually involves enlarging the overall estimate of economic values produced in the US, and probably reduces the relative proportion of the product statistically lost to alcohol misuse.

My central point, in any case, is that this calculation, whatever its other merits, is intended principally to establish that alcohol misuse is an economic interest that demands public attention. The calculation neither reflects a specific programme proposal nor stands in need of greater scientific precision or purpose. It has served as a model for deriving programme comparisons involving productivity gains as an output of occupational (employee assistance) programmes. More centrally, it has helped capture the attention and enthusiasm of legislators who would not otherwise find the public health rationales for government attention to alcohol misuse especially persuasive.

Behaviour

In Table 3.4, approximately 1 in 10 drinking adults in the US (about 10 million people) are classified as 'problem drinkers'; an additional 1 in 4 (25 million) are classed as 'potential problem drinkers'; while the other 65 million or so drinkers reportedly had 'no problems'. How can these figures be interpreted? In the original version of this table (Johnson et al., 1977), the authors listed the three problem categories as 'frequent problem-drinking systems', 'potential symptoms', 'no symptoms'. The most common of these symptoms ('frequently' or 'sometimes but not often': taking two or three drinks at one sitting, or going several days or weeks without taking a drink and then having several drinks at one time) are indistinguishable from criteria for moderate drinking patterns. The next most common symptoms (frequently or sometimes but not often: talking a lot about drinking, showing the effects of liquor more quickly than most people, taking a drink to feel better) are not, on their face, problems. Sixty per cent of the reported symptoms fall into one of the categories above.

What light do these data shed on the scope of alcohol misuse? The original authors warned that 'this problem index is presented for comparison purposes over time and should not be used as an absolute definition of problem drinkers'. A few categories of symptoms (not the common ones listed above) are markedly more prevalent among heavier drinkers than other drinkers. But the conglomeration of assorted causes, effects and frequencies associated with drinking, and the subsequent renaming of these categories as representing types of drinkers, add nothing to the observation that there was relative stability between 1973 and 1975 in reports of drinking patterns in the general population.

The significance of this analysis of psycho-behavioural patterns is that the number of adults in the US whom one might have to corral in order to segregate all, or at least the great bulk, of people who are 'at risk' of alcohol misuse is very large, on the order of 10 million to 35 million people. Of course, only a small minority of these tens of millions (a few million at most) actually create dangers or significant discomforts to themselves or others due to alcohol misuse in a given year. But to distinguish these few million from the pool of many million drinking brethren would be an enormously expensive proposition. In effect, this analysis tries to establish the size of the

60 *Programmes, Interests and Alcohol*

Table 3.4: Rates of Problem Drinking Among US Drinkers, by Drinking Population, 1973-5

	Percentages for each survey			
Drinking population	March 1973	January 1974	January 1975	June 1975
All drinkers				
No problems	64	70	65	63
Potential problems*	26	24	24	26
Problem drinkers**	11	6	10	10
Males				
No problems	57	66	62	57
Potential problems*	29	27	23	31
Problem drinkers**	14	8	15	13
Females				
No problems	74	77	70	73
Potential problems*	21	19	27	21
Problem drinkers**	5	4	3	6

* A potential problem drinker experienced two or three of sixteen problem drinking symptoms frequently or four to seven symptoms sometimes.
** A problem drinker experienced four or more of sixteen problem drinking symptoms frequently or eight or more symptoms sometimes.
Source: NIAAA (1978a, p. 15; adapted from Johnson *et al.*, 1977).

risk pool within which any programme of preventive measures would need to be broadcast in order to reach most alcohol misusers. These figures argue that from a demographic point of view, the interest in alcohol misuse is a broad one.

Conclusion

The principal aim of this chapter has been to identify and distinguish the purposes which govern the analysis of cost and benefit associated with alcohol use and misuse. Two distinct kinds of analysis were noted: first, comparison of alternative programmes meant to achieve certain limited sets of objectives; and second, calculation of the scope of interests demanding the generalised attention of collective policy-makers. In the first instance, the considerations guiding the analysis are prudent management of limited resources for the sake of a particular subset of acting units. Such programme comparisons stress precision, and imprecise results vitiate the analysis. In the second instance, the guiding consideration is how the calculation can affect the overall allocation of government attention and resources, given the full range of competing interests and issues. These calculations of interest-demand stress generality rather than precision; their governing principle is to translate the scope of the issue into a metric appropriate to the public interest.

In both cases, there are issues of measurement to be considered. In bringing these considerations to bear on some recent attempts to calculate the scope of interests derived from public health, economic and psycho-behavioural perspectives, this review tried to interpret the figures in terms of the ambiguities in measuring alcohol misuse, while emphasising the overall policy intentions that such calculations are designed to serve. It is appropriate to conclude that, notwithstanding specific problems in assessing needs or designing programmes, the evidence is persuasive that alcohol misuse generates a remarkable amount of trouble in the United States, and that the overall social interest in maintaining and improving measures to reduce this amount is substantial (cf. Moore and Gerstein, 1981).

Acknowledgement

The author is indebted to the Panel on Alternative Policies affecting the Prevention of Alcohol Abuse and Alcoholism (NIAAA contract No. ADM 281-78-0006) of the National Academy of Sciences, and especially to its Chairman, Mark H. Moore, for encouragement to explore such sinews of thought as are exposed in this chapter. Particular thanks go to Philip Cook, Thomas Schelling, Leonard Schifrin and Wolfgang Schmidt for some of the ideas used to direct this exploration.

4 SOCIETAL COSTS OF ALCOHOL ABUSE IN THE UNITED STATES: AN UPDATING

Leonard G. Schifrin

Introduction

In 1980 the Institute of Medicine (IOM) of the National Academy of Sciences issued a report on *Alcoholism, Alcohol Abuse, and Related Problems: Opportunities for Research*. Broadly stated, the purpose of the report was to 'review the research field and assess the scientific opportunities of particular research areas as viewed over the next five years'. The conclusions of that report can be stated in three ways:

First, alcoholism and alcohol abuse (hereafter simply referred to as 'alcohol abuse') impose large absolute societal costs in the forms of adverse health effects and psycho-social impacts, whether measured in terms of mortality, morbidity and other health criteria, or in terms of the real economic losses they generate. These economic losses for 1975 were estimated by Ralph Berry and others (Berry *et al.*, 1977) to be in the range of $39,898 million to $42,755 million. However, because of conservatism in their methodology and omissions from their calculations, the IOM report suggests that these costs may actually have been much larger, perhaps as high as $60,000 million for that year.

Second, the economic costs of alcohol abuse remain large when compared with the societal costs imposed by or associated with other major groups of disorders, such as cancer, heart and vascular disease, and respiratory disease. And third, comparing the research effort for each of these categories of disorder to its respective burden, research in alcohol abuse is seriously underfunded, particularly so in light of the progress already made in this area and the strong likelihood of significant incremental progress from incremental research endeavours. The economic cost-of-illness and research effort comparisons in the IOM report are reproduced in Table 4.1.

The numbers in Table 4.1 on their surface argue strongly for greater research effort in the alcohol problem area, but more perceptive readers rightfully have qualified, if not questioned, these data. For one thing, the economic cost measurements differ from one disease category to another in their inclusiveness; for another, all the respective research efforts probably are understated, perhaps unevenly, by the use of

Table 4.1: Health Research Dollars in Relation to Economic Cost

Disorder	NIH/ADAMHA Lead institute research effort 1978 $ in millions	Economic cost 1975 $ in billions (USA)	Research dollars per thousand dollars of cost $
Alcoholism/abuse	16	43	0.4
Cancer	627	19	30
Heart & vascular disease	284	46	6
Respiratory disease	69	19	4

Source: Institute of Medicine (1980).

budget figures from only the major federal research supporters — the National Institutes of Health and the Alcohol, Drug Abuse and Mental Health Administration. These criticisms are certainly valid; however, their effect is to modify slightly the above cost-of-illness comparisons and the research-to-economic cost ratios, rather than refute the general thrust of the data in Table 4.1 or the policy implications they offer.

A more serious criticism, though, rejects the Berry and IOM positions that $43,000 million is a 'conservative' estimate of the annual economic loss associated with alcohol consumption, and argues that this figure — which has become the conventional wisdom in the field — seriously exaggerates the economic dimensions of alcohol-related problems in the United States and, thus, is unreliable as a basis for policy decisions that allocate scarce health research funds. And if the $43,000 million is considered to be an exaggeration, it follows that the $60,000 million estimate suggested as a possible, if maximum, true annual cost in the IOM report is an implausible and unreliable figure.

Since the Berry work has come to occupy an important position in the literature on cost of illness in general and is the pre-eminent study on the cost of alcohol abuse, subsequent attempts to refine and update such estimates, including the effort of the IOM and this present work, necessarily draw heavily from it. In view of the criticisms of the Berry work, however, our use of it as the foundation on which to build current estimates of the societal costs of alcohol abuse must include a reconsideration of its strengths and limitations.

The objective of this chapter, then, is to offer an update of the Berry 1975 estimates to 1979, while taking into account the criticisms on both sides that have been aimed at it. Although this chapter does

64 Societal Costs of Alcohol Abuse in the United States

not offer a thorough, *de novo* recalculation, it does include previously omitted cost components, adjustments made to cost components included by Berry, some alterations in methodology, and accommodations to changes, particularly in the price level, in the economic environment between 1975 and 1979.

One main conclusion of this chapter is that when these inclusions and adjustments are made, the annual societal costs of alcohol abuse in the United States loom significantly larger than suggested by the Berry estimates for 1975, and even exceed the 'upper limit' estimated by the IOM.

Economic Costs of Alcohol Abuse: Methodology, Data and Revision

The societal costs related to alcohol abuse have been classified in various ways (Harwood and Cruze, 1980; Hodgson and Meiners, 1979), but four types of loss comprise most of what is quantifiable: (i) the loss in total production due to alcohol-related incapacity, absenteeism and deaths; (ii) the commitment of resources in the health care sector to the treatment of patients with alcohol-related problems; (iii) the various real losses to society from traffic accidents, fires and criminal acts in which alcohol is a factor; and (iv) the expenditure of resources by society to deal with the problems and effects of alcohol abuse through the social welfare network or public programmes in which alcohol abuse is the target.

Production Loss: Work Absenteeism

The largest economic cost associated with alcohol abuse is the lost production from diminished quantitative and qualitative participation in the work process. In 1975, $15,458 million, or about 36 per cent, of the total cost of alcohol abuse as calculated by Berry took this form.

Ideally, we would derive such estimates from the individual productivity differentials between alcohol abusers and non-abusers, compensating for all other differences between them. In the absence of such information, data on family *income* (which includes income from all sources, including labour, non-labour and transfer payments) have served as a proxy measure for individual productivity. Accordingly, the estimation of 'productivity' loss from alcohol abuse involves
(i) definition and measurement of the abuser population;

(ii) calculation of income differentials attributable to alcohol abuse between abuser and non-abuser families; and (iii) calculation of the aggregative income loss attributable to alcohol abuse for all abuser families in the population.

The basic 1968 survey data (Berry *et al.*, 1977) in this area provides estimates of the proportion of abuser families by age group and of the corresponding non-abuser-abuser family income differentials. These data have been updated to 1975 by Berry, and show an overall differential in excess of $2,700 in favour of households with no male alcohol abuser present. (The differentials by age group range from +$2,972 in the 40-49 age stratum to +$1,523 in the 50-59 age stratum) (Berry *et al.*, 1977). Harold Luft (1975), studying the relationships between health levels and earnings, attributes 24 per cent of earnings differentials between 'well' and 'sick' persons to characteristics other than health levels, and the remaining 76 per cent to differences in their health status categories. Accordingly, Berry, drawing on the Luft estimate, attributes 76 per cent of the abuser-non-abuser family income differential to alcohol abuse; on this basis he projects a population-wide productivity loss of $15,458 million.

The magnitude of this estimate warrants special attention. Admittedly, the data do not 'prove' alcohol-induced disability to be the cause of productivity loss of this magnitude; yet the estimate seems to fall far short of measuring the losses in output that are associated or related to alcohol abuse. For one thing, the definition of 'abuser' is a narrow one ('drinkers for whom drinking has high consequences'); further, it is limited to males, and only those between 21 and 59. Therefore, unless they happen coincidentally to be in a household where there already is a male alcohol abuser between 21 and 59, the productivity losses of (i) male abusers less than 21 or over 59, (ii) all female abusers, of all ages, and (iii) all males and females who are less than 'abusers' but incur some absenteeism or inefficiency related to alcohol use, are unrecorded.

Another rather obvious point is that comparisons of total *family income* differentials understate the respective *individual productivity* differentials, because employers may not reduce the incomes of workers (especially salaried employees) in proportion to productivity diminution, and because transfer payments and secondary worker entry into the labour force help sustain family income in the face of alcohol-related earnings declines. Still another important qualification of the data is that they totally exclude all losses in *non-market* production, i.e. household and community production, of both men and women, of all ages, resulting from or associated with alcohol consumption.

To what extent can these adjustments and eclusions be quantified, and what bearing would some approximation of their magnitudes have on the Berry estimates? Let us consider these several points in a slightly different order than presented above.

(1): Worker productivity losses from alcohol-related causes are borne, in part, in the form of income losses to others, that is, shifted to owners and fellow workers, as well as the alcohol-abusing worker. The losses from a reduction in the efficiency of a worker who is at work but suffering the health consequences of alcohol abuse are virtually impossible to determine. Lost output from lost work time may be only slightly less difficult to calculate; such losses also appear to be distributed, at least in part, among other factor providers in ways that defy accounting. Two hints that the losses of this nature to owners and management are large are the seemingly great corporate demand for alcohol treatment, counselling and other assistance services within the private sector, and evidence of the apparent cost-effectiveness of many of these programmes.

(2): The understatement of the alcohol-related productivity loss because of family income infusions from transfer payments and secondary worker entry into the labour force may well be the most serious source of understatement in the entire Berry analysis. Luft comments in that regard:

> While disability results in a 35 percent reduction in the earnings of the disabled, the family earnings of the disabled fall 'only' 16 per cent, reflecting the activity of other family members. (Luft, 1978)

Thus, it appears that the basic data on which the productivity loss estimate of $15,458 million is built may represent less than half of the true productivity loss from alcohol-related disability. On the basis of Luft's findings, the corrected estimate for 1975 lost production would be $33,814 million rather than $15,458 million, or an absolute increase of $18,356 million over the estimate from the previous method of calculation. Another way of stating the effects of this adjustment is that over $18,000 million of non-market production or activity was forgone by other family members, so that they could enter the labour market to restore, in part, the family income loss (and societal productivity loss) associated with male alcohol abusers, ages 21-59. This cost element previously has not been taken into account.

(3): What of the productivity loss from alcohol abuse among those below 21 or over 59 years of age? Here the evidence presents an odd mirror-image. Alcohol consumption among youths aged 20 and under seems to be a large and growing phenomenon, and this is particularly true for heavy drinking. Yet this age group also displays lower rates of 'alcoholism', much lower labour-force participation rates (about half as large as those for middle-age workers) and abnormal unemployment rates, which soften the productivity/income effects of any alcohol-related work problems of the young. (Heavy drinking among youths, though, may well have a decided hidden economic impact – a disinvestment in human capability by reduced productivity in the education process or by adverse effects on health – that will lead to sizeable revealed costs in later years, and which theoretically have a present value today.) For older drinkers, the reverse image appears, with the same result. Although they display lower levels of heavy alcohol consumption than young-to-middle-age workers, they have higher rates of alcoholism; further, a disproportionate number of alcohol-troubled workers are long-tenure (high wage) workers, thus indicative of a present productivity/income loss of possibly important proportions. However, on balance the data on income loss for alcohol-abuser families indicates a smaller loss for male workers in the age 50 to 59 category than in any other group, and the loss is likely to be even smaller for those 60 and older.

(4): The exclusion of women alcohol abusers from the data narrows the perspective very considerably. Male worker alcohol abuse, we have just calculated, resulted in a 1975 productivity loss of $33,814 million, a figure equal to about 5.7 per cent of total wage and salary disbursements paid to men. On the basis of a wide range of male:female alcohol-abuser prevalence ratios in the literature, ranging from 1:1 for private office practices and private hospitals to as high as 11:1 in prison populations (Greenblatt and Shuckitt, 1976), a 4:1 relative prevalence ratio seems plausible. Accordingly, we can assign to females a productivity/income loss associated with alcohol abuse one-fourth the rate of that for males, or 1.42 per cent of the female aggregate market-earnings base. For 1975, this loss, 1.42 per cent of total wage and salary disbursements earned by females ($260,000 million), comes to $3,692 million.

(5): The consideration of lost non-market production is also complex, and requires, at this point in our research, an equally broad brush. In the 'official' cost of illness literature produced by the Department of Health, Education and Welfare in the 1960s, household and community non-market labour effort for males was estimated at two hours per week, or about 5 per cent of the full-time work week of 40 hours (and a somewhat higher per cent of the average work week of 35 hours). Thus, an equivalent 5.7 per cent loss of this non-market contribution by males (itself equal, in total, to 5 per cent of the value of total male wage and salary earnings, or $30,250 million) adds another $1,728 million to the total 1975 alcohol-related productivity loss.

For females, although the proportion of household production lost to alcohol-associated factors is smaller than that for males due to their lower prevalence rates, their much greater volume of household production renders this source of loss a large one.

In a microeconomic perspective, housewives' production has been measured in various ways: at domestic worker hourly wage rates; by piecing together the various market wage rates for the respective functions performed in homemaking — nursing, meal preparation, cleaning, home decorating, chauffeuring, etc., weighted by the time spent on each; and by reference to earnings forgone by those who engage in homemaking and family care activities.

A macroeconomic perspective also can be used. Gronau, in a theoretical piece on the topic, reviews some of the literature in the field. He comments:

> Reconstructing the social accounts to generate a measure of economic welfare (MEW). Nordhaus and Tobin figured that the value of leisure and nonmarket work constituted in 1965 three-quarters of their measured MEW (the value of leisure accounting for about one-half and the value of labor inputs in home production accounting for one quarter of MEW). Morgan estimated that the inclusion of unpaid work in the national accounts would have increased gross national product in 1964 by 38 per cent. Sirageldin, using the same data as Morgan, states that had we measured the value of housework and home production, the average family's disposable income would have increased by 43 per cent. (Gronau, 1973)

The multiplicity of household services, their many providers, and the absence of market pricing mechanisms makes evaluation particularly difficult, but one may proceed with the Sirageldin estimate that non-market production equals 43 per cent of disposable income. In 1975, the aggregate disposable income, from the USA national income accounts, was $1,081,000 million, and 43 per cent of that figure is

$465,000 million. Of this, we already have calculated a share for males of $30,250 million; for females, then, the value of non-market output is estimated at $434,750 million. Earlier, the rate of productivity loss related to alcohol for women was estimated to be 1.42 per cent. Applying this to their share of non-market production, we obtain a loss estimate of $6,173 million.

Given the lack of data, we cannot calculate the productivity losses related to alcohol consumption at levels below those constituting 'abuse'. None the less, the additions we have made in this reappraisal loom large:

Berry's estimate of alcohol-related lost productivity in 1975, which is restricted to a narrow 'abuser population' definition and deals only with market activity, is $15,458 million. Raising the abuser-associated family earnings loss to account for the obscuring effect of secondary worker entry and transfer payment receipts adds $18,356 million to the 1975 societal cost of alcohol abuse. Including labour-force-participant women in the analysis raises the loss by another $1,311 million. Accounting for the non-market productivity losses of alcohol-abuser males adds $1,728 million; and the lost non-market productivity of alcohol-abuser females adds another $6,173 million.

The inclusion of the losses incurred by males below 21 and over 59 would increase the losses by an unknown amount, as would the losses incurred by all persons who are less than 'abusers' of alcohol.

Accordingly, the Berry figure of $15,458 million appears to be a very modest one. The calculations above would bring the estimated 1975 loss in the total civilian sector to $45,407 million, when all of the modifications in Berry's methodology and scope are accounted for.

Berry has calculated the productivity loss from alcohol abuse in the military as well, employing Cahalan's estimate that, in 1971, almost 19,000 man years were lost to military duty because of absences and reduced efficiency 'due to alcohol use'. This loss represents approximately 2 per cent of total man years available in the military, and thus 2 per cent of total military payroll is taken as the corresponding measure of the economic loss. This estimated cost for 1975 comes to another $411.3 million (Berry *et al.*, 1977).

Production Loss: Excess Mortality

While the excess mortality rates of both male and female alcohol abusers (abuser death rates expressed as multiples of non-abuser death

70 *Societal Costs of Alcohol Abuse in the United States*

Table 4.2: Estimated Excess Deaths for Males and Females Due to Alcohol Abuse, 1975

Age group	Males	Females
20-29	3,007	759
30-39	3,563	962
40-49	7,829	1,697
50-59	8,712	445
60-69	2,202	160
70 +	1,933	–
Total	27,246	4,023
Total male plus female		31,269

Source: Berry *et al.* (1977).

rates) range widely from one age group to another, the data indicate that alcohol abusers suffer above normal mortality rates at all ages (except possibly 60 and over); that the excess mortality rate tends to be higher for younger abusers than older; and that the relative mortality rates of female abusers, in general, exceed those of males (although the prevalence of female abusers is much lower within age groups than males, as noted earlier). The most reliable data put these excess mortality rates for all abusers at 4.18 for the age group 20-49 and 2.08 for ages 50-59. Disaggregating these data one level, the female excess mortality rate appears to be just about four times that of males (Berry *et al.*, 1977).

These excess mortality *rates* for abusers must be translated into an absolute *number* of excess deaths by reference to the alcohol-abuser prevalence rates. The resulting estimations of the number of such deaths in 1975 are provided in Table 4.2. As indicated by these data, 31,269 premature deaths were 'attributed' in 1975 to alcohol abuse (Berry *et al.*, 1977).

Using data on projected lifetime earnings[1] as calculated by the Social Security Administration and a discount rate of 6 per cent, the present value of future earnings (a proxy for output lost because of these premature deaths) has been calculated at $3,768 million for 1975.[2]

What can be said for the accuracy of this estimate, aside from the ubiquitous problems of measurement accuracy and the continuing caveat that economic effects 'associated with', 'related to', or even 'attributed to' alcohol use and abuse do not prove that they are necessarily *caused* by alcohol consumption? Lending to potentially sizeable understatement, as we have seen previously, is the omission of all non-market production of males (taken to have a value equal to 5 per cent of their market production), and some of that of women (in the Social Security calculations, housewives' services are given imputed values based on the market prices of such services). If only the 5 per cent non-market production of males is considered, the economic loss of premature mortality related to alcohol abuse rises from $3,768 million to $3,940 million, an increase of $172 million.

Lending to overstatement is the continuing problem of abnormally high unemployment rates in the USA, running about 2½–4 percentage points above 'normal'. If the present rates were to continue, our expected earnings data should be adjusted downward by an equivalent per cent. Four per cent of $3,768 million is $151 million, offsetting most of the upward adjustment from the inclusion of male non-market production loss. Accordingly, the Berry estimate for the present value of lost future production from the excess mortality of alcohol abusers is adjusted upward by a net amount of $21 million to $3,789 million.

Production Loss: The Excess Utilisation of Health Care Services Due to Alcohol Abuse

On the basis of (i) special studies estimating the level of utilisation by alcohol abusers of various components of the health care sector, namely hospitals, physician services, nursing home services and drugs and (ii) estimated population-wide prevalence rates for alcohol abuse, measurements of the *excess* utilisation of these four components and, by extension, other health services have been derived, and a proportionate share of the total expenditures for each component has been assigned as the cost of this excess utilisation. (This methodology has a unique twist: in calculating the per capita utilisation of each type of service by alcohol abusers and by non-abusers, the larger the estimate of the abuser prevalence rate, the smaller the per capita use by abusers and the greater that of non-abusers, and thus, the lower the level of excess or abnormal utilisation by abusers.) While the utilisation-of-services breakdown between alcohol abusers and non-abusers is based on a fairly narrow collection of special studies, in virtually every case the disproportionate use of either hospital capacity, physician services, mental health services or drugs is the observed result. As expected, the excess utilisation rates vary from one component to another, but where there are several studies of the same service (e.g. hospital care), the results, though not identical, are reasonably close, and all of the studies, as a whole, are mutually supportive.

As indicated, these results were extended to most of the other types of health service expenditure, and the overall estimate of excess health care utilisation 'due to alcohol abuse was . . . [$12,743 million] for 1975 or about 12 per cent of national health expenditures by or for adults' (Berry et al., 1977).

This estimate is certainly not a firm one, due to the narrowness of the underlying data base, but an examination of those data — which rely heavily on patient identification by type of health problem, and use proportionate assignments of health care costs to adult alcohol abusers and non-abusers — gives no particular indication of being an understatement or overstatement. But as long as alcohol abusers are believed to use the relatively more costly hospital services, assigning them a cost factor proportional to their share of total hospital days of inpatient care may tend to understate their use of all hospital provided care. Additionally, to whatever extent a stigma is attached to alcohol-related problems, they may be under-reported in the patient population.

Motor Vehicle Accidents

There are two main sources of data on the economic losses due to all motor vehicle highway accidents, the National Highway Traffic Safety Administration (NHTSA) and the National Safety Council (NSC). Due to differences in inclusiveness, assumptions and discount rates, the larger of the two estimates, that of the NHTSA ($36,837 million) runs about 75 per cent above that of the NSC ($21,200 million) for 1975 (Bureau of the Census, Statistical Abstract of the US, 1976; Berry et al., 1977). The contention that the lower figure is excessively conservative because of its numerous omissions and high discount rate is generally valid; but the other estimate is too high at least in comparison with the other costs associated with alcohol abuse, because of its inclusion of rather peripheral impacts. Accordingly, a figure approximately (but coincidentally) just about equally between the two, representing a range of economic impacts consistent with other facets of their study, is used. That figure for 1975 is $28,717 million. Of this, only a part is related to alcohol abuse, of course.

The extent to which alcohol abuse is considered a factor in motor vehicle accidents rests in large part on the Blood Alcohol Concentration

(BAC) level taken as the indicator of impaired driving ability. While many factors contribute to motor vehicle accidents, studies that have eliminated the effects of many other variables have found an association between high BAC levels (perhaps mixed in with any remaining variables) and motor vehicle crashes. These studies generally support the acceptance of a 0.10 per cent BAC as a valid benchmark for an increased likelihood of involvement in motor vehicle crashes both in *frequency* and *severity*, although in several studies a still lower BAC, 0.05 per cent, seems to make a difference in accident frequency.

While multicausation makes it difficult to identify alcohol consumption as the 'cause' of a given crash where a high BAC is present, a practical solution to the question of alcohol as a contributing factor is to calculate the difference between the rate of accident 'involvement' at BACs above the 0.10 per cent level and the rate at the 0.10 per cent level. The difference in 'involvement' rates thus gives dimension to the association of 'high' levels of alcohol presence and vehicular accidents, a so-called excess motor vehicle accident or crash level.

In Table 4.3, the 'estimated net percentage of crashes attributed [*sic*] to alcohol abuse' by Berry for 1975 are presented. The data support two conclusions: alcohol is a factor in all four accident categories, and the more so the more serious the crash. Applying these percentages to the modified 'compromise' estimate of the 1975 costs of crashes ($28,717 million), the total costs 'due to alcohol abuse' at BAC levels of 0.05 per cent and 0.10 per cent come to $6,047 million and $4,350 million respectively. At the 0.05 per cent level or above, alcohol abuse can be said to be related to 21 per cent of the total cost of vehicular crashes; at the 0.10 per cent level or above, it is related to 15 per cent of the total cost of vehicular crashes.

How do the arguable peripheral inclusions by Berry — funeral costs, legal and court costs, insurance administration and accident investigation — compare with the exclusions — the loss in non-market production from accidents, 'loss to others' not involved in the crashes, and traffic delay, all of which are counted by the NHTSA? The inclusions represent $2,175 million, or 6 per cent of all costs of crashes in the NHTSA report. The exclusions, on the other hand, would represent $8,120 million, or an amount equal to 22 per cent of the NHTSA total.

Again, there is the issue of causation to consider. The presence of alcohol appears to be reasonably well isolated from other contributing factors such as weather conditions, time of day, driver personal

Table 4.3: Estimated Net Percentage of Crashes Attributable to Alcohol Abuse, By Type of Crash

	Estimated net percentage of crashes due to alcohol abuse at or above	
Type of crash	BAC = 0.05%	BAC = 0.10%
Fatality	41.5	32.5
Personal injury		
Minor/moderate	13.0	8.5
Severe/critical	12.0	7.5
Property damage only	7.0	3.0

Source: Berry et al. (1977).

characteristics and driving experience, and can stand on its own as a factor significantly associated with motor vehicle crashes. But this does not mean that alcohol is the *cause* of these crashes. Other factors, intimately involved with alcohol abuse, may well be present and may be the true causal agent, if indeed there is one. But the data show an association between high levels of alcohol use and vehicular crashes, and methods and assumptions that meet the test of plausibility put these costs at $4,350 million to $6,047 million for 1975. Accordingly, the Berry figure of $5,143 million is accepted.

Alcohol Abuse and Fire

There are few studies of the relationship between alcohol abuse and fires, and the only evidence we have is piecemeal. However imperfect, this evidence points towards a contributing role for alcohol in the starting of fires from smoking and in mortality from fires. Perhaps the most recurring themes in the data are that alcohol is present disproportionally in fire victims; that alcohol abusers appear to have a very high relative mortality rate from fires; and that alcohol abusers have a higher predisposition to burn injury than non-abusers. These phenomena stem, presumably, from alcohol's role in the starting of fires (e.g. in falling asleep while smoking) and in impeding escape once a fire is underway. On the basis of this thin but complementary evidence, a part of the total 1975 cost of fires has been assigned to alcohol abuse.

The essential findings of the Berry study, in respect to the estimated cost of fires by type of loss and the respective portions of each type

Table 4.4: Tentative Estimates of the Economic Cost of Fire in 1975 That Might Be Attributable to Alcohol Abuse

Type of loss	Estimated cost of fire (millions)	Proportions that might be attributable to alcohol abuse	Tentative estimate of economic cost due to alcohol abuse (millions)
Present value in 1975 of lost future production due to premature death	$ 435.5	59.7	$260.0
Medical treatment of personal injuries	712.7	16.8 35.0	119.7 249.4
Lost production due to personal injury	89.9	16.8 35.0	15.1 31.4
Property damage			
Building fires	3,436.6	6.1	209.6
Non-building fires	734.0	0.0	0.0
Total	$5,408.6		Low estimate $604.4* High estimate $750.4

* When adjusted to eliminate double counting, the low estimate is $434.
Source: Berry *et al.* (1977).

tentatively attributable to alcohol abuse are shown in Table 4.4. The total 1975 economic cost of fires is $5,409 million; the amount associated with alcohol abuse ranges from $604 million to $750 million. Net of double-counted items, the lower figure is reduced to $434 million. Given the fewness and limitations of the various supporting empirical works, the question of accuracy here is moot. But, at present, the numbers appear to be small relative to other economic costs of alcohol abuse, and even sizeable errors in either direction do not change the general picture that is emerging. However, since these figures include neither the deaths of non-abusers from fires where alcohol may have been a factor, nor the property loss to abusers from fires not caused by alcohol abuse (which, if included, would exaggerate the alcohol-related fire losses), the errors of omission seem to lean in the direction of understatement. The present state of the art, however, permits us to say little more than that.

Alcohol Abuse and Crime

We know little about the extent to which alcohol abuse is related to criminal activity and virtually nothing about any connection that might exist. Yet, what limited evidence there is suggests that alcohol is present disproportionally among sexual abusers of children, and among both the perpetrators and victims of homicide and other personal injury crimes such as assault, rape and many robberies. And since criminal incidents probably are under-reported, the volume of crime, particularly crimes of personal violence, associated with alcohol abuse may be considerably larger than inferred from the present data. Further, while we attach no societal cost to the money and property taken in thefts of various kinds because these crimes essentially are redistributions rather than net losses of wealth, there are real and large psychological costs resulting from such crimes and the fear of such losses. To whatever extent alcohol may be a contributing or associated factor in all crimes, it is thus not fully reflected in the 'economic cost' frame of reference.

Given these many qualifications, what can be said about the economic dimensions of this association, that is, the economic cost of crimes associated with alcohol or where alcohol is 'present'? This cost represents the lost production of persons killed or injured in crimes, and the medical care utilised by those injured. The total (1975) as calculated by Berry comes to about $3,300 million, approximately 95 per cent of which is the present value of the lost future production of homicide victims (Berry *et al.*, 1977). Based on estimates of the proportion of alcohol association in each type of criminal offence, almost 65 per cent of this loss, or $2,098 million, is identified as associated with alcohol consumption. This is a very tenuous estimate and, at present, we probably are best off taking it only as a loose approximation of the association between two phenomena whose clear connections we do not yet understand well enough: alcohol consumption and crimes of personal violence.

Societal Responses to Alcohol Abuse

In addition to productivity losses, property losses and health care costs associated with alcohol consumption, additional resources are expended in what is termed the 'social response' to alcohol abuse. Berry defines this response as (1) indirect programmes of a welfare nature, such as various forms of social insurance and public assistance, and (2) direct programmes to mitigate alcohol abuse through 'detection, prevention, treatment, rehabilitation, research and education'.

The indirect programmes are aimed at alleviating economic distress, and such distress is disproportionately associated with alcohol abuse. Although a large component of these transfer payment programmes might be related to alcohol abuse, because they are transfer payments they impose no net costs on society, except for their administrative costs. Direct programmes which provide services and utilise economic resources in doing so, are a real social cost, however. Thus, the part of direct services and all administrative expenses attributable to alcohol abuse is one more element in the societal cost of alcohol abuse.

It is estimated that alcohol abusers are 4 (to 8) per cent of the labour force and have an unemployment rate 3 times that of non-abusers (Berry *et al.*, 1977). Hence they raise the unemployment level at least one-twelfth higher than it would be if no workers were alcohol abusers and, correspondingly, at least 8 per cent of the unemployment compensation programme administration costs are assignable to alcohol abuse. Similar calculations of the excess representation of alcohol abusers among accident victims and of their families among the lower income groups provide comparable estimates of the excess proportion of other income maintenance programmes that can be associated with alcohol abuse. All together, the share of total administrative costs (and of direct services) thus attributed totals $1,274 million for 1975.

The second category, 'direct response', includes the expenditures on alcohol programmes and for highway safety, fire protection and law enforcement. Separating from the latter three of these the proportion of real costs associated with alcohol abuse (based on the proportionate roles of alcohol associated with accidents, fires and crimes) and adding the alcohol programme costs not counted elsewhere in the analysis, another $1,426 million enters into the 'social response', for a total, for 1975, of $2,699 million.

The social discussion of Berry's estimates of the 1975 societal cost of alcohol abuse in the United States and the revisions made to them are summarised in Table 4.5. The Berry estimates total $42,755 million, while the revised estimates total $74,724 million. Also in the table are brief reminders of the bases of the respective revisions as presented in the discussion.

Table 4.5: Societal Costs Related to Alcohol Abuse, 1975, Berry and Revised Estimates ($ millions)

Category	Berry et al.	Revised	Basis
Lost production			
lost market production (male, civ.)	$15,458	$33,814	Luft earnings loss estimates
lost market production (female, civ.)	–	3,692	Male/female earnings and abuse-prevalence ratios
lost non-market production			
(male, civ.)	–	1,728	Government estimates of non-market production by males; male/female earnings ratios; Sirageldin (cf. Gronau) estimate of value of non-market production
(female, civ.)	–	6,173	
total lost civilian production	$15,458	$45,407	
lost military production	411	411	
excess mortality 1975	3,768	3,789	Inclusion of non-market production of males; adjustment for excess unemployment
Total lost production	$19,637	$49,607	
Health care costs	$12,743	$12,743	unchanged
Motor vehicle crash losses net of double counting	5,143	5,143	unchanged
Fire losses net of double counting	434	434	unchanged
Costs associated with violent crime (including social responses to crime)	2,857	2,857	unchanged
Other social responses	1,940	1,940	unchanged
Total	$42,755	$72,724	

Source: Adapted from Berry et al. (1977).

The Costs of Alcohol Abuse in 1979

To update the estimates to 1979, further adjustments are required, as shown in Table 4.6. The largest category of loss, civilian production, is increased by 56.7 per cent, which is the extent of the growth in the current-dollar value of total employee compensation from 1975 to 1979. The value of lost military production is increased by 10.5 per

Table 4.6: Estimated Societal Costs Related to Alcohol Abuse, 1979 ($ millions)

Category	Revised 1975 estimate	Updated 1979 estimate	Basis for update
Lost production			56.7% increase in total
(civ.)	$49,196	$77,090	employee compensation
(mil.)	411	454	10.5% increase in total military payroll
Health care costs	12,743	20,465	60.6% increase in total national health care expenditures
Motor vehicle crash costs	5,143	6,768	31.6% increase in total cost of highway accidents
Fire losses	434	647	49.1% mean increase in total employee compensation, health care expenditures, and general rate of inflation (GNP deflator index)
Violent crime	2,857	4,477	56.7% increase in total employee compensation
Social response	1,940	3,467	78.7% increase in government receipts less transfer payments
Totals	$72,724	$113,368	

Source: Adapted from Berry *et al.* (1977).

cent, reflecting the growth in the total military payroll, itself the result primarily of higher pay rates rather than greater size of the military force. Health care costs associated with alcohol abuse are 60.6 per cent higher in 1979 than 1975, corresponding to the growth in total national health care expenditures in that period. The 1979 cost of motor vehicle crashes where alcohol is a factor is 31.6 per cent higher than 1975, representing an assumed constant proportion of alcohol-related accidents in a larger total highway accident cost. The cost of fire losses in 1979 is 49.1 per cent above the 1975 level, reflecting the mean influence of higher employee compensation, larger health care expenditures and the general inflationary trend (as a measure of property valuation changes) since 1975. The 1979 economic loss from violent crimes where alcohol is a factor is 56.7 per cent above that of 1975, which, again, is the increase in total employee compensation in that period (since 95 per cent of the economic cost of violent crimes is attributed to the lost output of its victims). Last, the 1979 social response is 78.7 per cent greater than the 1975 response, which is the increase in total governmental 'activity' expenditures (receipts less transfer payments) over that period. The 1979 totals, thus adjusted and updated in Table 4.6, indicate the current dollar 1979 societal costs related to alcohol abuse in the United States to be on the order of $113,000 million.

Three points should be emphasised in respect to this result. (1) The present annual costs related to or associated with alcohol abuse in the USA calculated in this report are not offered as precise measures, although they seem to be defensible, plausible estimates. Perhaps they are best considered as acceptable order of magnitude indicators of the 'true' costs. (2) These costs do not represent the costs *of* alcohol abuse, *due to* it or *caused* by it. The cost figures in this report suggest the dimensions of a pool of negative impacts related in one way or another to one form or another of alcohol abuse. This pool also may be viewed as the potential resource savings to society from additional resource outlays of a mitigating nature, which include alcohol-related research, treatment and prevention. And since alcohol is not totally the cause of these societal costs, alcohol-related research is not the only path towards their mitigation. Other pathways, perhaps many, may also lead to reduction of these costs, but efforts closely related to the physical and behavioural aspects of alcohol consumption seem to offer an excellent potential for large net social gains. (3) The costs discussed here are not presented in the framework of a cost-benefit analysis of alcohol use, and thus considerations of consumer surplus and any positive health and productivity benefits of moderate alcohol use have not been included. The implications thus relate not to questions of abstinence versus consumption of beverage alcohol, but the benefits and costs of efforts to reduce the adverse effects related to it.

Accordingly, one main conclusion of this chapter, as noted in the introduction, is that the annual societal costs related to alcohol abuse are larger, seemingly very much larger, than indicated by the Berry estimates for 1975; the second and more important conclusion is that, in view of the magnitude of the costs calculated herein, the great potential societal savings they represent, and the very modest level of effort currently made towards realising these savings, additional societal resources would be well spent if directed toward the economic, social and personal problems related to alcohol abuse.

Notes

1. The Social Security Administration projections assume an annual productivity increase of 2 per cent, based on historical trends. Recently in the USA (1975 to 1979) the average annual productivity increase has been 2.15 per cent. Thus far, then, the Berry present-value output loss represents a fairly accurate projection of productivity increments through time.
2. This figure represents the present value of future earnings of those who constitute the excess deaths of alcohol abusers in 1975. An alternative method, discussed by Berry *et al.* but not employed by them, would be to calculate the output loss in 1975 resulting from the premature deaths of alcohol abusers up to and including 1975.

5 CALCULATING THE COSTS OF ALCOHOL: THE SCANDINAVIAN EXPERIENCE

Esa Österberg

Introduction

Each Scandinavian country has a language of its own and this — coupled with the obscurity of the Finnish language in particular — has prevented the Scandinavian debate on the economic costs and benefits of alcohol use from attracting greater attention. Nevertheless, the Scandinavian debate poses a variety of questions which are relevant to the current dialogue about how the costs of the use or abuse of alcohol should be computed. The main purpose of this chapter is to bring the Scandinavian experience before a wider public, and to present some critical views on the calculation of the costs of alcohol use.

The Early Committees

The Scandinavian committees on alcohol which sat at the beginning of this century did have some ideas about the calculation of the economic costs and benefits of alcohol. These committees did not, however, calculate the economic costs and benefits of alcohol use in actual monetary units and neither did they try to compile a societal profit and loss account for drinking. But most of them did consider the economic aspects of the use of alcohol. Their reports also gave thought to how the passing of a Prohibition Act would be likely to affect the government coffers, trade policies, the alcohol industry and the national economy as a whole (*Indstilling*, 1915; Brock, 1916; *Komiteanlausunto*, 1926; *Betænkning*, 1927). Some of the committees also addressed themselves to analysing consumer expenditure on alcohol, the value of alcohol production and tax revenue; certain outlays to the public sector caused by drinking were considered as well (Rygg, 1914; *Indstilling*, 1915; *Komiteanlausunto*, 1926).

It was only in Sweden that the foundations laid down by the early committees led on to wider debate about the economic costs and benefits of drinking. This was partly due to the fact that the Swedish temperance committee of 1911 had commissioned research on the national economic aspects of prohibition. The study which resulted approached the question of the likely effects of prohibition in three ways. One, the effect of prohibition on the economic harm due to alcohol misuse; two, prohibition's effect on industry; and three, the manner in which prohibition would affect state finances (Brock, 1916). The study emphasised that the economic harm attributable to alcohol misuse was far from being the most serious injurious aspect of drinking. Secondly, the study reached the conclusion that to enforce prohibition, thereby forfeiting alcohol revenue, and nevertheless to keep public expenditure at the same level as before would mean that other taxation would have to be drastically increased (Brock, 1916).

Dahlgren and Khennet

In itself, Brock's study did not lead on to wider debate. It did, however, serve as a model when the chapter on the effects of alcohol use on the national economy and state finances was written by Thorild Dahlgren in 1924, in the *Handbook of the Alcohol Issue*, a book for teachers. Dahlgren's approach differed from Brock's: Dahlgren was concerned with the effects of alcohol, not the effects of the enforcement of prohibition. Furthermore, Dahlgren made a deliberate attempt to compile a societal profit and loss balance for alcohol. The credit column of his ledger listed the importance of the manufacture of alcohol to agriculture; the alcohol industry; and alcohol sales. The list of debit items was longer: reduced work performance; a greater likelihood of accident; more sickness; shortened life expectancy; increasing crime; lower living standards; a weakening of future generations; the destruction of property; and weakened capital formation (Dahlgren, 1924). It is hardly surprising that Dahlgren proved unable to transcribe the items on his balance sheet into monetary units and that he could not mould them into one figure demonstrating how profitable or unprofitable alcohol use was to the national economy either. Nevertheless, Dahlgren expressed the opinion that, on both quantitative and qualitative grounds, the alcohol balance sheet was in the red and that a fall in the use of alcohol or its cessation would be advantageous from the point of view of the national economy (Dahlgren, 1924).

Like Brock, Dahlgren considered the effects of alcohol on the national economy and state finances separately. Looking at the effects of alcohol on state finances, Dahlgren pointed out that apart from bringing in revenue, alcohol affected the public purse through the harm wrought by drinking – a point which Brock did not make quite as clearly. Dahlgren emphasised that alcohol causes the state expenditure in two different ways. First, it makes it necessary for the state to take measures to prevent alcohol problems. Secondly, in spite of these preventive measures – or perhaps because of their insufficiency or inefficacy – alcohol use causes diverse, widespread harm and injury, which the state is then obliged to alleviate (Dahlgren, 1924).

There were only run of the mill reviews of the manual at first (Handboken... 1924; Handboken... 1925; Handboken... 1926). Dahlgren's review received little attention. Nevertheless, even at this stage, one political economist, Professor Emil Sommarin, did write a fairly long review of Dahlgren's work and the approach it implied. First, Sommarin (1925) emphasised that the production of alcoholic beverages, the alcohol trade, the use of alcohol and its consequences could and should be examined from an economic point of view. He maintained that this would make it possible to clarify and support temperance work. Secondly, the article put forward ideas to demonstrate that it is impossible to calculate the profit and loss which the use of alcohol causes the national economy: the matter lies outside the realm of serious economics. Thirdly, even though a political economist himself, Sommarin maintained that the alcohol issue is predominantly a matter of social policy. According to Sommarin, drawing up profit and loss figures to serve the cause of temperance would defeat its own aims: alcohol policy might come to be reviewed in terms of pure economics and this would work against the goals of the temperance movement (Sommarin, 1925).

A further edition of the manual appeared in 1928, containing a revised and shortened chapter by Dahlgren. The fundamental points were still the same, however, and Dahlgren stressed the extent to which the societal balance sheet for alcohol was now even deeper in the red. He even questioned the advantageousness of the items which he had entered on the credit side of his ledger. The fact that Dahlgren's chapter was cut was not due to Sommarin's criticism, but rather to Dahlgren having been so busy that he had passed the job of revising his original chapter over to Hans Gahn and Gahn's article, which appeared in the same year, conscientiously adhered at length to the guidelines laid down by its predecessor. The article is noteworthy for the fact that the author, despite strenuous effort, was unable to demonstrate that alcohol constitutes a financial loss to the state (Gahn, 1928).

Both Dahlgren's chapter and Gahn's article came in for adverse criticism (Khennet, 1929). Khennet's main argument was that Dahlgren and Gahn had each obfuscated matters by treating the revenue obtained from the alcohol industry and the employment which alcohol provided as beneficial to society. Khennet also showed that Dahlgren had compiled the debit columns of his ledger in such a way that certain items were computed twice over. After criticising the procedures used by Dahlgren and Gahn, Khennet then went on to present his own societal profit and loss balance sheet for alcohol.

The entries in the debit column of Khennet's balance sheet were composed of the production and distribution costs of alcoholic beverages, and also of secondary alcohol costs. There are seven of these secondary costs: the direct costs which alcohol causes the government and local authorities (the treatment of alcoholics and alcohol education); the indirect costs which alcohol causes the government and local authorities (outlay engendered by courts, medical services and alleviating the distress of the poor); reduced revenue brought about by weakened working performance; the monies lost because of increased sickness and mortality; the financial loss brought about by increased crimes; the financial loss brought about by the weakening of futu generations; and the work of supporters and opponents of temperance. The right-hand side of Khennet's accounts listed the value with which consumers viewed those alcohol beverages they had bought. He pointed out that the value of alcoholic beverage sales consistently underestimated this factor as alcohol was strictly rationed in Sweden at that time. Khennet also stated that the value of alcohol sales might overestimate the advantageousness of alcohol, because some consumers, he said, do not drink because of the pleasant effects of alcohol but rather because they are dependent upon it – and, in fact, would probably be happy if they were freed from its grip (Khennet, 1929).

Myrdal's and Ohlin's Contribution

Dahlgren (1930) and Khennet (1931) proved unable to resolve their differences. This prompted *Tirfing* – the journal in which the discussion mainly took place – to seek a solution by turning to political economists. And this was how Professors Gunnar Myrdal and Bertil Ohlin came to take part in the controversy.

The tone of Myrdal's remarks was particularly vehement (Myrdal, 1930). He did not dispute the feasibility of compiling a profit and loss balance for the user of alcohol. He did, however, think that it would be futile to do so. He gave two reasons for this view. First of all, Myrdal pointed out that, from the point of view of policy decision-making, it is senseless to compile a societal cost-benefit analysis of the use of alcohol unless one is comparing two policy options. In other words, it would — perhaps — make sense to compare post-prohibition Sweden with the state of affairs which would pertain if Sweden unwaveringly held to the alcohol policy restrictions then in force. Conversely, there would be no point at all in comparing present-day Sweden to a hypothetical completely dry Sweden, unless one could lay down actual policy measures which, with a high degree of probability, would rid Sweden of alcohol altogether. In short, it is hard to imagine what kind of a country Sweden would be without alcohol when one is unable to demonstrate the measures which would banish alcohol here and now. Secondly, Myrdal also doubted the wisdom of comparing the usefulness of different alcohol policy measures solely from an economic standpoint. On the one hand, he would appear to believe that measures taken to regulate the production and consumption of alcoholic beverages and to alleviate alcohol problems should not be judged on exclusively economic grounds. But, on the other hand, he also seemed to be opposed to compiling balance sheets for the national economy for the added reason that these kind of calculations force one to rely on values and assumptions which are not generally accepted. And the fact that these values and assumptions are not usually made explicit when results are presented, filled Myrdal with particular alarm, especially in cases where the results depend heavily on initial value-related assumptions (Myrdal, 1930).

Ohlin began his article by asking himself just what 'economic views' entail. He emphasised three points. First, a given economic phenomenon may be measured by observing its effect on the per capita national income. Secondly, he stressed that, in the final resort, the consumer must have the right to decide how he spends his own money; the question of what kind of consumption is useful and justified should be left to the consumer, too. Thirdly, Ohlin still believed that society need not — indeed, where certain commodities are concerned, must not — accept consumer sovereignty. Neither should society accept the existing distribution of income as a matter of course (Ohlin, 1930).

Just commenting on the debate was not enough for Ohlin. He went further and tried to analyse the economic profit and loss standing of alcohol himself. In his opinion, there were two kinds of economic costs. On the one hand, there were direct costs — the production and distribution costs of alcoholic beverages; on the other, there were indirect costs. These latter all had to do with the part which drinking played in lowering productivity, and Ohlin listed increased sickness, a greater risk of accidents, the impoverishment of various social strata, lower living standards, higher crime rates, the poorer upbringing and standards of nutrition which future generations would receive, the tendency for people to squander their leisure, and the energy which supporters and opponents of the temperance cause spent in attacking one another. But higher mortality did not, in Ohlin's view, constitute a loss to the national economy since it simultaneously lowered both production and consumption alike and did not, therefore, affect the per capita national income (Ohlin, 1930).

Ohlin reckoned that the direct costs of alcohol ran to 150 million crowns in 1930, and estimated that indirect costs lowered national income by 10 per cent, about 600 million crowns. This estimate was based, first, on the views of Irving Fisher according to which the enforcement of prohibition had boosted the US GNP by 10 per cent, and, secondly, on the fact that Swedish alcohol consumption figures in the late 1920s were slightly higher than US figures had been just before the prohibition. On the other hand, Ohlin maintained that the national economic worth of alcoholic beverages was synonymous with the value with which the consumers viewed their drinks. It proved impossible for Ohlin to estimate the economic benefits of alcoholic beverages with any great precision, but he did, however, reach the opinion that the value of alcoholic beverages to the consumers might well be double or more what consumers spent on alcohol (Swedish consumers spent about 300 or 400 million crowns a year on alcohol at that time). Ohlin therefore concluded that the national economic benefits of alcohol use might well exceed its national economic costs. Hence, from a purely economic standpoint, the question of whether or not the existence of alcohol should be accepted was unanswerable. It is very interesting to note that Ohlin nevertheless proceeded to follow his analysis of alcohol and the economy with a call for prohibition. His justification was that social policy – and Ohlin counted alcohol policy as one aspect of social policy – cannot be allowed to rest on free consumer choice and a desire for the maximum national income. Aesthetic and cultural considerations prompted Ohlin to urge prohibition (Ohlin, 1930).

When considering the national economic importance of alcohol use, Ohlin took pains to distinguish between the national economy proper and state finance. The revenue which the state obtains from alcohol and the costs of alcohol misuse did not figure independently on the societal profit and loss account of drinking (Ohlin, 1930). Ohlin's article also included a short section on the manner in which the use of alcohol affects state finance. In this section he pointed out that the immediate consequence of the passing of a Prohibition Act would be that the state would lose revenues accruing from alcohol taxation, some 130 million crowns in 1930. Changes would also occur in public spending as the Budget would no longer need to consider the role which alcohol plays in crime, deprivation and sickness. Though, by the same token, prohibition would increase public spending as the enactment and enforcement of the Act would entail expense, too. Taking these factors into account, Ohlin estimated that the state would have to cope with a budgetary deficit of about 100 million crowns were a Prohibition Act to be passed. Nevertheless, the fact that the GNP would rise by 10 per cent would result in the state receiving additional taxation revenue to the tune of slightly over half the 100 million crowns deficit. Ohlin also thought that the state could easily compensate for the reduced income which prohibition would bring about by levying new taxes or raising existing taxation (Ohlin, 1930).

Professor Sommarin also took part in this discussion; his comments stress the importance of scrutinising alternative processes. He pointed out, for instance, that all the profit and loss computations which had figured in the debate were based on the assumption of full employment, in other words on the assumption that discharged labour and increased production potential could always be used by the economy. As he topically – writing in the 1930s – pointed out, people who had previously been employed by the alcohol industry and then found themselves out of work as a result of prohibition would not be greatly consoled by the fact that according to economic theory unemployment was an impossibility (Sommarin, 1930).

In 1931 the debate flagged and then died. Nevertheless, Ohlin took up the topic again in 1939 when he published an abbreviated version of his 1930 article. The basis of his thinking had remained unchanged, but he revised his estimate of the manner in which prohibition would be likely to affect the national income. His revised figures were that the use of alcohol decreases the national income by at least 3 to 4 per cent and that the maximum corresponding value lies somewhere between 7 to 8 per cent (Ohlin, 1939).

The Origins of Estimates

It was not until well into the 1960s that the subject of the costs of alcohol misuse became an important issue in Scandinavia once more. Finland viewed the matter with quite particular interest. Notwithstanding, the subject had cropped up from time to time between the early 1930s and late 1960s. For instance, in Finland Pekka Kuusi had dealt quite extensively with the topic in the 1950s (Kuusi, 1952). Kuusi first emphasised that, historically speaking, alcohol control has always been a social issue, not an economic one. Secondly, he contended that it would be easy to keep the state alcohol ledger in such a way as to show a profit, arguing that the tax revenue which the state receives from alcoholic beverages is far greater than the costs engendered by drinking. Thirdly, Kuusi claimed that it is impossible to give precise figures for the economic harm wrought by the use of alcohol; consequently, the idea of compiling a national economic balance sheet for the use of alcohol should be forgotten. And fourthly, he pointed out that the production, buying and selling, use and control of alcoholic beverages affect the economic interests of diverse groups, and that an understanding of this fact is essential for a true appreciation of the way in which alcohol control operates (Kuusi, 1952).

The debate which began in Finland in the late 1960s was started by groups who supported temperance. Their primary aim was to procure estimates of the economic costs of alcohol use which could then be employed to back harsher legislation. One of their arguments was that Ohlin in Sweden and Fisher in the United States had already made such calculations. In the 1970s, the main arguments advanced in the Finnish debate were of the following nature. 'Irving Fisher has estimated that the use of alcoholic beverages cuts the US national income by approximately ten per cent. Bertil Ohlin's estimate of the corresponding figure for Sweden is three to eight per cent' (Parliamentary Bill 317/1971) and 'Drinking costs society three times as much as it brings in. The work of the Swedish research scientist, Ohlin, demonstrates that the social costs of drinking are almost three times greater than the revenue resulting from alcohol taxation and sales.'

As has already been pointed out, Ohlin's estimates owed a great deal to the analysis by Fisher. How, then, did Fisher come to estimate that alcohol use lowers national income by 10 per cent? Simplifying matters somewhat, Fisher began with the experiment conducted by Ashaffenburg in 1896, in which four typists were given 35 grammes of alcohol each. In conjunction with certain other data, this very small experiment prompted Fisher to speculate that a glass of beer a day — about twelve grammes of alcohol — has the effect of reducing productivity by between 2 and 4 per cent. He then proceeded to estimate that the pre-prohibition consumption of alcohol per capita in the US was equivalent to five glasses of beer, or 60 grammes of alcohol a day. Computing on the same basis as before, this implies a reduced productivity rate of between 10 and 20 per cent. Fisher maintained that the lower figure formed a safe minimum. He also suggested that a 10 per cent rise in labour productivity would push the national income up by 5 per cent and, furthermore, that socially useful production would increase an additional 5 per cent as resources previously deployed in the alcohol industry became available to other sectors of the economy (Fisher, 1927). One major difficulty with Fisher's calculation — which should be mentioned right away — is that the US per capita consumption of alcohol prior to the enforcement of prohibition was closer to six grammes a day than sixty grammes a day. If one corrects this slip, Fisher's safe minimum then drops to 1 per cent (Österberg, 1981b).

Fisher did not — as we have seen — actually claim that the US national income would grow by 10 per cent if people were to stop drinking or prohibition were to be implemented. Five per cent was the figure he mentioned. What is interesting is the fact that Fisher's estimate of a 10 per cent drop in productivity managed to surface as a 10 per cent drop in national income when it was transferred to Swedish soil. Neither did the chopping and changing stop there; the original US estimate was converted into a Swedish estimate of 10 per cent at first, the 10 per cent then being revised to 3 to 8 per cent. Fisher's and Ohlin's figures later surfaced in Finland without any reference to the year they concerned becoming, in Finland, part of the stock in trade in the debate on the costs of alcohol use which took place in the 1970s. The figures, although clearly very dubious, were widely regarded as authoritative at that time and, indeed, are still thought to be valid by some people to this day.

Recent Calculations

The main countries in Scandinavia to urge that research should aim at calculating the costs of alcohol use have been Finland, Norway and Sweden. The matter has also been discussed in the Nordic Council. As a result, there has been some discussion about both the theoretical and practical problems involved in cost analyses, and the practical worth of such calculations from the point of view of alcohol policy (Österberg, 1976; Horverak, 1976; Mäkelä and Österberg, 1979; Köpniwsky, 1979; Nordiska, 1979; Kosonen et al., 1980; Österberg, 1981a; Köpniwsky, 1981; Österberg, 1981b). Furthermore, in the 1970s parliamentary committees on alcohol in both Finland and Sweden have participated in the discussion (*Statens*, 1974:90; *Komiteanmietintö*, 1978). The claims of policy research have also led to the production of calculations. Jorma Purontaus (1970), for instance, tried to employ cost-benefit analysis to gauge the effect of the 1969 revision of Finnish alcohol legislation. Aarno Salaspuro (1978) investigated the costs of the harmful effects of alcohol use to the hospitals in Finland in 1972, and in 1976, Johannes Virolainen, a former Minister of Finance, drew attention to the financial burden which the misuse of alcohol causes the Finnish state. Virolainen's calculations were based on a rough estimate of the share of the costs caused by the use of alcohol in the main categories of public spending. He claimed that the costs caused to the state by alcohol use ran to 900 million marks in 1975 and that the state received 2,257 million marks from alcohol in the same year (Table 5.1). Using as his point of departure the minimum and maximum figures of Ohlin's article, Virolainen assumed that alcohol use cut taxation income by 6 per cent which amounted to about 1,500 million marks, and thus demonstrated that the state alcohol balance sheet stood slightly in the red (Virolainen, 1976).

In Finland Klaus Halla has also attempted to gauge the public financial costs of drinking in 1975; the most important of his findings are given in Table 5.2. Virolainen estimated the role that alcohol played in various administrative sectors; Halla, on the other hand, proceeded by counting the number of various alcohol problems and then multiplying that number by the sum of money spent on each single problem. This is one of the reasons why Halla's estimate is markedly lower than Virolainen's (Halla, 1977; Halla, 1978). A similar study — albeit much more comprehensive and detailed — has been made in Denmark. This Danish research also looks at matters on a sector basis. It includes the following fields: hospital costs and daily allowances; disability pensions; traffic accidents; the money spent on research; police and court costs; and a variety of other costs brought about by the use of alcohol. All in all, costs related to alcohol problems ran to some 1,700 million Danish crowns in 1972/3. This represented 52 per cent of the tax revenue obtained from alcohol (Olesen, 1976; Olesen, 1977).

An article written in 1980 by the Norwegian, Hans Olav Fekjær, featured a brief account of the way in which alcohol use affects public finance. The methodology was the same as the procedure followed by Virolainen. According to Fekjær, the state was receiving through alcohol taxation only 2 of every 3 crowns it was paying out because

92 Calculating the Costs of Alcohol in Scandinavia

Table 5.1: Finnish State Alcohol Costs by Administrative Sectors in 1975 as seen by Johannes Virolainen, million Marks

Administrative sector	
Ministry of Justice (includes gaols)	83
Ministry of the Interior (includes police)	110
Ministry of Finance (includes pensions)	15
Ministry for Social Affairs and Health (includes social security, accidents, unemployment insurance, disability insurance, care of the disabled, treatment of alcoholism, alcohol prevention, medical costs)	700*
Total	908

* Medical costs account for 250 million marks.
Source: Virolainen (1976).

Table 5.2: Public Economy Costs Arising from Alcohol Problems in Finland in 1975 as seen by Klaus Halla, million Marks

Sector	
1. Medical costs	161.0
2. Policing costs	37.6
3. Gaol costs	78.6
4. Social welfare	61.1
5. Social insurance	24.0
6. Hospital and administrative costs arising out of road traffic	4.0
Total	366.3

Source: Halla (1978).

of alcohol use (Fekjær, 1980). Another Norwegian, Asbjørn Borg (1970) has attempted to assess the cost that alcohol misuse causes society and industry, and Tore Sager (1974) has gauged the societal effectiveness of fines and gaol sentences meted out for drunken driving. There are also two Finnish studies which have addressed themselves towards the burden which problem drinkers cause society and to the usefulness of rehabilitation programmes in the city of Espoo (Kolari, 1978; Kolari, 1980).

The most comprehensive study conducted recently in the Nordic countries was commissioned by the Finnish State Alcohol Monopoly (Kasurinen, 1980). The main purpose of the study was to ascertain the present standing of the alcohol industry and its significance to the

Table 5.3: Cost of Damage Caused by the Use of Alcohol in 1978 as seen by Veikko Kasurinen, million Marks

Real Costs	
Medical and welfare costs	290
Forensic medicine costs	3
Compensation paid for occupational disability	218
Material damage from accidents	198
Social welfare	140
Law enforcement	159
Administration of justice	35
Administration of prisons	118
Administration of alcohol affairs	2
Alcohol control measures	29
Educational and temperance activity	29
Research activity	4
Total	1,225
Alternative Costs	
Value of work lost due to fatalities	295
Value of work lost due to illness or injury	372
Value of work lost due to absenteeism or similar cause	19
Value of work lost due to imprisonment	92
Total	778
Total Real and Alternative Costs	2,003

Source: Kasurinen (1980).

national economy. Veikko Kasurinen also gauges the economic costs of the harm wrought by the misuse of alcohol. They amounted to 2,003 million marks in 1978, a figure equivalent to 1.5 per cent of the Finnish gross national product. The costs caused by alcohol use are classified as either real or alternative costs (cf. Table 5.3). The distinction is based on the principle that real costs create money transactions, give rise to cash flows, whereas alternative costs are based on the concept of alternative action and describe forfeited opportunity (Kasurinen, 1980). Kasurinen also addressed himself to the benefits brought about by drinking. The study estimated the benefits accruing to the economy as a whole at 5,736 million marks. This figure includes the concept of state alcohol revenue in the sense in which the term is generally understood, the effect of alcohol-related employment on the gross national product, and the direct and indirect taxes paid by the alcohol industry.

Conclusions

The idea of calculating the costs of alcohol use from the point of view of state finance and the national economy is not a new one. The subject first began to be dealt with in the Scandinavian countries in the early years of this century. The discussion about the costs of alcohol use was particularly animated in Sweden in the late 1920s; the debate, however, flagged and ceased in the 1930s. But within the last ten or fifteen years the subject of the economic costs of alcohol has been revived anew in most Scandinavian countries.

What can the Scandinavian debate teach us? No agreement has been reached on how the costs which alcohol misuse causes the state or the national economy should be calculated or even on what attitude one should take to such costs calculations. Indeed, there is still quite deep dissension over the advisability of analysing alcohol costs and about the usefulness of cost calculations. Furthermore, even those who make it their business to calculate the economic costs arising out of the use of alcohol would appear to rely more on once-and-for-all solutions of their own than on the lessons of the past. Notwithstanding, a perusal of the debate does lead one to some important questions about calculating alcohol-related costs.

The first point to be noticed is that it was prohibition and the effect which it was likely to have which was to the forefront of the debate early in this century. More recent calculations, on the other hand, have tended to concentrate on the consequences of alcohol use or alcohol misuse or alcoholism. This shift in emphasis, from comparing opposed alcohol policy options – whether a Prohibition Act should be passed or not – to analysing the economic effect of an existing phenomenon, alcohol use, alcohol abuse or alcoholism, creates difficulties in interpreting these calculations, especially from the policy-making perspective. One might well ask how the recent cost calculations serve policy-making by comparing the existing situation with the hypothetical non-alcohol situation (the counterfactual) which, according to our present knowledge, is out of reach of actual policy alternatives. Is all that cost calculations have to say that life would be better if alcohol or alcohol problems did not exist or that governments should begin to do something about alcohol? If so, nobody would be much the wiser. Furthermore, analysing the economic effect of an existing phenomenon may create problems. Calculation methods, for instance cost-benefit analysis, have been developed as tools for the specific task of making comparisons between two or more policy options or projects. One is also tempted to ask whether the use of alcohol or different alcohol policy measures should be judged on the basis of a single general profit and loss balance. Might it not make better sense to calculate the costs and benefits in relation to some specific organisation or budget or to some accepted book-keeping system such as system of national accounts (Mäkelä and Österberg, 1979)? The Scandinavian debate would seem to suggest that at least the financial consequences to the state of alcohol use or certain alcohol policy measures should be regarded as an entity of their own.

It has been pointed out that separating cost calculations from policy options creates problems especially as far as gauging official alcohol economy is concerned (Kosonen et al., 1980). It is not, for instance, always remembered that the balance sheet includes items which are qualitatively different. On the one side, there are the sums which are employed in preventing alcohol problems (e.g. alcohol education); on the other, the money which the government spends in attempting to alleviate existing alcohol problems. The point is that an increase in the money devoted to preventing alcohol problems may well cause the state's overall alcohol costs to drop since prevention lessens the harmful effects of alcohol use. Consequently, cutting prevention spending may well lead to an increase in total alcohol costs because decreased prevention activity is connected with greater alcohol problems. Secondly, those policy measures which attempt to alleviate alcohol problems are based on conscious decisions of their content and expenses. Cutting down these activities does not decrease alcohol problems but it certainly alters the way in which people have to pay and suffer from these problems. One could for instance imagine what would happen if a state-financed hospital for problem drinkers were to be closed. Alcohol costs are not a negative phenomenon and minimising them need not be advisable, because the state is not a commercial enterprise and preventing and coping with alcohol problems is not a business.

It is nothing new to speak about the dangers of double counting or inexact or totally wrong estimates. Even here the Scandinavian calculations offer good examples, even if this chapter has not been the right place to deal with them (cf. e.g. Österberg, 1981b). One should, however, note the view of Sten Köpniwsky (1979) according to which the economic calculus should always aim at the most probable cost estimates rather than, as has often been the case, minimum estimates of costs.

The Scandinavian debate raises some interesting points about the political aspects of calculating the costs of alcohol use. It has usually been the case that the temperance movement has either made the calculations or been to the forefront in urging for them. Barring a few rare exceptions, the temperance movement has been disappointed: it has proved almost impossible to demonstrate that alcohol costs are greater than alcohol benefits and even doctoring the books has not produced high enough cost figures. At the same time as those who support cost calculations have run into difficulties while trying to use cost figures to support their line, many of the opponents of cost calculations have stressed that economic considerations are not relevant enough and that one must look elsewhere to find arguments to support a tightening up of alcohol policy.

The Scandinavian debate also leads one to ask how the economic phenomena attendant upon alcohol use should be approached. The practice of compiling various types of balance sheets would not seem to be the best way, as is shown by the balancing approach's inability to reconcile opposing points of view. Looked at from the balance sheet perspective, it is obvious that the resources which are deployed in manufacturing alcoholic beverages can only be thought of as costs. But this does not do away with the fact that those who obtain their livelihood through alcohol feel that alcohol production is beneficial to their private economy and exert real pressure on alcohol policy. One might say that the philosophy underlying balance sheets is one of acceptance of policies aimed at general good. The view, however, is fallacious: alcohol policy is a matter of reconciling conflicting interests − often social policy and economic considerations.

6 THE COSTS AND BENEFITS OF ALCOHOL IN ONTARIO: A CRITICAL REVIEW OF THE EVIDENCE

Eric W. Single

The Ontario Context

Alcohol consumption in Ontario has grown at a relatively rapid pace during the post-war period (Single *et al.*, 1981); per capita consumption of alcohol, expressed in terms of 100 per cent ethanol, has increased from 5.4 litres in 1950 to 9.0 litres in 1978. Beer is the most popular type of alcoholic beverage, but preferences are changing in the direction of greater spirits and wine consumption. In 1978 beer accounted for 48.0 per cent of total alcohol consumption, spirits 38.5 per cent and wine 13.5 per cent.

The locus of alcohol control policy is at the provincial level. The province regulates the marketing and distribution of alcoholic beverages, while the federal government has jurisdiction over the manufacture, importation, exportation and interprovincial trade in alcoholic beverages. The province operates a monopoly on the off-premise sale of all spirits, imported wines and imported beer. Domestic wine and beer are sold through monopoly outlets as well as private stores which are closely regulated by the province. In 1979 there were 7,131 licensed on-premise establishments (10.9 per 10,000 adults). It is estimated that about one sixth of alcohol consumption occurs in on-premise locations (Single *et al.*, 1981).

All three parts of the alcohol industry are highly concentrated. The brewing industry is dominated by three large companies – Molson's, Labatt's and Carling-O'Keefe. Together they account for over 95 per cen of the Ontario market. Prices are uniform and are not determined by competitive market mechanisms but rather by government control. Barriers to entry into the industry are high, and the number of breweries has diminished from more than 30 in 1960 to only 11 in 1979. It is noteworthy that all three major breweries are part of international conglomerates.

The distilling industry is also highly concentrated in a few firms which are mainly subsidiaries or affiliates of multinational corporations. Although there are 34 firms which supply products to the provincially operated monopoly stores, 85 per cent of these are controlled by six multinational corporations. The three largest multinationals — Hiram Walker, Seagrams and National Distillers — accounted for 74.3 per cent of the market in Ontario in 1975. A major difference between the brewing and distilling industries is that the distillers have a large export market. Indeed, in 1975 Seagrams received 94 per cent of its income from exports and Hiram Walker received 82 per cent of its income from exports. The major market for these exports was the United States. Canada's 1975 exports to the US exceeded domestic sales by 50 per cent (Gay, 1979).

The wine industry is much smaller than the brewing or distilling industries. It consisted of ten wineries in Ontario in 1980, supplying about half of the total wine consumption for the province, with only a negligible export market. The industry survives primarily because of government protection. Local wineries are given a preferential mark-up compared with imported wines, their products are more prominently displayed, and wineries have been permitted to sell their products through special outlets (recently expanded to include winery outlets in department stores). Two companies (Chateau-Gai and Jordan) are owned by major breweries (Labatt's and Carling-O'Keefe, respectively). Although it is generally expected that sales of table wine will continue to increase, high costs of land and labour give the wine industry a low profit margin. As a result, the major barrier to growth is not political but economic (Gay, 1979). Unlike the other sectors of the alcohol industry, government is actively promoting domestic wine, but the relatively poor economic performance of the wineries has scared off capital investment.

Estimates of the Costs and Benefits of Alcohol in Ontario

The most frequently cited attempt to quantify the costs associated with alcohol consumption in Ontario is the study by Holmes in 1976, entitled 'The Demand for Beverage Alcohol in Ontario, 1953 to 1973, and the Cost-Benefit Comparison for 1971'. Prior to that time, there had been at least one attempt to estimate the costs and benefits of alcohol for Canada. In a study commissioned by the Brewers Association of Canada, Johnson (1972) applied the findings of two American studies and one study in the province of New Brunswick to Canada. Johnson himself was clearly aware of the inadequacies of this procedure, but none the less concluded that revenues exceeded costs by about 50 per cent ($900 million to $600 million in 1969). He also concluded that the costs associated with alcohol use were substantially less for beer than for other types of alcoholic beverages.

Holmes, an economist, was commissioned by the Addiction Research Foundation to examine many of the same issues within the province of Ontario (Holmes, 1976). He divided costs and benefits into 'private' and 'non-private' categories. Private costs consisted of (i) production and distribution, i.e. the costs of raw materials, manufacturing and transportation costs; (ii) wage and salary losses attributable to heavy alcohol consumers, estimated from a Canada-wide study; and (iii) property damage resulting from alcohol-related auto collisions. Non-private costs consisted of (i) medical treatment for alcohol-related health problems; (ii) labour productivity losses; (iii) law enforcement costs attributed to alcohol-related crimes; and (iv) alcohol research, namely, the Addiction Research Foundation. For ten different health conditions, the excess morbidity attributable to alcohol was computed by comparing the rate of illness occurrence in heavy consumers with a general population sample of equivalent age and sex composition. These treatment costs were estimated to be approximately $116 million in 1971. Labour productivity costs were estimated to be $124 million in that year, but the highest costs in Holmes's scheme were those of production and distribution, estimated at $369 million.

According to Holmes's accounting, the benefits of alcohol consisted of the values of sales plus a consumer 'surplus', which was equal to the difference between what consumers paid and what would have been spent if alcohol were priced to maximise dollar sales. In this scheme, non-private benefits were assumed to be negligible; tax revenues were already included as part of the sales value. Thus, the model assumed a perfectly rational consumer, and Holmes was well aware of the problems posed by addictive or compulsive consumption. The total benefits were estimated to be $1,267 billion. Thus, in the model proposed by Holmes, benefits exceeded costs by $500 million in 1971, the same amount as the consumer 'surplus'.

The Holmes study, particularly the work on estimating alcohol-related health costs, became the basis for subsequent estimates of the costs of alcohol. Giesbrecht modified Holmes's estimates and compared the resultant costs with the revenues which the Ontario government received from alcohol taxation in 1971 (Giesbrecht, 1977). Giesbrecht took Holmes's estimate of $116 million for health costs and added $8.5 million for welfare costs attributed to alcohol, based on a study of case loads in two cities, and $11.1 million for children's aid costs attributed to alcohol. The method by which these costs are apportioned to alcohol is not stated. In any event, public health costs were estimated to be $135 million. Giesbrecht added to this figure the costs attributed by Holmes to labour productivity losses and law enforcement plus his own estimate of cost of motor vehicle accidents based on the amount of fines and penalties for alcohol-related driving infractions ($18 million). The total of these estimated costs attributed to alcohol use in 1971 was $327 million, compared with $196 million in provincial revenues from alcohol sales.

A task force investigating the adequacy of alcoholism treatment services (Marshman et al., 1978) used Holmes's basic model for estimating the costs of treating alcohol-related health problems and applied it to 1976 data. The per adult consumption increased from 10.5 litres of ethanol in 1971 to 11.6 litres in 1976, and the resulting impact on the proportion of drinkers consuming alcohol at hazardous levels (deemed to be greater than or equal to 10 centilitres of ethanol per day) was taken into account. Treatment costs were estimated to be $332 million for 1976. No attempt was made to assess other costs or benefits.

Adrian (1978) similarly updated Holmes's estimates in the 1977-8 Statistical Supplement to the Addiction Research Foundation Annual Report. She indicated $320 million for medical treatment in 1976, $75 million lost to reduced labour productivity in 1977, $3 million lost wages due to alcohol-related illness in 1977 and $40 million for law enforcement costs due to heavy alcohol consumption in 1975-6. No explanation is offered for why these figures differ from those of Marshman with regard to health costs, nor is there any explanation for the marked decrease in estimated labour productivity and law enforcement costs. Despite the lower rates of consumption in 1971, Holmes's estimates were much higher for these alcohol-related costs.

There have been no further attempts to quantify the costs of alcohol in Ontario, but the health ministry of the federal government did provide estimates of the magnitude of alcohol-related health and social problems for the country as a whole (Health and Welfare Canada, 1981). Thus provincial studies of the costs of alcohol consist entirely of Holmes's work plus some brief updates or revisions of his estimates.

There is an equal paucity of research with regard to the benefits of alcohol. Only one detailed study has been conducted on this topic. In a report commissioned by the Addiction Research Foundation, Gay estimated that over 1.87 billion dollars were generated through the manufacture and sale of alcoholic beverages in Ontario in 1975 (Gay, 1979). Spirits contributed 52 per cent of this sum, beer accounted for 37 per cent, and wine production and sales contributed 11 per cent of the total. The major recipient was the government. The Ontario government received a total of $532 million dollars from sales taxes, corporate taxes, personal income taxes and profits attributed to alcoholic beverage sales. The federal government received $409 million from excise taxes, import taxes, corporation taxes, licence fees and personal income taxes of alcohol industry employees in Ontario. The second largest recipients were the related industries and services, such as the Ontario corn and grape-growing industries, packaging industry and transport. Gay estimated that of the $601 million received by the Ontario alcohol industry in receipts, over $500 million were spent on these related industries. A total of 35,711 persons were employed in the production, sale and service of alcoholic beverages, with net incomes of over $343 million. In addition, licensed establishments earned $116 million after expenses and wages. Finally, Gay noted that the alcohol industry itself earned $114 million.

Conceptual Problems With Cost-benefit Accounting

It is beyond the scope of this chapter to consider all of the problems associated with cost-benefit accounting (see Kosonen *et al.*, 1981). However, even a cursory examination of the efforts in this area indicates major conceptual and methodological problems. First, those authors who attempt to compare estimates of the costs of alcohol with the benefits do little to resolve the basic policy issues surrounding alcohol control. Even if there were no theoretical or methodological problems involved in quantifying the costs and benefits of alcohol, the crucial issue from a policy perspective is not whether alcohol should be prohibited but rather the impact of marginal increments or decreases in consumption. What one ought to focus upon is therefore not the total costs or total benefits of alcohol but the costs and benefits of say, a 10 per cent decrease or increase in consumption.

A second major problem is that there is no consensus as to what constitutes a 'cost' and what constitutes a 'benefit'. As Österberg has noted (1978), even in the debates surrounding the cost of cost-benefit accounting in the alcohol policy area in the 1920s, the first and foremost issue was what should be considered to be a gain and what would be deemed a loss. The classic illustration of the problem concerns premature death due to alcohol use. From a social and moral point of view, such deaths are clearly undesirable, but from a strictly economic point of view, they benefit the economy by relieving society of the need to pay for pensions or health expenses in old age. As Österberg has stated, 'strictly speaking, a decent person would thus be a person who performs productively to his or her greatest capacity and who passes away on the day of his or her retirement' (Österberg, 1978).

The conceptual problems with the notion of 'costs' and 'benefits' are evident from the few available studies. Although Gay cites employment data as 'benefits' of the alcohol industry (Gay, 1979), these data might be viewed from another perspective as costs to the economy because they involve resources which, in the long run, could be otherwise employed. A redevelopment of resources could not be accomplished immediately or without cost, but the potential to redirect these resources should be kept in mind in evaluating the economic significance of the alcohol industry. The conceptual difficulty is further illustrated by the manner in which Holmes treats the value of raw material used in alcohol production as a 'cost' while Gay treats the same data as a 'benefit'. Many economists (as noted by Leu in Chapter 1) would consider factors such as the income of alcohol industry workers as 'transfer payments' which are not relevant to a cost-benefit accounting.

Methodological Problems with Cost-benefit Accounting

As all of the authors cited above are keenly aware, a major problem in the use of cost-benefit accounting in the policy area is the assumption that one can quantify the major costs and benefits with reasonable accuracy. It is obvious that certain key costs and benefits are not quantifiable. The usual justification for proceeding anyway is that some empirical data is better than making policy judgements solely on the basis of speculation or moral considerations (e.g. Johnson, 1972).

Even in those cases where it may be possible to estimate the dollar value of a cost or benefit, there are many technical problems and necessary assumptions. By way of illustration, let us consider just one of the many steps involved in arriving at an estimate for almost any health or social problem associated with immoderate alcohol use, namely, estimating the number of 'alcoholics' or 'heavy drinkers'.

The first problem with estimating the number of 'alcoholics' is that there is very little consensus as to what exactly is meant by this term.

Jellinek's classical description of the alcoholic involved a progressive development of well-defined phases and symptoms (Jellinek, 1960). This conceptualisation was based mainly on populations of clinical alcoholics in the United States.

As several writers have pointed out (e.g. Room, 1977), since the time of Jellinek's formulation there has been considerable evidence which indicates that the extent and nature of alcohol-related problems are quite different in the general populations as compared with clinical alcoholics. Most clinical alcoholics are well past 30 years old, whereas in general population surveys it is young men under the age of 30 who consistently score the highest on various indices of problem drinking.

There is also a major discrepancy with respect to the number of problem drinkers identified in surveys and the number of clinical alcoholics. Edwards (1973) found that the number of persons defined as 'problem drinkers' in a general population survey was nine times the number of persons identified as alcoholics by clinical or agency data. Room has interpreted these findings as indicating that the problem of the 'alcoholic' is in part due to a labelling process by which problematic drinking which is normal and tolerated among young men is deemed inappropriate among the relatively few middle-aged drinkers 'who retain their youthful heedlessness and drinking style' (Room, 1977).

Given the existence of at least two distinct sets of problematic consumers of alcohol, one in the general population and ? special group of older, chronic drinkers who appear in treatment settings, it is not surprising that there are a wide variety of methods used to estimate numbers of 'alcoholics'. The prevalence of alcoholism has been measured by treatment data (Walsh and Walsh, 1973), survey techniques (Manis and Lunt, 1957; Mulford and Miller, 1959; Bailey *et al.*, 1965; Cahalan *et al.*, 1969; Cahalan and Room, 1974), consumption data derived from aggregate sales or tax records (Ledermann, 1956; de Lint and Schmidt, 1968; Schmidt and de Lint, 1970; Single and Giesbrecht, 1978), and from data on alcohol-related mortality (Jellinek, 1947; Jellinek and Keller, 1952; Keller and Efron, 1955; Schmidt and de Lint, 1970; Celentano, 1976; Single, 1979).

Each of these methods has its advantages and disadvantages. Treatment data are frequently more an indicator of availability of facilities rather than alcoholism incidence, as an unmeasurable number of alcoholics never enter the treatment system. Even under the best of circumstances, however, treatment agencies only come into contact with the older, classical clinical 'alcoholic'.

The indirect measure of alcoholism prevalence based on consumption data (Ledermann, 1956) attempts to estimate the number of persons with rates of consumption similar to that of clinical alcoholics, based on the theory that aggregate consumption data enable one to predict the distribution of consumption in a society. Holmes's estimates of alcohol-related health costs were based on this method. The indirect measures based on mortality data, such as the Jellinek estimation formula (Jellinek, 1947) similarly use data concerning the incidence of alcohol-related mortality among clinical alcoholics to generate an estimate of the total number of alcoholics in a society. The raw data in indirect estimation procedures are typically statistics which are routinely collected. Thus, the use of these methods is relatively inexpensive.

Despite this advantage, there are a number of drawbacks concerning the use of indirect estimation procedures. Most notably, the alcoholic population which is being estimated is not clearly defined. The Ledermann procedure attempts to estimate the number of persons consuming alcohol at levels equal to the minimal levels among clinical alcoholics. Many such persons may not have any social or behavioural problems associated with alcohol use and, by the same token, there are undoubtedly many persons who consume lower amounts of alcohol and experience alcohol-related problems. The well-known Jellinek estimation procedure (Jellinek, 1947; Jellinek and Keller, 1952) similarly assumes the clinical alcoholic to be typical of all alcoholics, in that certain key elements in the estimation formula are estimated from studies on clinical populations.

Further, both the Ledermann and Jellinek formulae have been criticised on technical grounds. The Ledermann equation has been criticised frequently for not providing an adequately close fit to the true distribution of alcohol consumption (e.g. Parker and Harman, 1978). In the original formulation of the Jellinek procedure, the rate of death due to cirrhosis among alcoholics and the proportion of all cirrhosis deaths attributable to alcoholism were treated as constants (Jellinek, 1947). Popham (1970), Seeley (1959) and others have noted that these rates are in fact variable.

There is a long and extensive literature on the use of surveys to measure alcohol consumption and drinking problems (e.g. Room, 1977). In surveys, problematic consumption is generally operationalised in terms of a high self-reported intake, using a quantity-frequency scale such as the Strauss and Bacon scale (Strauss and Bacon, 1953), or alternatively, the researcher uses a set of questions intended to tap the basic behavioural and social problems associated with 'alcoholism'. Such problems vary according to the setting and the characteristics of the drinker, and thus it is virtually impossible to develop a measure which would be reliable in every setting at any time. The use of a quantity-frequency scale suffers from an even more serious problem. Namely, it is typically the case that alchol consumption is generally highly underestimated in surveys (Mäkelä, 1969; Room, 1971; Pernanen, 1972). Further, the extent of under-reporting is not random but related to volume of intake (Popham and Schmidt, 1981).

Given these problems, it is perhaps not surprising that alternative survey methods have provided discrepant results. Celentano (1976) examined five different indicators of alcoholism from survey data in Washington County, Maryland, and found very divergent results, ranging from a rate of 3.1 per cent using the Mulford and Miller Social Problems Scales to 15.2 per cent using a revised version of the Strauss and Bacon quantity-frequency scale. Despite these problems, survey techniques remain a common method for ascertaining the nature and extent of alcohol-related problems.

Thus, no single estimate of the prevalence of alcoholism is entirely satisfactory. Whatever measurement error is inherent in the use of a particular technique, such as the use of the Ledermann equation by Holmes, is then compounded by any error in the estimates of the proportion of a particular problem attributable to immoderate alcohol use.

Conclusion: A Proposal to Substitute Terms

Given the conceptual and methodological problems inherent to cost-benefit accounting, an alternative terminology is suggested. In place of the term 'cost', it would be preferable to think of factors such as the contribution of alcohol to morbidity as simply indicating the 'magnitude of alcohol-related problems'. This would offer certain advantages. There would be less tendency to ignore those problems which cannot be quantified. The inclusion of alcohol-related problems which cannot be estimated in dollar terms would also diminish the tendency to sum up the dollar costs and compare the result with the dollar benefits. The policy issues are too complex to be reduced to such a simplified accounting procedure.

In place of the term 'benefit', the term 'economic significance' would be a preferable alternative. Gay's study is thorough and in many ways, exemplary. However, as noted earlier, it is highly contentious whether she has examined the 'benefits' or the 'costs' of alcohol. The detailed accounting of raw materials, production employment, distribution networks, tax revenues from sales and employment income, etc., would be better described as indicators of the economic significance of the alcoholic beverage industry.

In conclusion, there are enormous problems involved in estimating the costs and benefits of alcohol and it is clearly over-reaching to attempt to deal with complex policy issues by comparing necessarily crude and incomplete estimates of dollar costs versus dollar benefits. None the less, if we think of factors such as excess absenteeism among heavy drinkers as indicators of the magnitude of alcohol-related problems rather than as 'costs' to society, and we think of factors such as employment in the production and distribution of alcoholic beverages as indicators of the economic significance of the industry rather than as 'benefits', then we have performed a worthwhile exercise and helped clarify the likely impact of policy options.

7 ALCOHOLISM: AN ECONOMETRIC MODEL OF ITS CAUSES, ITS EFFECTS AND ITS CONTROL

Stuart O. Schweitzer, Michael D. Intriligator and Hossein Salehi

Introduction, Purpose and Findings

Alcoholism and alcohol-related deaths are significant social problems in many nations, particularly the advanced industrialised nations of North America and Western Europe. Alcoholism and alcohol-related deaths account for a significant part of morbidity and mortality. Alcoholism is also an important factor in work days lost, traffic accidents and fatalities and family and societal disruption (Luce and Schweitzer, 1978). Despite its obvious social significance, alcoholism has not been treated to a detailed econometric analysis.

Most previous econometric studies in this area have focused on consumption of alcoholic beverages. Such a focus is understandable in terms of the well-established literature in econometric studies of demand. It is also a first step to the study of alcoholism, but only a first step. It must be emphasised that econometric studies of demand for alcoholic beverages provide only partial and indirect insights into the problems of alcoholism, since one of the principal findings of this chapter is that the relationships between demand for alcoholic beverages and both alcoholism and alcohol-related mortality are rather indirect and weak.

The purpose of this chapter is to specify, to estimate and to use an econometric model of alcoholism which would incorporate its causes, its effects and its possible control. Such a model should give more complete and more direct insights into the problems of alcoholism than previous demand studies.

Some findings emerge from this study, on the basis of the estimation of the econometric model using 1975 data on 35 US states, concerning the relation between consumption of beer and spirits; the role of standardising variables that influence alcohol consumption, alcoholism and alcohol-related mortalities; and the role of control variables influencing these variables.

As to the relation between beer and spirits, it is found that they have some opposite effects and that they may offset one another. For example, raising the price of spirits lowers alcoholism, but raising the price of beer appears to *increase* alcoholism, possibly because of the shift from beer to other alcoholic beverages as the price of the other beverages falls relative to that of beer. As to the role of standardising variables, those exerting the largest and most significant influence on alcoholism and alcohol-related mortality are income and tourism. For example, the elasticity of alcoholism with respect to income is 1.01, so that a 10 per cent increase in income leads to a 10.1 per cent increase in alcoholism, as measured by the number of alcoholics per 1,000 population. As to the role of control variables, those exerting the largest and most significant influence on alcoholism and alcohol-related mortality are prices (which, of course, are to a large extent determined by taxes), minimum drinking age and unemployment. While unemployment may not be considered as a control variable for alcoholism *per se*, it is treated as an object of general economic policy and it does have an important effect on alcoholism. Hence, it is useful to consider the effect of this macro-policy variable upon alcoholism and alcohol-related deaths. For example, the elasticity of alcoholism with respect to unemployment is 0.57, while the elasticity of alcohol-related mortality with respect to unemployment is 0.41, so a 10 per cent increase in the unemployment rate (e.g. from 8 per cent to 8.8 per cent) increases alcoholism by 5.7 per cent and alcohol-related mortality by 4.1 per cent. Thus an important policy conclusion is that, in addition to being concerned about unemployment for social and economic reasons, policy planners should also be concerned about unemployment for its significant effects in promoting alcoholism and alcohol-related mortality.

The remainder of this chapter consists of a survey of the relevant literature, a summary of the data used in the study, a presentation of the econometric model and its estimation, a discussion of the use of the estimated econometric model to simulate various policy conclusions, and a conclusion.

Previous Studies

Most previous studies of issue relating to alcoholism that use an econometric approach are, rather, studies of the demand for alcoholic beverages. A major focus of these studies is that of estimating the price and income elasticities of demand for beer, wine and distilled spirits (Ornstein and Hanssens, 1981). Tables 7.1 and 7.2, based on Ornstein

(1980), summarise some of the resulting estimated elasticities. These studies provide inconsistent evidence on the influence of prices and income on alcohol consumption. They provide no evidence, however, on the determinants of alcoholism or alcohol-related mortality. An exception is the recent paper by Cook and Tauschen (1981) which estimates separate relationships for the demand for spirits and the prevalence of alcoholism. As such, it comes closest of any of the previous studies noted in considering demand as only one stage in the process by which alcohol produces social costs. Unfortunately the Cook and Tauschen study is limited to spirits and omits beer and wine, despite the fact that more ethanol is consumed via beer than via spirits.

Data

The study is a cross-section analysis of alcohol consumption patterns, economic and social characteristics and alcohol control programmes in 35 states in the continental United States in 1975. Fourteen states (and the District of Columbia) were excluded either because of the influence of neighbouring states (New Hampshire, Massachusetts, Connecticut, New York, New Jersey, Maryland and Virginia) or because of missing data (Illinois, Louisiana, North Carolina, North Dakota, Oklahoma, Alaska and Hawaii).

Arkansas was excluded from the data set because of an anomaly in that state's reported alcoholism rate. Its reported rate is nearly three standard deviations below the mean value for the sample, although other variables in the model, including the rate of alcohol-related mortalities, are not outliers.

Table 7.3 presents statistics relating to the data, divided into endogenous variables (of the econometric model), standardising exogenous variables and policy variables.[1] Table 7.3 also presents the means, standard deviations and minimum and maximum values for the sample of 35 states in 1975. Where relevant the data are expressed in per capita terms; this generally means per population age 14 and older in order to take primary account of the population group likely to consume alcoholic beverages. One result using per capita variables is that the problem of heteroskedasticity is minimised.

The endogenous variables of the model are consumption of beer and spirits, alcoholism and alcohol-related mortality. It would have been desirable to have a consumption equation for wine as well as the

Table 7.1: Price and Income Elasticities of Demand for Alcoholic Beverages

	Place and time	Method		Beer	Price Wine	Distilled spirits	Beer	Income Wine	Distilled spirits
Niskanen (1962)	USA, 1934-54	Simultaneous equations (3-stage least squares, linear)		-0.50a,b	-1.59a	-2.027a,b	-0.33a,b	1.45a	0.61a,b
		Ordinary least squares (linear)		-0.33a,b	-0.35	-0.93a	-0.27a,b	0.80a	0.62a
Hogarty & Elzinga (1972)	USA, 1950-9 and by states	Ordinary least squares (log)		-0.89a			0.43a,b		
Norman (1975)	USA, 1946-70	Ordinary least squares (log)		-0.87a			0.35a,b		
Comanor & Wilson (1974)	USA, 1947-64	Ordinary least squares	(SR)c	-0.56a	-0.68a,b	-0.25	-0.18	0.41	0.18
			(LR)c	-1.39	-0.84	-0.30	-0.46	0.50	0.21
Stone (1945)	UK, 1920-45	Ordinary least squares (log)		-0.73		-0.72	0.14		0.54
Stone (1951)	UK, 1920-48	Ordinary least squares (log)		-0.60a,b	-1.17a	-0.57a,b		0.98a	0.60a,b
Prest (1949)	UK, 1870-1938	Ordinary least squares (log)		-0.66a,b		-0.57a	0.23a,b		0.70a
Nyberg (1967)	Finland, 1914-62	Static model		-0.49	-0.83	-0.13 Vodka,	0.22	0.97	0.42
						-0.95 Other,			1.30
		Dynamic model	(SR)	0.003	-0.99	-0.60 Vodka,	0.19	0.39	0.25
						-1.10 Other,			0.49
			(LR)	0.01	-3.28	-2.00 Vodka,	0.64	1.29	0.84
						-3.65 Other,			1.62
Walsh & Walsh (1973)	Ireland, 1953-67	Ordinary least squares (log and linear)		-0.17		-0.17	0.79a		2.04a
Lau (1975)	Canada, 1914-69	Ordinary least squares (log and linear)		-0.03	-1.65a,b	-1.45a,b	0.20	1.43a,b	0.68a,b
Johnson & Oksanen (1977)	Canada, 1955-71	Ordinary least squares (linear)	(SR)	-0.22a,b	-0.50a,b	-0.91a,b	0.04	-0.01b	0.23a,b
			(LR)	-0.38	-1.30	-1.60	0.06	-0.02	0.40
		(with error components analysis)	(SR)	-0.27a,b	-0.67a,b	-1.14a,b	0.00b	0.04b	0.11a,b
			(LR)	-0.33	-1.78	-1.77	0.02	0.04	0.17
Huitfeldt & Jorner (1972)	Sweden, 1963-8				-.09	-0.8 Vodka,			
						-3.2 Other,			

Table 7.1: Continued

Study	Location, Period	Method			
Labys (1976)	France, 1954-71	Ordinary least squares (log)	-0.06[b]		0.15[a,b]
	Italy		-1.00[a]		0.28[a,b]
	Portugal, 1954-71		-0.68		0.05[b]
	Spain, 1954-71		-0.37[a,b]		0.14[a,b]
	F.R. Germany, 1954-71		-0.38[a,b]		0.51[a,b]
	USA (domestic price), 1954-71		-0.44		2.35[a,b]
	USA (import price), 1954-71		-1.65[b]		3.34[a,b]
E.E.C.9	Belgium, 1954-71	Ordinary least squares (log)	-1.14		1.81
Malmquist (1948)	Sweden, 1923-39	Calculation of arc elasticities	-0.37		0.30
Simon[h]	USA, 1955-61	Ordinary least squares (linear)	-0.79		
Wales (1963)	USA, 1960	Ordinary least squares; seemingly unrelated regressions (linear)	0.084		1.69[a]
Smith (1976)	USA, 1970		-1.95[a]		1.75[a]
Lidman (1976)	California, 1953-75	Ordinary least squares (log and linear)	0.02[b]		1.017[a]
Barsby & Marshall (1977)	USA, 1970-5	Ordinary least squares (log)	-1.06[a]		1.23[a]
Ornstein & Hanssens (1981)	USA, 1974-8	Ordinary least squares (log and linear)	-0.677[a] to -0.999[a]	-0.065 to -0.312[a]	0.432[a] to 0.597[a]
Cook & Tauchen (1981)	USA, 1962-77	Analysis of covariance	-0.96	-0.009 to -0.067	0.43

[a] Significantly different from 0, p < 0.05.
[b] Significantly different from 1, p < 0.05.
[c] (SR) = short-run; (LR) = long-run.
[d] As reported by Lau (1975); test statistic not provided.
[e] Price elasticity estimates in these studies are not comparable to those of others since the own-price variable is included twice (alone and in the substitute price variable) in the estimate equation.
[f] As reported by Lidman (1976); test statistic not provided.
[g] As reported by Labys (1976); test statistic not provided.
[h] Simon used a special arc-elasticity formula based on the definition of price elasticity.
Source: Ornstein (1980).

Table 7.2: Estimates of Cross-price Elasticities

	Place and time	Method	Beer on wine[a]	Wine on beer	Beer on spirits	Spirits on beer	Wine on spirits	Spirits on wine
Malmquist (1948)	Sweden, 1923-39	Ordinary least squares (log)						
Walsh and Walsh (1970)	Ireland, 1953-67	Ordinary least squares (log and linear)			-0.21 to -0.33	-0.64 to -1.01 0.19 to 0.22		
Lau (1975)[b]	Canada, 1914-69	Ordinary least squares (log and linear)		-0.73 to -0.86	1.27	1.00[c]	-0.31 to 0.19	
Johnson and Oksanen (1974)	Canada, Pooled time series and cross section, 1955-71	Ordinary least squares (linear)	-0.03	0.23[c]	-0.11	-0.13	0.14	0.21[c]
Johnson and Oksanen (1977)	Canada, 1955-71	Ordinary least squares (linear) (with error components analysis)	—	+[c]	—[c]	—	+	+
Niskanen (1962)	USA, 1934-54	3-stage least squares Ordinary least squares	-0.39 -0.44[c]	2.55[c] 0.24	0.36 0.42	0.29 0.65[c]	1.33[c] -1.54	-0.05 -0.41
Lidman (1976)	California, 1953-75	Ordinary least squares (log and linear)			0.28			

a The cross elasticities are classified by dependent:independent variables; the first beverage listed is the dependent variable and the second the independent variable.
b These studies use relative price variables, e.g., beer price divided by spirit price, in log form. The ratios were not deflated by a consumer price index and t statistics could not be calculated.
c Significantly different from 0, $P < 0.05$.

consumption equations for beer and spirits, but the absence of a price index for wine prevented this. The level of per capita consumption of wine is, however, included as one of the standardising exogenous variables. Though on the average beer is 4.5 per cent alcohol (ethanol) while distilled spirits are 45 per cent alcohol and wine is 15 per cent alcohol, most alcohol consumption in the 35 states in the sample is via beer (Furst *et al.*, 1981). On average the population age 14 and older drinks 1.32 gallons of alcohol via beer consumption and 1.17 gallons via spirits consumption, but only 0.29 gallons via wine consumption, providing some justification for not including a wine consumption equation directly in the model.

Of all the data for the model, the greatest doubts arise for those pertaining to alcoholism, which rely on the Jellinek method. The problems with this method result from its reliance on historical relationships between alcoholism and cirrhosis deaths and its inconsistency across small areas (see Jellinek, 1959; Brenner, 1959; Seeley, 1959a; and Furst *et al.*, 1981). Data using this method have well-known deficiencies, but it was felt that the data are the best available measure of the extent of alcoholism and that their use is warranted in areas as large as states. There are also problems with the data on alcohol-related mortality because of the differences within and between different regions in the incidence and quality of autopsies.[2] As in the case of alcoholism, however, it was felt that the data are the best available and that their use is warranted in regions as large as states. The standardising exogenous variables are included in the model to adjust for state-to-state differences that influence the endogenous variables. Income is expected to determine consumption, as expected from demand theory. Tourism should affect demand since it usually entails greater consumption of alcoholic beverages. Urbanisation would influence both the level and composition (i.e. beer v. spirits) of consumption. Temperature and religion have also been used in previous studies as variables influencing consumption; they can be interpreted as standardising variables. Finally, consumption of wine is also introduced, as noted, as a standardising exogenous variable since it could not be included as an endogenous variable.

Policy variables of the model include the price of beer and spirits, which, as retail prices, would be affected by taxes at the federal, state and local levels. Outlets include both on-premise and off-premise outlets for alcoholic beverages. Advertising is included as a dummy variable, taking the value 1 if prohibited and 0 if any alcoholic beverage advertising is allowed. Minimum drinking age is that for beer, and it is

114 Alcoholism: An Econometric Model

Table 7.3: Statistics Relating to Variables of the Model

Endogenous variables	Mean	Standard deviation	Minimum value	Maximum value
CB = Consumption of beer (in gallons per-capita)[a]	29.26	6.079	19.465 (Alabama)	44.318 (Nevada)
CS = Consumption of spirits (in gallons per-capita)[a]	2.597	1.299	1.385 (Utah)	9.122 (Nevada)
ASM = Alcoholism (in number of alcoholics per 1,000)[a]	39.608	11.884	21.445 (Mississippi)	69.976 (Nevada)
ARM = Alcohol-related mortality (in number of deaths per 100,000)[b]	46.06	11.611	31.300 (Iowa)	82.100 (New Mexico)
Standardising exogenous variables				
I = Income (thousand dollars per-capita)[c]	5.466	0.611	4.035 (Mississippi)	6.575 (Nevada)
TR = Tourism (thousand of dollars per-capita)[a]	0.044	0.121	0.007 (Rhode Island)	0.735 (Nevada)
UR = Urbanisation (population in SMSA per-capita)[c]	0.563	0.245	0.099 (Vermont)	0.929 (California)
TM = Temperature (annual average temperature °C × 10)	127.7	45.01	67.0 (Wyoming)	250.0 (Florida)
RG = Religion (number of people belonging to Christian churches per 1,000 population)[c]	515.029	117.16	325.000 (Washington)	836.000 (Utah)
CW = Consumption of wine (in gallons per-capita)[a]	1.931	1.207	0.68 (West Virginia)	5.990 (Nevada)
Policy exogenous variables				
PRB = Price of beer (cents per gallon)	322.79	35.474	267.000 (Utah)	416.520 (Georgia)
PRS = Price of spirits (cents per gallon)	3098.0	227.583	2660.000 (Vermont)	3540.000 (Washington)
OL = Outlets (outlets per 1,000)[a]	1.327	1.007	0.149 (Tennessee)	4.412 (Nevada)

Table 7.3: *Continued*

Policy endogenous variables	Mean	Standard deviation	Minimum value	Maximum value
BAN = Advertising ban (1 if prohibited; 0 if any is allowed)	0.229	0.426	0.000 (27 of the states)	1.000 (Alabama, Georgia, Kansas, Missouri, Montana, S. Carolina, Utah, Vermont)
MDA = Minimum drinking age for beer (years)	19.057	1.327	18.000 (19 of the states)	21.000 (10 of the states)
EX = Alcoholism rehabilitation expenditures (state budget on alcohol control per 1,000 population)[a]	3403.96	2227.09	479.823 (Georgia)	9981.030 (Oregon)
UN = Unemployment rate (per cent)	8.026	2.322	3.700 (South Dakota)	12.500 (Michigan)

[a] Per-capita of the population age 14 and older, 1975.
[b] Per-capita of the population age 15 to 75, 1975-7 average.
[c] Per-capita of the total population.

set by the states, ranging from 18 to 21.[3] Alcoholism rehabilitation expenditures include both state-funded rehabilitation programmes and the state portion of federal grants allocated through the National Institute on Alcohol Abuse and Alcoholism. The unemployment ratio is included both as a proxy for general social and economic conditions in the state and as a major object of economic policy.

The Model

The econometric model that represents the variables summarised in Table 7.3 is a system of simultaneous equations shown in the following four equations:

116 *Alcoholism: An Econometric Model*

$$CB = ASM^{a_1}\ I^{a_2}\ TR^{a_3}\ UR^{a_4}\ TM^{a_5}\ RG^{a_6}\ PRB^{a_7} \quad (1)$$
$$PRS^{a_8}\ OL^{a_9}\ e^{a_{10}BAN}\ MDA^{a_{11}}\ UN^{a_{12}}\ e^{a_0}\ e^{u_1}$$

$$CS = ASM^{b_1}\ I^{b_2}\ TR^{b_3}\ UR^{b_4}\ TM^{b_5}\ RG^{b_6}\ PRB^{b_7} \quad (2)$$
$$PRS^{b_8}\ OL^{b_9}\ e^{b_{10}BAN}\ MDA^{b_{11}}\ UN^{b_{12}}\ e^{b_0}\ e^{u_2}$$

$$ASM = CB^{c_1}\ CS^{c_2}\ CW^{c_3}\ UR^{c_4}\ OL^{c_5}\ EX^{c_6}\ UN^{c_7} \quad (3)$$
$$e^{c_0}\ e^{u_3}$$

$$ARM = ASM^{d_1}\ CB^{d_2}\ CS^{d_3}\ CW^{d_4}\ UR^{d_5}\ EX^{d_6}\ UN^{d_7} \quad (4)$$
$$e^{d_0}\ e^{u_4}$$

where u_1, u_2, u_3 and u_4 are the error terms that capture the effects of all omitted variables and other errors in the specification of the model or in measuring the variables.

By taking the logarithms of equations (1) through (4) the system is transformed to a system of log-linear (constant elasticity) equations:

$$\ln CB = (a_1\ \ln ASM) + (a_2\ \ln I + a_3\ \ln TR + a_4\ \ln UR + \quad (1')$$
$$a_5\ \ln TM + a_6\ \ln RG) + (a_7\ \ln PRB + a_8\ \ln PRS +$$
$$a_9\ \ln OL + a_{10}\ BAN + a_{11}\ \ln MDA + a_{12}\ \ln UN) +$$
$$a_0 + u_1$$

$$\ln CS = (b_1\ \ln ASM) + (b_2\ \ln I + b_3\ \ln TR + b_4\ \ln UR + \quad (2')$$
$$b_5\ \ln TM + b_6\ \ln RG) + (b_7\ \ln PRS + b_8\ \ln PRB +$$
$$b_9\ \ln OL + b_{10}\ BAN + b_{11}\ \ln MDA + b_{12}\ \ln UN) +$$
$$b_0 + u_2$$

$$\ln ASM = (c_1\ \ln CB + c_2\ \ln CS) + (c_3\ \ln CW + c_4\ \ln UR) + \quad (3')$$
$$(c_5\ \ln OL + c_6\ \ln EX + c_7\ \ln UN) + c_0 + u_3$$

$$\ln ARM = (d_1\ \ln ASM + d_2\ \ln CB + d_3\ \ln CS) + (d_4\ \ln CW + \quad (4')$$
$$d_5\ \ln UR) + (d_6\ \ln EX + d_7\ \ln UN) + d_0 + u_4\ .$$

In each of these equations the right-hand side of explanatory variables has four sets of variables: a set of explanatory endogenous variables, a set of standardising exogenous variables, a set of

Table 7.4: Estimation of the Reduced Form

Exogenous variables	Endogenous variables			
	ln CB	ln CS	ln ASM	ln ARM
Standardising				
ln I	0.4299	0.8041	1.0061	0.1532
	(0.3812)	(0.6388)	(0.6379)	(0.5645)
ln TR	0.1033***	0.2889***	0.0607	0.1309**
	(0.0367)	(0.0615)	(0.0614)	(0.0544)
ln UR	-0.0347	0.0260	-0.0074	-0.2259*
	(0.0739)	(0.1239)	(0.1237)	(0.1095)
ln TM	0.0526	-0.0026	-0.1079	0.3019*
	(0.1008)	(0.1689)	(0.1687)	(0.1493)
ln RG	0.1332	0.0197	0.1952	0.0280
	(0.1415)	(0.2371)	(0.2368)	(0.2096)
Policy				
ln PRB	-0.2664	0.3331	0.2829	-0.5593
	(0.2921)	(0.6806)	(0.4888)	(0.4326)
ln PDS	0.1581	-0.1307	-0.4783	0.9243
	(0.3819)	(0.6399)	(0.6391)	(0.5655)
ln OL	0.0852*	0.0907	0.0111	0.0233
	(0.0471)	(0.0790)	(0.0789)	(0.0698)
BAN	-0.1068*	0.0598	-0.1411	0.0137
	(0.0592)	(0.0993)	(0.0992)	(0.0878)
ln MDA	-0.7360**	-0.9245	0.4342	-0.2028
	(0.3517)	(0.5894)	(0.5886)	(0.5209)
ln EX	0.0616	0.0745	-0.0340	-0.1098
	(0.0441)	(0.0740)	(0.0739)	(0.0654)
ln UN	0.0869	0.2511	0.5692***	0.4082**
	(0.1125)	(0.1886)	(0.1883)	(0.1667)
Intercept	3.7079	1.2583	1.5378	-1.3116
	(3.2254)	(5.4047)	(5.3977)	(4.7763)
R^2	0.7766	0.7739	0.6731	0.6089
$\bar{R}^2$ (adjusted R^2)	0.6547	0.6506	0.4950	0.3956
F	6.37***	6.28***	3.77***	2.85**

Note: Numbers in parentheses are standard errors.
 ***: Significant at the 1% level.
 **: Significant at the 5% level.
 *: Significant at the 10% level.

(exogenous) policy variables and an intercept. Equations (1) and (2) are demand equations for beer and spirits respectively, where, for example, a_2 and b_2 are income elasticities, a_7 and b_7 are (own) price elasticities and a_8 and b_8 are cross price elasticities. These equations differ from the more usual demand equations in including alcoholism as an explanatory endogenous variable and unemployment as a policy

Alcoholism: An Econometric Model

Table 7.5: Estimates of the Structural Form

	Endogenous variables			
Endogenous variables	ln CB	ln CS	ln ASM	ln ARM
Standardising				
ln CB	–	–	-0.0778	0.2656
			(0.2740)	(0.2447)
ln CS	–	–	0.1259	0.1497
			(0.1574)	(0.1625)
ln ASM	-0.1021	0.3389	–	0.0116
	(0.1305)	(0.2049)		(0.1892)
ln ARM	–	–	–	–
Standardising exogenous variables				
ln I	0.5415	0.4761	–	–
	(0.4134)	(0.6493)		
ln TR	0.1013 **	0.2562 ***	–	–
	(0.0382)	(0.0600)		
ln UR	-0.0749	-0.0298	0.0754	-0.1280 *
	(0.0697)	(0.1093)	(0.0706)	(0.0718)
ln TM	0.0604	0.0619	–	–
	(0.1039)	(0.1631)		
ln RG	0.1479	-0.0542	–	–
	(0.1478)	(0.2322)		
ln CW	–	–	0.1689	0.0098
			(0.1226)	(0.1301)
Policy variables				
ln PRB	-0.4715 *	-0.1092	–	–
	(0.2446)	(0.3842)		
ln PRS	0.3269	0.3537	–	–
	(0.3629)	(0.5699)		
ln OL	0.1016 **	0.1096	0.0998	
	(0.0470)	(0.0739)	(0.0643)	
BAN	-0.1097	0.1246	–	–
	(0.0633)	(0.0995)		
ln MDA	-0.7437 *	-1.1487 *	–	–
	(0.3647)	(0.5729)		
ln EX	–	–	-0.0904	-0.1142 *
			(0.0627)	(0.0667)
ln UN	0.2084	0.1521	0.2962 **	0.3459 **
	(0.1256)	(0.1972)	(0.1427)	(0.1534)
Intercept	3.8162	0.6649	3.8710 ***	2.8401 **
	(3.3251)	(5.2227)	(1.0068)	(1.1192)
R^2	0.7635	0.7897	0.6166	0.3834
$\bar{R}^2$ (adjusted R^2)	0.6345	0.6750	0.5172	0.2235
F	5.92***	6.88***	6.20***	2.40**

Note: Numbers in parentheses are standard errors.
   ***: Significant at the 1% level.
   **: Significant at the 5% level.
   *: Significant at the 10% level.

Alcoholism: An Econometric Model 119

variable. Equations (3) and (4) explain alcoholism and alcohol-related mortality, respectively, in terms of alcohol consumption, standardising variables and control variables. The coefficients in all four equations are expected to be positive with the exception of a_6, a_7, a_{10}, a_{11} in (1); b_6, b_7, b_{10}, b_{11} in (2); c_6 in (3) and d_6 in (4).

The reduced form of this model explains each of the endogenous variables as a function of all exogenous (standardising and policy) variables. It thus accounts for all direct and indirect effects of each of the exogenous variables on each of the endogenous variables, and it therefore yields the appropriate set of elasticities to be used in studying policy initiatives (Intriligator, 1978). For example, the number of outlets (OL) has both a direct and indirect effect on consumption of beer since it enters directly equation (1) but it also affects alcoholism in (3) and thus influences ASM in (1). As another example, MDA has no direct effect on ASM but it has two indirect effects via its effects on both CB and CS.

Table 7.4 summarises the least squares estimates of the reduced form equations of the model, obtained by estimating these equations using the data on the 35 states in 1975. Table 7.5 summarises the least squares estimates of the original (structural form) model (Intriligator, 1978).

The results shown in these tables indicate that the endogenous variables are reasonably well explained by the explanatory variables in both the reduced form and the structural form. The relatively high R^2 for cross-section studies, especially for the equations for consumption of beer and spirits, indicate high explanatory power. At the same time, however, the fact that the coefficients are generally not significant indicates the presence of multicollinearity, in which groups of explanatory variables tend to move together.

Because of the log-linear specification, all of the coefficients shown in Tables 7.4 and 7.5 other than those for advertising, which was entered directly as a dummy variable, and for the intercept, have the interpretation of elasticities. For example, the income elasticity of beer is estimated as 0.4299 and that of spirits is estimated as 0.8041 in the reduced form equations, which change the estimated values of 0.5415 and 0.4761 respectively in the structural form to account for indirect effects of income, via the effects of alcoholism in the structural form. Of particular importance to note is the significance of tourism in alcohol beverage consumption and the size and significance of the elasticity with respect to minimum drinking age, especially in the beer equation.[4] According to this result, an 11.1 per cent increase in the minimum drinking age, from 18 to 20, would reduce beer consumption by 8.17 per cent, or, on average, from 29.26 to 26.87 gallons per capita. The large and significant effects of minimum drinking age on consumption also appear in the structural form estimates of Table 7.5. Overall, the explanatory variables that appear to be most important to consumption of beer and spirits, in terms of the size and significance of the estimated elasticities in either the reduced form or the structural form equations, are tourism, minimum drinking age, income, outlets, advertising and the price of beer. While previous studies, as summarised in Table 7.1, have focused on the effects of price on alcohol consumption, this study finds that the price of spirits is insignificant in influencing consumption of spirits in both the reduced form and structural form, while the price of beer is significant in influencing consumption of beer in the structural form (where the estimated elasticity is −0.475) but insignificant in the reduced form. In fact, these results are consistent with those reported in Table 7.1, as most previously estimated price elasticities for spirits in the US are not significantly different from zero.

The other two equations, for alcoholism and alcohol-related mortalities, did not perform quite as well as the equations for consumption in terms of R^2 or F, but their explanatory power is still very large, especially for cross-sectional studies. Furthermore, they indicate an important role for several policy variables. Unemployment is an important determinant both of alcoholism, with an elasticity of 0.57, and of alcohol-related mortalities, with an elasticity of 0.41. Prices of beer and spirits appear to have opposite effects on alcoholism and mortality, with the price of beer increasing alcoholism and decreasing mortality but the price of spirits having exactly the opposite effect − decreasing alcoholism and increasing mortality. Previous studies have assumed explicitly or implicitly that consumption of alcoholic beverages would increase alcoholism and/or alcohol-related mortality. Our findings are that average statewide consumption has no significant effect on either alcoholism or alcohol-related mortality. Alcoholism and alcohol-related mortality are apparently determined by the entire distribution of alcohol consumption, particularly its upper tail, rather than merely its mean value (Bales, 1946). We also found that, for the reduced form, neither number of outlets nor minimum drinking age affect alcoholism or alcohol-related mortality.[5] The alcohol-related mortality equation demonstrates the significant role of tourism in increasing the alcohol-related mortality rate. Urbanisation, on the other hand, tends to be associated with lower alcohol-related

Alcoholism: An Econometric Model 121

mortality rates, perhaps because of the availability of treatment programmes, while mean temperature is inversely related to alcohol-related mortality.

Simulation of Policy Initiatives

Several policy initiatives that could influence the level of alcoholic beverage consumption, alcoholism and alcohol-related mortality were simulated using the estimated reduced-form equations of Table 7.4. The simulations analysed the potential impact of changes in the policy variables of the model, specifically, taxes on alcoholic beverages, that influence retail prices; minimum drinking age; advertising, rehabilitation expenditures and unemployment. Two types of simulations were conducted. The first type allowed for different changes in the policy variables in each of the 35 states in the sample, while the second assumed the same changes in the policy variables in all of these states.

An example of the first type of simulation is that for a change in the minimum drinking age, currently with most at 18 or 21 but some at 19 or 20. The simulation used the estimated reduced form to determine the effects of raising all states in the sample that have a minimum drinking age of less than 21 up to one of 21. A second example of this type of simulation is that for unemployment, where the unemployment rates for states above the average unemployment rate in the sample, 8.067, are lowered to this average by suitable economic policies. A third example is that for advertising for alcoholic beverages, where states not now prohibiting such advertising are assumed to establish such prohibitions. A fourth simulation allowed for *both* an increase in the minimum drinking age to 21 and a prohibition of all advertising for alcoholic beverages. The result of these four simulations are shown in Table 7.6.

The first column of Table 7.6 shows that an increase in the minimum drinking age to 21 would lower beer consumption by 8.39 per cent, would lower spirits consumption by 7.28 per cent, would reduce alcoholism by 0.37 per cent and would reduce alcohol-related mortalities by 3.23 per cent. Thus there are significant reductions in consumption of alcoholic beverages but not in alcoholism due to an increase in the minimum drinking age to 21.

The second column of Table 7.6 shows that a reduction in the unemployment rates of those states with above-average unemployment to the sample average of 8.067 per cent would lead to small reductions

Table 7.6: Simulations of Policy Initiatives Affecting States Differently

Effect on	Minimum drinking age raised to 21 (MDA = 21)	Unemployment rate lowered to 8.067% (UN = 0.08067)	Advertising ban (BAN = 1)	Minimum drinking age raised to 21 and advertising ban (MDA = 21) (BAN = 1)
Consumption of beer, CB (% change)	26.47 (-9.39%)	27.95 (-3.25%)	25.69 (-11.08%)	24.05 (-16.75%)
Consumption of spirits, CS (% change)	2.242 (-7.28%)	2.352 (-2.73%)	2.564 (-6.04%)	2.365 (-2.19%)
Alcoholism, ASM (% change)	43.26 (-0.37%)	38.70 (-10.87%)	36.70 (-15.48%)	38.10 (-12.25%)
Alcohol-related mortality ARM (% change)	44.31 (-2.23%)	42.31 (-6.64%)	45.63 (0.68%)	44.84 (-1.06%)

Note: % change shows percent change relative to the actual levels of
CB = 28.89 gallons per-capita (of the population age 14 and older).
CS = 2.418 gallons per-capita (of the population age 14 and older).
ASM = 43.42 alcoholics per 1,000 (of the population age 14 and older).
ARM = 45.32 alcohol-related mortalities per 100,000 (of the population age 15 to 75).

These actual levels differ from the average values reported in Table 7.2 since the average values in Table 7.2 are averages of state per-capita levels, while the actual levels here are average per-capita levels for the entire 35-state sample. For example, the average consumption of beer of the 35-state sample is 29.26 gallons (in Table 7.2), while average consumption per-capita across all 35 states is 28.89 gallons.

in alcohol consumption (3.25 per cent and 2.73 per cent respectively for beer and spirits) but to substantial reductions in alcoholism, amounting to 10.87 per cent, and in alcohol-related mortalities, amounting to 6.64 per cent. While it takes a number of years of hard drinking to become an alcoholic, differences in unemployment rates across the states frequently persist over long periods, leading to greater alcoholism problems in states with above-average unemployment. In addition, one would expect in any population a number of individuals who, because of past drinking problems, are at high risk of developing alcohol-related health problems. These people, when confronted with the stress of unemployment, may well become alcoholics. These results suggest that unemployment has manifold effects on society, including alcoholism, so reducing unemployment would be of substantial value in combatting alcoholism over and above its general economic value to society.[6]

The third column of Table 7.6 shows that a prohibition on advertising for alcoholic beverages leads *not* to a general reduction in alcoholic beverage consumption but rather a *shift* from beer consumption to spirits consumption. Alternatively, it can be inferred that advertising of alcoholic beverages results in a shift from spirits to beer consumption. This may be related to the presently high ratio of beer advertising relative to that of other beverages. The prohibition of advertising and the resulting shift to spirits consumption significantly decreases alcoholism — by over 15 per cent. In particular, alcoholism appears to be related to total alcohol consumption, and reducing beer consumption by 3.20 gallons reduces alcohol consumption by 0.14 gallons, while increasing spirits consumption by 0.146 gallons increases alcohol consumption by 0.066 gallons, resulting in a net decrease of 0.074 gallons. At the same time, alcohol-related mortality increases slightly, since it appears to be more closely related to spirits consumption, which has increased.

The fourth column of Table 7.6 shows the effect of combining two policy instruments — changing the minimum drinking age to 21 and prohibiting advertising. The result is a very substantial reduction in beer consumption and in alcoholism, but only small reductions in spirits consumption and in alcohol-related mortality.

Each column of Table 7.6 refers to a different policy strategy for attempting to reduce alcohol consumption, alcoholism and alcohol-related mortalities. The results indicate the complexity of the relationships because similar reductions in consumption are not necessarily accompanied by similar reductions in alcohol or alcohol-

Table 7.7: Simulations of Policy Initiatives Affecting States Uniformly

Effect on	Price of spirits increased by 10% (PRS = 3407.8)	Outlets per-capita decreased by 10% (OL = 1.194)	Rehabilitation expenditures increased by 10% (EX = 3744.36)
Consumption of beer, CB (% change)	29.35 (1.58%)	28.64 (−0.85%)	29.07 (0.62%)
Consumption of spirts, CS (% change)	2.386 (−1.31%)	2.396 (−0.91%)	2.436 (0.74%)
Alcoholism, ASM (% change)	41.34 (−4.78%)	43.37 (−0.11%)	43.27 (−0.34%)
Alcohol-related mortality ARM (% change)	49.51 (9.24%)	45.22 (−0.23%)	44.82 (−1.10%)

Note: % change shows percent change relative to the actual levels of
CB = 28.89 gallons per-capita (of the population age 14 and older).
CS = 2.418 gallons per-capita (of the population age 14 and older).
ASM = 43.42 alcoholics per 1,000 (of the population age 14 and older).
ARM = 45.32 alcohol-related mortalities per 100,000 (of the population age 15 to 75).

related mortality. For example, alcohol consumption is reduced by raising the minimum drinking age and also by banning advertising. But one notes that the former approach produces a much smaller reduction in alcoholism than does the latter. One possible explanation is that raising the minimum drinking age affects primarily younger drinkers, while banning advertising affects *all* drinkers, including those who are older and therefore at greater risk of alcoholism.

The second type of simulation is one in which the effects across the states are uniform. An example is a tax on alcoholic beverages, specifically an increase in the federal excise tax on spirits from the current level of $10.50 (which has prevailed at the same level since 1951) to a new level, which could have the effect of raising the price of spirits by, say, 10 per cent − from $30.98 per gallon to $34.08. This new tax level would be $17.40.[6] A second example is a decrease of 10 per cent in the number of per capita outlets from an average of 1.327 to 1.194. A third example is an increase in rehabilitation expenditures of 10 per cent from an average of $34.04 to $37.44 per 100,000 population. The results of these simulations are shown in Table 7.7, using the estimated (reduced form) elasticities reported in Table 7.4.

The first column of Table 7.7 shows the effects of a 10 per cent increase in the price of spirits. Consumption of spirits drops, as expected, by 1.31 per cent, while consumption of beer rises, beer substituting for spirits, by 1.58 per cent, to the new levels shown in the table. While these changes are relatively small, there are more substantial effects on alcoholism and alcohol-related mortality, alcholism falling by 4.78 per cent and alcohol-related mortality rising by 9.24 per cent.

Columns 2 and 3 of Table 7.7 show similar, though less dramatic, results for two other policy changes, reducing the number of on-premise outlets by 10 per cent and increasing state expenditures on alcoholism rehabilitation programmes by 10 per cent. As expected, reducing the number of outlets decreases beer and spirits consumption and also reduces both alcoholism and alcohol-related mortalities. Raising rehabilitation expenditures, however, is associated with *rising* rates of beverage consumption and alcoholism (though the increases are small). It is plausible that these results are due to reverse causality, i.e. rehabilitation expenditures are increased in response to high rates of alcoholism. Once in place, however, these rehabilitation programmes do appear to reduce alcohol-related deaths.

Conclusion

As a result of formulating a simultaneous equations econometric model of alcohol consumption, alcoholism and alcohol-related mortality and estimating this model using cross-section data for US states in 1975 the following four major conclusions emerge:

1. It is important to study alcoholism and alcohol-related mortality directly — as opposed to making inferences indirectly via the demand for alcoholic beverages alone. The usefulness is demonstrated of estimating separate relationships for alcoholism and alcohol-related mortality in addition to the more frequently estimated demand relationships for alcoholic beverages. These relationships are sufficiently complex to warrant the use of a systems approach to aid in understanding the ways in which consumption of alcoholic beverages, alcoholism and alcohol-related mortality are related to one another.
2. The equations have a high degree of explanatory power, in spite of our use of data on one of the endogenous variables, alcoholism, which many have questioned.
3. The model is useful in analysing policy variables to show their

126 Alcoholism: An Econometric Model

relative levels of importance not only in influencing consumption of alcoholic beverages but also in reducing the social cost of alcoholism.

4. Several policy variables are seen to be significant determinants of consumption, alcoholism and alcohol-related mortality. These include the rates of taxation, the number of outlets, advertising and the minimum drinking age. Of particular importance, however, is the role of unemployment as a determinant of alcoholism and alcohol-related mortality.[7] It is apparent that elevated rates of unemployment produce significant social costs, including alcoholism and alcohol-related mortality, in addition to the more commonly measured direct economic losses.

Notes

1. In fact, the econometric model uses logarithms of these variables rather than the variables themselves.
2. The alcoholism measure relies upon cirrhosis deaths while the alcohol-related mortality variable includes a large number of causes of death, only one of which is cirrhosis. The correlation between alcoholism and alcohol-related mortality was found to be relatively low (less than 0.3).
3. Some states have different drinking ages for beer and spirits. For example, some set 18 for beer and 21 for spirits (in Colorado, Kansas, Missouri, Ohio, South Carolina and South Dakota). Nevertheless it was found in practice that the minimum drinking age for beer tends to be more important, and in the regressions it was found that using only the minimum drinking age for beer gave more valid results than treating both minimum drinking ages separately. It may be the case that where there are different minimum drinking ages, outlets only enforce the lower of the two minimum ages, treating those old enough for beer as also old enough for spirits.
4. Table 7.2 shows that Nevada is an outlier in many respects, with the maximum reported values for CB, CS, ASM, I, TR, CW and OL. Of particular interest was TR, for which Nevada is furthest away from the mean value (over 16) times the mean). The model was therefore re-estimated, omitting Nevada from the data set. Only one coefficient changed sign (though remaining insignificant) and most of the others were little changed, either in magnitude or level of significance. The only R^2 that changed appreciably was that for CS, where it fell from 0.7739 to 0.6102. The estimated elasticity of CB with respect to TR omitting Nevada rose from 0.1033*** to 0.1512*** while the elasticity of CS with respect to TR fell from 0.2889*** to 0.2078**. The elasticity of ARM with respect to TR rose from 0.1309** to 0.1867**. The other significant coefficients did not change by more than 10 per cent.
5. These results are consistent with part of those of Colon (1981), namely the lack of influence of minimum drinking age on alcoholism, but they are inconsistent with the Colon result that outlets do affect alcoholism.
6. The new tax level of $17.40 represents an increase of $6.90 per gallon, which, times the 45 per cent alcohol in spirits, yields the increase of $3.10 per gallon of spirits.

7. M.H. Brenner (1973) reached a similar conclusion on the effect of unemployment on alcoholism using an entirely different set of data and a different methodology. He found that admissions to New York state hospitals for alcohol-related problems varied with the business cycle, increasing in periods of high unemployment and decreasing in those of low unemployment.

8 MODELLING ALCOHOL CONSUMPTION AND ABUSE: THE POWERS AND PITFALLS OF ECONOMIC TECHNIQUES

Alan Maynard

Introduction

The chapter is divided into three parts. The first brief section is concerned with the nature of scientific analysis in economics: forming a hypothesis and testing it. In the second section the problems of scientific inquiry are discussed in relation to alcoholism in general and the chapter by Schweitzer *et al.* in particular. The final section examines the question of whether speculative econometrics in a world characterised by uncertainty about causal relationships and all too naive policy-makers, is useful.

The Methodology of Economics

The debate amongst economists about the methodology of their discipline has been long and, at times, quite heated (for further details of its nature see Blaug, 1980). The economist adopts the deductive way of theorising, i.e. if X is true, then Y is true. The central aim of economics is to predict and not merely to explain. A 'good' theory is one which gives good (i.e. accurate) predictions and theories will be disregarded if their predictions prove inferior to those of their rivals.

Unfortunately economics, like all the social sciences, is in an early stage of its development. The economist has no universal laws like those in chemistry, physics or mechanics; unlike the 'hard' physical sciences, economics is 'soft'. Furthermore economic theories are inherently difficult to test because the data are usually very poor and the basic econometric techniques are not without their limitations. The difficulties of testing economic theories often tempt economists from the path of science and the pursuit of falsificationist precepts. In many areas of economics, different practitioners reach conflicting conclusions and, given the inadequate data, it is sometimes impossible to decide which conclusion is correct. Thus it is common for contradictory hypotheses to coexist for many years (e.g. 'monetarism' and 'Keynesianism').

Such outcomes may tempt economists to abandon their avowed methodology. However this temptation has to be resisted as it would leave the economist with no way of choosing between the alternative explanations of economic events. The only way in which we can move on to identify efficient theories (in terms of predictive quality) is to improve the theoretical basis of econometrics and invest considerably more resources in the collection of data which can be used to test the competing theories.

Economics is thus concerned with the formulation of theories which give good predictions. The economist is concerned with the testing and retesting of theories and discarding those whose predictive performance is inferior to their rivals. The construction of any economic model should start out with a clearly articulated set of relationships which identify cause and effect ('if X, then Y'), and, where possible, the linkages between the cause and the effect. The testing of such models should adhere closely to the articulated structure and avoid the common mistake of testing relationships not contained in the theoretical model! The results of such tests should be set out clearly and related to results elsewhere, that is, to the outcomes of the testing of competing models.

To emphasise the tentative nature of economic analysis it is useful to set out some of Mayer's (1980) suggestions to 'harden up' economic science. First, he emphasises the need for more data collection: at present many data series to test economic theories about alcohol abuse are noticeable by their absence. Secondly, he repeats the requirement for scientific inquiry that tests must be repeated and periodic surveys of the 'state of the arts' carried out. Thirdly he advocates that academic journals assess submissions not on the basis of the sophistication of the techniques used but on the likely accuracy of the results. Fourthly Mayer suggests that to avoid 'data mining and results selection', journals require authors to provide the results of all regressions for publication, not just those that happen to support their hypothesis! Fifthly, he argues that journals should also publish insignificant results and require all authors to submit their unpublished data so that verification by others can be facilitated.

These suggestions highlight some of the limitations of published econometric work. Economics is an 'infant industry' but its methodology is explicit and scientific. Like all angels, economists can be tempted from the path of scientific rigour but these temptations and the responding 'soul reclamation' by colleagues may sometimes tell us something useful about how the economic environment works.

130 *Modelling Alcohol Consumption and Abuse*

The Modelling of Alcoholism

Problems of Estimating and Interpretation

The objective of this section of the chapter is to use the preceding review by Schweitzer, Intriligator and Salehi as a framework to illustrate some of the problems of modelling alcoholism and testing economic relationships. Chapter 7 is an innovative and interesting attempt to move away from conventional econometric analysis of the problems and policies associated with alcoholism, which is usually concerned with estimates of demand equations, and to divert econometric effort into the domain of acquiring explanations of alcoholism. Thus the chapter is concerned with the outcomes of the consumption of alcohol, not merely with the factors which influence consumption *per se*.

The authors provide four equations, all estimated in log linear form. The first two are concerned with the consumption of beer and spirits respectively, and the second two are concerned with alcoholism (numbers per thousand) and alcohol-related mortality (deaths per 100,000). Each equation has a set of explanatory endogenous variables (V_1), a set of standardising exogenous variables (V_2), a set of exogenous policy variables (V_3) and an intercept (V_4). These are summarised as follows:

(1) Beer consumption = V_1 (alcoholism) + V_2 (income, tourism, urbanisation, temperature and religion) + V_3 (price of beer, price of spirits, number of outlets, advertising, minimum drinking age and unemployment) + V_4

(2) Spirits consumption = as for (1)

(3) Alcoholism = V_1 (beer consumption and spirits consumption) + V_2 (consumption of wine and urbanisation) + V_3 (number of outlets, alcoholism rehabilitation expenditures and unemployment) + V_4

(4) Alcohol-related mortality = V_1 (alcoholism, beer consumption and spirits consumption) + V_2 (consumption of wine and urbanisation) + V_3 (alcoholism rehabilitation expenditures and unemployment) + V_4

In all the equations the right-hand variables are explanatory, i.e. they explain the magnitude of the dependent variable on the left-hand side of the equation. The subsequent discussion of these equations will be under three headings: data, equation construction and omitted variables, and cause-effect relationships.

The data, as the authors indicate, are not without their limitations, e.g. they accept the reservations about the Jellinek formula. The dependent variables are generally defined in a rather narrow and limited way. For instance income is measured in terms of millions of dollars of personal income per capita but consumption may be affected by variations in taxation levels between the states and variances in the distribution of that income within the state. The effects of using alternative alcoholic beverage consumption measures, quantities and expenditures, could also be explored, as a marginal gallon of spirits may do more harm than a marginal gallon of beer! Inevitably the alcoholics and alcoholic-related mortality data will be inaccurate due to errors and omissions in reporting: a man may be killed in a road traffic accident today and would have died of liver disease tomorrow if he had lived.

These problems are familiar to all researchers, be they economists or epidemiologists, in the alcohol field. Many of the data series could be improved substantially but in the meantime we must all massage the available data as best we can.

The second problem associated with econometric work in the field of alcohol abuse is related to the construction of the equations and the problems that arise from the omission of relevant variables.

Let us discuss the problem of omitted variables first. The following relationship is postulated:

$$E_t = f(S, P, E)$$

i.e. earnings in time t (E_t) are determined by schooling (S), parental background (P), and ethnic origins, black, white or whatever (E). If this equation is estimated we can estimate the coefficients on S, P and E and from them make conclusions about the extent to which differences in schooling, parental background and ethnic origin, 'explain' differences in earnings. However these estimates may be biased upwards if a significant explanatory variable, for instance 'ability', was omitted. The omitted variable, ability, may affect earnings but this effect in the above equation will only be picked up indirectly by other variables whose coefficients will be affected.

Similarly in any other field, omitted variables may bias estimates

132 *Modelling Alcohol Consumption and Abuse*

and lead to false impressions about the relationship between dependent and explanatory variables. Thus, for instance, cultural antecedants may affect consumption and harm, e.g. Spanish Americans may drink more heavily than non-Spanish Americans. A failure to include variables such as this may bias estimates.

This omission of a possibly relevant variable shows that equation construction is essentially *ad hoc*. We are not starting from an explicit and carefully reasoned model from which we identify explanatory variables, rather we are asking crude questions such as 'what factors affect beer consumption?'. Our response to this question leads to the selection of a list of 12 variables in the case of the Schweitzer, Intriligator and Salehi chapter and this selection is based on subjective criteria of plausibility: 'Well, maybe tourist levels and temperature variations affect consumption. Let's put it in and see.'

The problem which arises from using this starting-point is that it gives rise to ambiguities in the nature of the cause and effect which is being implied to exist in the model. This is the third major problem involved in econometric modelling and let us analyse it with reference to particular points in the study in question. The variables discussed are ones which dominate the scientific and policy debate and the problems associated with the results show how it is difficult to identify cause and effect let alone the appropriate remedial policies.

Tourism and Outlets. The authors put tourism in their consumption equations. Although it is not clear, the inference is that those states with more tourism do more drinking. However the estimation of this relationship may be biased because they also include an outlets variable in these same equations. This practice generates the possibility of collinearity existing (i.e. states like Nevada, with high tourist rates, have many outlets too) and generating biased estimates. Furthermore the alcoholics recorded in Nevada are not tourists and the adverse health effects of Nevada's alcohol regulation show up in the statistics of other states. If increased indigenous alcoholism is due to increased access due to tourism, this factor might usefully be included in the 'harm' equations ((3) and (4)).

Advertising. The analysis of advertising effects concentrates on prohibition/no prohibition effects only, i.e. a dummy variable is used. The simulation of policy changes in the chapter shows that the imposition of prohibition leads to substitution out of beer and into spirits with a fall in alcoholism. These results are unusual: the causality is not clear. Ideally the analysis of advertising effects would use expenditure data to give estimates of the elasticities, i.e. the responsiveness of demand to differing levels of expenditure on advertising. This might enable us to determine the efficient type of advertising policy.

Urbanisation. The authors found a negative relationship between population density and alcoholism and its associated mortality, i.e. higher urbanisation reduced abuse and deaths. This is strange as we might expect urbanisation to lead to more outlets, more abuse and more harm. Also the urbanisation, income and unemployment variables may interact. Thus we have problems defining causality and the possibility that estimates will be biased due to collinearity.

Unemployment. It is not clear why this variable is included. Maybe the hypothesis is that more unemployment leads to more abuse. But this effect would be picked up with the income variable. The authors found that unemployment had only small effects on consumption but significant effects on alcoholism and associated mortality. The causation is unclear and this result is similar to that in the Brenner hypothesis which, as Gravelle, Hutchinson and Sterne (1981) have shown, is not statistically robust and unclear as to causation. What is required is careful identification of the links between unemployment, consumption and abuse, and this is absent.

Minimum Drinking Age. The results of the analysis show that increasing the drinking age reduces consumption, and the equations indicate that reduced consumption leads to less harm. Even if we accept these results, the policy implications are not obvious. Even if our policy objectives are reduced consumption and harm, trying to achieve these objectives may not be easy by the drinking age route because of compliance problems. The costs of imposing and enforcing this policy to politicians in particular may be intolerable!

Rehabilitation Expenditure. The results to equation (3) and (4) seem to indicate that increased rehabilitation expenditure reduces the number of alcoholics and alcoholic deaths. However it is plausible that the causality runs the other way, i.e. the numbers of alcoholics and alcoholic deaths affect the level of rehabilitation expenditure. This result is interesting also because of the lack of evidence at the micro level of many rehabilitation programmes having any beneficial effects.

There is a clear need to reconcile this conflict between macro and micro evidence with more evaluative research of treatment programmes (Maynard and Kennan, 1981a).

Religion. The religion variable analyses the effects of differing levels of Christians in the local community. The religion-consumption-abuse linkages are not clear but presumably related to the ethic amongst some Christian groups of abstinence or restricted use of alcohol. However not all Christian groups share the same ethic with the same vigour and more careful elaboration and investigation of these linkages, if any, is called for.

Thus the major areas of debate about an approach using equations such as those above ((1) to (4)) are the problems of collinearity (linked variables in the same equation biasing estimates) and the implications of the results, especially with regard to cause and effect. This latter problem is of vital importance for policy purposes in particular.

The Problems of Identifying Efficient Policies

Having identified, perhaps not fully but certainly quite extensively and very provocatively, the variables with significant effects on the consumption and harm indicators used, Schweitzer, Intriligator and Salehi discuss the choice between competing policies.

The first obvious set of policy variables which can be manipulated is prices. The authors of this American study find that the price elasticity of demand for beer is -0.2 and for spirits -0.13, i.e. a 1 per cent increase in the price of beer would reduce consumption by 0.2 per cent whilst a 1 per cent increase in the price of spirits would reduce consumption by 0.13 per cent. These elasticities are low by UK standards where the equivalent elasticities provided by the government are -0.2 and -1.6 (Central Statistical Office, 1980). All elasticity estimates are concerned with small changes in the price of alcoholic beverages, i.e. they give no indication of the effects of large price increases. It is possible that large price increases would have larger effects on consumption. So, although the price-tax option seems of little use in the American case, it has to be remembered that the consumption effects of a large price increase might be quite different.

However these small price and consumption effects do have substantial results in terms of the harm indicators, e.g. a 10 per cent increase in the price of spirits seems to reduce alcoholism by 4.78 per cent and alcohol-related mortality by 9.24 per cent. Consequently the

Modelling Alcohol Consumption and Abuse 135

authors conclude that even if price elasticities are low, the 'harm elasticities' are greater, and price movements generated by tax changes may be an effective way of reducing the social costs associated with alcohol abuse.

A variety of alternative policies are available for use in the pursuit of policy targets such as reduced consumption and reduced harm. Raising the minimum drinking age to 21 years would apparently reduce US beer consumption by 8.39 per cent, spirits consumption by 7.29 per cent, alcoholism by 0.37 per cent, and alcohol-related mortality by 3.23 per cent. It is not clear why, in comparison to the tax-price policy, the significant effects on consumption do not generate very substantial effects on harm.

Changes in advertising policy in the US would lead to shifts out of beer consumption into spirits consumption presumably because of the at present high level of beer advertising relative to spirits. These switching effects seem to have little effect on the harm indicators.

Two other policies, reducing the number of outlets and increased rehabilitation expenditure, have muted effects on consumption and harm. However, reducing unemployment appears to have quite spectacular effects on harm but not very significant effects on consumption. This again leads to speculation about the nature of the unemployment-harm linkage. If the intervening variable in the relationship is not consumption, what is it? Again we return to the cause-effect problems discussed above and, in relation to the Brenner hypothesis, by Gravelle *et al.* (1981).

The conclusion of this policy analysis is hardly surprising. Those having faith in some sort of Ledermann relationship have argued that alcohol abuse could be reduced by policies which were directed at consumption levels. The most obvious of these policies is the tax-price policy instrument which seems effective in relation to reducing consumption and harm but is unattractive to policy-makers for reasons not unassociated with the political popularity of ministers and their sensitivity to the use of this policy instrument because of its effects on political support and the cost of living index.

The Lessons of the Economic Analysis of Alcohol Abuse

Economic analysis in the field of alcohol abuse, as in any other field, will never give the policy-maker a complete picture of causal relationships and efficient policies. Economics is a way of thinking about things and the precision of its 'tool-kit' is limited by the paucity of good theories and good data with which to test these theories. Provided theory is constructed with care and tested repeatedly whenever new data are available, the process of scientific inquiry is likely to result in the slow evolution of a better understanding of the society in which we live.

The chapter by Schweitzer, Intriligator and Salehi is no exception to this. Its approach is novel and provocative. It is easy to criticise some aspects of the process of formulating the equations, testing the relationships and interpreting the results, but what the authors have provided is a starting block from which future runners in the race to understand the economics of alcoholism can take off. What is required now is that their lead should be followed by other researchers using improved methods of analysis and better data sources.

The policy implications, and their associated problems of this work and other economic analyses of alcohol abuse, should not be ignored. If the objective that policy-makers are seeking to achieve is reduced alcohol abuse and if they believe that abuse and consumption are related, then most of the relevant economic analysis that is available seems to indicate that the use of taxation policies may be an efficient way of reducing harm. The same elasticities vary across products, being related negatively to market share: thus beer, the most popular UK alcoholic drink, has a lower elasticity than wine. The price elasticities vary through time as tastes and market shares alter, and they seem to vary across income groups.

The identification of the most efficient tax-price option is not easy. Income elasticities are quite high (see Maynard and Kennan, 1981b for further discussion) and thus in periods of income growth the real price of alcoholic beverages will have to rise faster than the cost of living (price) index if consumption is to be stabilised. The values of the cross elasticities are relatively under-researched but it seems that a more rapid relative increase in the price of beer, for example, leads to a shift in demand to other alcoholic products. Another problem associated particularly with the vigorous use of the tax instrument is that it may create incentives for consumers to make their own alcoholic beverages either legally or illegally.

Despite these difficulties, the efficient pursuit of health objectives indicates that the taxation and the retail price of alcoholic beverages in many countries, e.g. Britain, the United States and Sweden, has fallen behind movements in the price level. Furthermore during this period, the last 20 years or so, incomes rose rapidly and substantially.

The case for a large increase in the price of alcoholic beverages seems strong as the main cause of increased consumption and harm in the last 20 years seems to be the significant fall in the real price of alcohol. However if this policy was successful and consumption was reduced, the effect on the producer groups might be quite sharp. It is likely that governments would be sensitive to such employment and profit effects. Consequently governments will have to make harsh choices between alcohol-induced deaths and employment in an industry whose products apparently damage and kill its citizens. The harsh nature of this trade-off is likely to induce governments to raise tax levels slowly but consistently. Such a policy of 'gradualism' is also attractive politically because it will reduce the effect of the tax hikes on the retail price index.

The evidence about outlets and advertising on consumption seems to indicate that its effects are small but positive. Elsewhere in this volume Tony McGuinness presents results for the effects of advertising in the UK (Chapter 16). The elasticities are quite small but statistically significant, indicating that curbs on advertising would reduce consumption and, assuming some causal link, harm. One cost of curbing advertising is that the flow of resources that maintain the media would be curtailed. The volume of drinks advertising is such that once again policy-makers are faced by harsh trade-offs. A policy of gradualism in advertising reduction would seem sensible if it was decided to attack alcohol abuse by this method. Some might argue that if the elasticities are so low, it is sensible to leave the advertising activity intact. Perhaps the sociologists who are concerned with the culture of drinking patterns portrayed in the media would not agree. However their concern is with drinking behaviour on the screen through all viewing hours and not just in the advertising slots.

The economists have presented an extensive set of estimates of elasticities, or responsiveness of demand to small changes in price, income, the price of other alcoholic beverages and advertising, and policy-making is thus quite well informed on these issues (these estimates are summarised in Schweitzer, Intriligator and Salehi, and Maynard and Kennan, 1981a and 1981b). However, little is known about the costs and benefits of rehabilitation and treatment programmes. In all countries governments who have been unwilling to curb consumption have felt obliged to throw resources at the treatment of the problems this consumption creates. This allocation of treatment resources has not been based on any scientific evidence that the treatment of alcoholics is clinically effective or cost-effective.

That governments can spend money in the knowledge that they are having no observable effects on health outcomes but useful effects on political support, is a fact of life which should be subject to continual criticism. A large research effort is required to identify the costs and benefits of alternative ways of treating and rehabilitating alcoholics. If governments are not prepared to reduce the harm arising from alcohol abuse, they should ensure that the meagre resources they allocate to treatment are used efficiently.

Such a research effort in evaluation will require a large investment of resources. These resources will be used to improve the data base and this will have a variety of spin-offs. One benefit from such an investment is that we will be able to investigate more thoroughly the pathways of alcohol abuse, e.g. who harms himself? How? When? How is he treated? At present we have little knowledge about, for instance, how much it costs to treat a drunken driver who is involved in a road accident. We have little knowledge about the NHS, police, probation and social work inputs which may be put into his case. Only if we acquire such information, will we obtain more knowledge of the social costs of alcohol abuse, the nature of resource allocation, and the ability to consider whether such resources could be allocated more efficiently.

At present the estimates of the social costs of alcohol abuse in the United Kingdom are tentative and incomplete (see Holtermann and Burchell, 1981). However these estimates show that the resource losses are not insignificant, perhaps as much as £1,000 million in 1981 (Maynard and Kennan, 1981b). The magnitude of these estimates and the fact that they are incomplete (how, for instance, can you value the lives forgone due to excess alcohol consumption?) highlights the need for an active prevention policy.

Whilst price increases may reduce consumption, the effects of prevention campaigns are unknown. Typically governments allocate small budgets to health education and other prevention activities. There is no professional group with an incentive to prevent illness: doctors are mainly concerned with the cure and care of the ill. It is often asserted, sometimes by doctors, that spending on prevention is uneconomic. The fact of the matter is that much of the spending on the NHS (present budget £12,000 million) may be uneconomic. Cochrane (1972) has argued that many therapies have not been evaluated scientifically and McKeown (1976, 1977) has argued that the principle cause of the modern rise of population is not health care but better nutrition arising from greater affluence. So doctors who assert that prevention resources could be better spent should take care: we know as little about the efficiency of prevention as we do about many types of medical care and cure.

Prevention policies imply that behaviour must be changed: like prices, information alters the consumer's perception of the costs and benefits of particular activities. Such 'manipulation' is often rejected as paternalistic, but this position implies an acceptance of the harm excess alcohol consumption generates. The freedom of the individual to damage himself and others is circumscribed in many areas of activity and it seems unavoidable that more resources will have to be put into alcohol-abuse prevention if the costs of alcoholism are to be reduced.

The political costs of adopting active prevention policies are quite clear. The UK alcohol production and related trades employ about 700,000 people in breweries, distilleries, distribution, bars, clubs and restaurants. The producers contribute generously to the political support of political parties. Like all economic policies, a policy of reducing alcohol abuse would have costs and benefits: 'there is no such thing as a free lunch.' It is to be hoped that in the near future these costs and benefits will be clarified by further research by economists and alcohologists, and that governments will grasp the thorny problems associated with the reduction of alcohol abuse.

So the lessons to be drawn from the economic analysis of alcohol abuse seem to be that if the policy objective is the reduction of abuse by reducing consumption:

1. Policy 1: raise the real price of alcohol gradually over 2 or 3 years so that at least 1960 real prices are restored. Based on this experience, manipulate real prices upwards over the next period until consumption targets are reached.
2. Policy 2: curtail advertising, although the effects of this policy may be small and will affect the finance of the media.
3. Policy 3: set up carefully constructed (randomised control trials) to evaluate alternative prevention and treatment programmes.

It will be interesting to monitor the performance of successive governments in the years to come!

9 THE RELATIONSHIP BETWEEN TAXATION, PRICE AND ALCOHOL CONSUMPTION IN THE COUNTRIES OF EUROPE

Phil Davies

The role of fiscal and price manipulation in controlling alcohol consumption and preventing alcohol problems has been stressed repeatedly in the alcohol research literature (cf. Bruun *et al.*, 1975; Popham, Schmidt and de Lint, 1976, 1978; Moore and Gerstein, 1981). Alcohol researchers, however, are by no means unanimous in their appraisal of the relationship between alcohol taxation, prices and consumption. In the present volume, for instance, McGuinness and Cook are agreed that alcohol consumption is generally responsive to the price of alcoholic beverages, though they appear to differ in their estimations of the strength of this relationship and on whether the manipulation of alcohol taxes and prices is warranted. Walsh (this volume) also offers a cautious note by pointing out that in Ireland alcohol consumption and alcohol problems have continued to increase despite fairly regular and sizeable tax increases on alcoholic beverages.

This chapter examines the relationship between alcohol taxes, prices and consumption in the countries of the European Economic Community. In addition, the relationship between per capita alcohol consumption and deaths from cirrhosis of the liver is examined. A two-fold approach is employed. First, a cross-sectional analysis is offered of these variables amongst the countries of the EEC. Second, the trends in the price and taxation on alcohol beverages are examined as well as in per capita consumption over time in each of these countries. These two approaches provide contrasting perspectives on the relationship between alcohol taxation, prices and consumption, and it is concluded that a deterministic model of the effectiveness of alcohol taxation and price manipulation is untenable. The role of other prevention measures, and the cultural, historical and sociological contexts in which they and drinking practices develop, are briefly discussed.

The Data

In order to undertake international comparisons of price mechanisms and their impact on consumption and alcohol-related harm, one would ideally want regularly monitored data on taxation and price changes, patterns of alcohol consumption and various indices of alcohol-related harm in different countries. Taxation data would include the amounts of special levies on each beverage type (beers, wines, spirits), the level of general or sales taxes, and the total tax burden on a litre of each beverage type. Price data for each beverage type are also important, adjusted for changes in the level of real disposable incomes over time. The proportion of consumer expenditure on alcoholic beverages over time is an additional valuable indicator of price and income factors on alcohol consumption.

The amount of alcohol consumed per capita in a country is a useful summary measure of alcohol consumption, though ideally one would also require carefully monitored data on changes in the amounts consumed by different groups of drinkers. These data would also contribute to the measurement of alcohol-related harm in different communities over time, for it is important to know whether a given change in the price of, or taxation on, alcoholic beverages only affects the drinking behaviour of heavy drinkers, moderate drinkers, or both. Using liver cirrhosis death rates as an outcome measure of alcohol control policies is a convenient practice, though inadequate for a number of reasons. The proportion of liver cirrhosis deaths caused by alcohol consumption will almost certainly vary from country to country, and variations in diagnostic and death certification practices further undermine cirrhosis mortality data. Also, deaths from liver cirrhosis only represent one extreme of the broad range of problems and disabilities now commonly acknowledged to be associated with alcohol use. Not all of these problems and disabilities are the consequence of heavy or excessive alcohol use. For instance, car involvements in fatal and serious accidents, drivers with over the legal blood alcohol concentration limit killed in accidents, drinking and driving prosecutions, and alcohol-related accidents at work and in the home are examples of alcohol-related harm that occur to people who may be classified as 'moderate' or 'occasional' drinkers.

This chapter relies heavily on two sources of data: *Alcohol Taxation and Control Policies* by Mavis Brown (1978), and *Developments in the Availability of Alcoholic Beverages in the EEC Countries*, by Pekka Sulkunen (1978). The data provided by these studies fall short of the ideals mentioned above. Brown's work is probably the most comprehensive source of data on taxes levied on alcoholic beverages in different countries. Even so, it does not provide continuous data for some countries (e.g. Italy), nor does it relate tax levels to overall price structures. Sulkunen's study provides data on trends in the price of alcoholic beverages *vis-à-vis* per capita consumption during the period 1950-72, but not beyond. Moreover, these data are derived from an indirect measurement procedure, the expenditure on alcohol by households divided by total annual consumption of alcohol, which Sulkunen acknowledges is a rather crude indicator. Other data on price are calculated by different procedures. Walsh (1980), for instance, calculates the real price of alcoholic beverages by dividing the index of alcoholic drink in the consumer price index by the 'all items' index. Another procedure is to divide the price index of alcoholic drink by the index of disposable incomes. It is not that any of these procedures is wrong, nor that they are without their own merits. Rather, the problem is that for some countries and for certain periods of time the available data are collected by different means which make international comparisons hazardous.

Alcohol Taxation and Prices in the EEC

A comparison of levels of taxation on alcoholic beverages in 1977 (Table 9.1) indicates that there is considerable variation amongst the countries of the EEC. The newer member countries of the EEC, Denmark, Ireland and the United Kingdom, have much higher levels of taxation on all three beverage types than is the case in the older member countries. In France and Italy, where 71 per cent and 80 per cent of total alcohol consumption respectively is consumed in the form of wine, the special taxes levied on this beverage type are either negligible (in France) or zero (in Italy). Similarly, there are no special taxes on wine in West Germany, and a comparatively low rate of taxation is levied on beer despite the fact that beer consumption accounts for the majority (52 per cent) of alcohol consumed in West Germany. The same rank order of countries is obtained when data on special taxes are taken for 1975 (Brown, 1978).

Bruun *et al.* (1975) have suggested that in periods of inflation especially, there will be a tendency for the price of alcohol to lag behind disposable incomes unless governments adjust taxes on alcoholic beverages from year to year, if not month to month. The available data

Table 9.1: Special Taxes on Alcoholic Beverages in Canadian Dollars, per litre of 100% Alcohol, 1977

Beers		Wines		Spirits	
Ireland	14.4	UK	12.4	Denmark	31.8-48.8
Denmark	13.4	Denmark	11.9	UK	21.8
UK	7.4	Ireland	8.8	Ireland	20.9
Belgium	2.6	Belgium	3.2	West Germany	10.2
Netherlands	2.3	Netherlands	1.7	Netherlands	10.1
Italy	1.8	France	.2	France	7.2-.3.5
West Germany	1.6	West Germany	0	Belgium	10.0
France	.4	Italy	0	Italy	2.6-3.5

Source: Brown (1978).

suggest that monthly adjustments are not made in any of the EEC countries, and that there is considerable variation in the frequency and magnitude with which beverage alcohol taxes are adjusted. Between 1972 and 1977 the United Kingdom adjusted its taxes on alcoholic beverages more frequently than any of the other countries of the EEC, averaging at least one increase each year. By way of contrast, France, Italy, Luxembourg, West Germany and the Netherlands did not change the taxes levied on their principal beverage types at all between 1972 and 1977. In Ireland, where excise duties on beer and spirits were adjusted six times between 1970 and 1980, Walsh (1980) points out that the tax increases introduced in the 1980 budget only restored the relative prices of the two beverages to their 1970 levels.

Some idea of the magnitude of changes in taxation by beverage type is given in Table 9.2. Each beverage type in Table 9.2 is rank ordered in terms of the percentage increase in taxation levels between 1972 and 1977. Again, it is the newer EEC countries that have made the largest adjustments in alcohol taxes. Where adjustments have been made in the older EEC countries, it is on spirits, reflecting the overall tendency in Europe to tax spirits more heavily than beers and wines regardless of the country's principal beverage type.

Taxation, however, constitutes a larger proportion of the retail price of alcoholic beverages in some countries than others. This is indicated in Table 9.3 which demonstrates the differential role of taxation on the price of alcohol in the countries of the EEC. These data again indicate that the average retail price of alcohol is higher in the newer member countries of the EEC than in the older ones. However, this is attributable to a much higher level of taxation on alcohol in Denmark,

Table 9.2: Percentage Change in Taxation on Alcoholic Beverages in the Countries of the EEC 1972-7

Beers	%	Wines	%	Spirits	%
Ireland	108	UK	229	Denmark	106
UK	52	Belgium	100	UK	75
Denmark	43	Denmark	25	Ireland	69
Belgium	18-38	France	0	France	68
Netherlands	0	Netherlands	-5	Belgium	39
West Germany	0	West Germany	0	West Germany	30
France	0	Ireland	N/A	Netherlands	24
Luxembourg	N/A	Italy	N/A	Italy	N/A
Italy	N/A	Luxembourg	N/A	Luxembourg	N/A

Source: Brown (1978).

Table 9.3: Price of Spirits and Taxes Levied on Spirits in the Countries of the EEC, 1973

Country	Price per hectolitre without tax (units of account)	Taxes per hectolitre of pure alcohol (units of account)	Average price + taxes (units of account)
Denmark	26-28	1808	1835
Ireland	12-30	1293	1314
United Kingdom	12-30	1290	1311
France	72	475	547
Netherlands	42-46	494	538
West Germany	79	410	489
Belgium	36-40	440	478
Luxembourg	36-40	340	378
Italy	99	133	232

Source: Maurel (1974).
Note: A unit of account is the administrative currency of the EEC.

Ireland and the United Kingdom than in the other member countries. The price per hectolitre of alcohol before tax is appreciably lower in Denmark, Ireland and the United Kingdom than in the other EEC countries. Sulkunen (1978) points out that whereas price fixing by state monopolies is the major price control mechanism on spirits in France and West Germany, heavy taxation is the method used to control the consumer price of alcohol in the newer EEC countries. Taxation also constitutes a higher proportion of the price of beer in the newer countries of the EEC than in the older ones, as is indicated in Table 9.4.

Table 9.4: Percentage of Taxation in the Price of Beer, the Countries of the EEC, 1973

Country	% of tax in price
Denmark	57
Ireland	53
United Kingdom	40
Netherlands	35
Italy	23
Luxembourg	21
West Germany	19
Belgium	19
France	18

Source: Guildstream Research Services (1973).

Against this pattern of prices and taxes on alcoholic beverages one would anticipate alcohol consumption and liver cirrhosis deaths to be higher in the older EEC countries than in Denmark, Ireland and the United Kingdom, and highest in the EEC countries which have the lowest taxes on alcohol and percentage adjustments over time. This is largely confirmed by the data in Table 9.5. Denmark, Ireland and the United Kingdom are amongst the lowest consumers of alcohol in the EEC, and they have lower cirrhosis mortality than the other EEC countries. Those countries with low or zero taxes on alcohol, and the smallest adjustments between 1972 and 1977, i.e. France, Italy, West Germany and Luxembourg have the highest rates of per capita alcohol consumption and of liver cirrhosis deaths. Belgium, which has above average alcohol taxes and percentage adjustments amongst the older EEC countries, occupies the middle position in the rank order of EEC countries for alcohol consumption and liver cirrhosis deaths. One slight anomaly is the Netherlands which has amongst the lowest per capita alcohol consumption and liver cirrhosis mortality in the EEC, despite having only average alcohol taxes and lower than average percentage adjustments between 1972 and 1977. This suggests that the relationship between alcohol taxes and prices on the one hand and consumption and cirrhosis deaths on the other is not an exact or deterministic one. Taxes and prices on alcoholic beverages are only two variables in a complex web of economic and non-economic control measures. It is quite possible, indeed probable, that other factors, including cultural, religious and historical values towards alcohol use, as well as other control measures, such as health education and licensing arrangements,

146 *Taxation, Price and Alcohol Consumption in Europe*

Table 9.5: Alcohol Consumption per Person Aged 15 Years and above, and Deaths from Liver Cirrhosis, the Countries of the EEC, 1976

Country	Consumption (litres pure alcohol)	Rank	Cirrhosis (per 100,000 population)	Rank
France	22.3	1	32.9	1
Italy	17.3	2	31.9	2
Luxembourg	17.2	3	29.6	3
West Germany	16.7	4	28.1	4
Belgium	12.8	5	14.4	5
Denmark	11.6	6	10.6	6
Netherlands	10.9	7	4.5	7
United Kingdom	9.1	8	3.8	8
Ireland	9.1	8	3.6	9

Source: Davies and Walsh (1979).

operate with or without taxation and price measures to restrict or exacerbate both alcohol consumption and alcohol problems. In general, however, those countries which have higher taxes and prices on alcoholic beverages tend to have lower alcohol consumption and cirrhosis deaths, and vice versa.

Price and Consumption Over Time

The data presented so far provide a rather limited and static view of alcohol taxation and prices, and their relationship to alcohol consumption and cirrhosis deaths, at a particular point in time. This section examines the relationship between price and consumption over time in the different countries of the EEC. The data in Table 9.6 indicate that although the rank order of EEC countries by per capita alcohol consumption remained fairly constant between 1950 and 1976, the rate of increase during this period was as high or higher in the new EEC countries than in some of the older ones (e.g. France, Italy, Belgium), despite the higher levels of alcohol taxation, percentage adjustments and prices in the newer member countries. Indeed, in France there was a continuous, though small, decline in per capita alcohol consumption between 1950 and 1976 despite low alcohol taxation and infrequent tax adjustments. A similar decline was evident in Italy between 1970 and 1976, where there is also minimal alcohol taxation, infrequent tax adjustments and low retail prices. These data

Table 9.6: Per Capita Consumption of Pure Alcohol in Litres per Person aged 15 Years and over in the Countries of the EEC

	Consumption			Percentage change		
	1950	1970	1976	1950/ 1970	1950/ 1976	1970/ 1976
France	23.9	22.9	22.3	-4	-6	-3
Italy	12.9	18.7	17.2	+45	+33	-8
Luxembourg	8.4	13.0	17.2	+55	+105	+32
West Germany	4.3	14.9	16.7	+246	+388	+12
Belgium	6.8	11.7	12.8	+72	+88	+9
Denmark	5.2	8.3	11.6	+60	+123	+40
Netherlands	2.8	7.7	10.9	+175	+289	+42
Ireland	5.8	7.2	9.1	+24	+57	+26
United Kingdom	4.9	7.0	9.1	+43	+86	+30

Source: Davies (1979).

suggest that alcohol consumption may develop independently of trends in alcohol taxation and prices. To examine this in more detail, reference is made to data provided by Sulkunen (1978) on price and consumption trends in the EEC countries over varying time spans between 1950 and 1972.

The evidence provided by Sulkunen indicates that a variety of relationships between the price of alcoholic beverages and per capita alcohol consumption are observable within and between the EEC countries. The strongest evidence for a continuous inverse relationship between the price of alcoholic beverages and per capita alcohol consumption is found in the Netherlands between 1952 and 1967 (Figure 9.1(a)). A similar relationship existed in West Germany between 1955 and 1965, though after 1965 consumption in West Germany fell despite a continued fall in the price of alcoholic beverages (Figure 9.1(b)). An inverse relationship between alcohol consumption and the real price of alcoholic beverages can also be found in the United Kingdom (1966-72) and in Denmark (1958-60, 1962-6, 1967-9) (Figure 9.2), though during certain years a pattern of price and consumption moving in the same direction can also be observed in both these countries. In these countries, however, these exceptions to the rule tend to be fairly short term.

A rather different and mixed pattern of alcohol prices and consumption is evident in Italy between 1951 and 1966, and in Belgium between 1953 and 1967. Sulkunen (1978) characterises these countries as having stable average prices during this period. This is perhaps more so in the case of Belgium than Italy, where between

Figure 9.1: The Relationship Between the Price of Alcoholic Beverages and Alcohol Consumption in the Netherlands and in West Germany

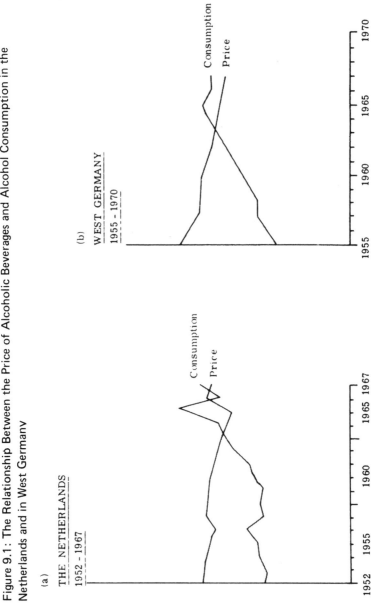

Figure 9.2: The Relationship Between the Price of Alcoholic Beverages and Alcohol Consumption in the United Kingdom and in Denmark

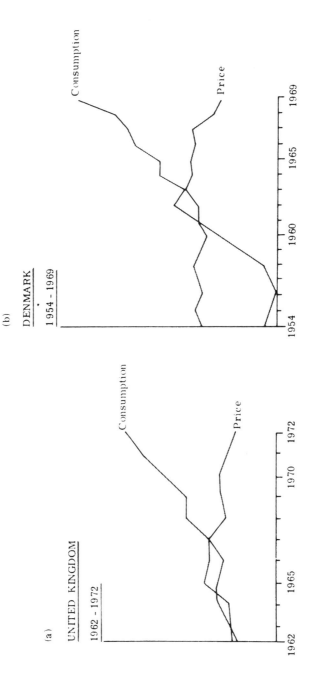

Figure 9.3: The Relationship Between the Price of Alcoholic Beverages and Alcohol Consumption in Belgium and in Italy

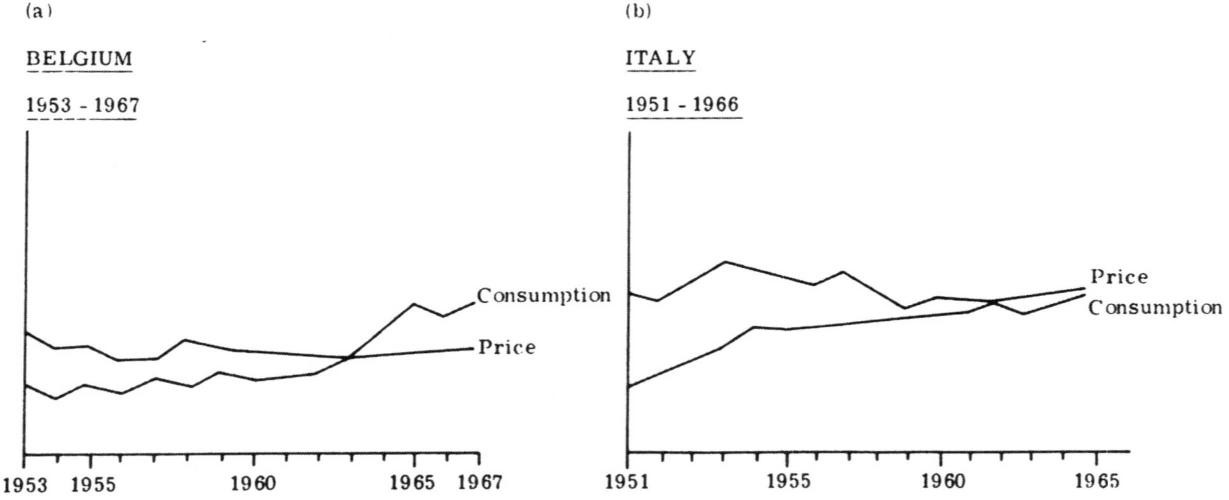

(a)

BELGIUM
1953 - 1967

(b)

ITALY
1951 - 1966

1953 and 1962 there was an overall fall in the price of alcoholic beverages, albeit with intermittent fluctuations. Consumption in Italy increased marginally against this pattern of prices. Beer prices in Italy increased during this period while wines and spirits fell (not indicated in Figure 9.3(b)). Despite these price rises for beer its consumption in Italy grew strongly. The relationship between price and consumption in Italy, then, is mixed and differs according to beverage types. In Belgium, overall consumption fluctuated between 1958 and 1962 and then increased appreciably despite fairly stable alcohol prices. In both countries there are certain years when alcohol consumption and the price of alcoholic beverages have increased or decreased together.

The strong evidence that alcohol consumption may develop independently of trends in the price of alcoholic beverages is provided by Ireland between 1960 and 1970, and by France between 1959 and 1972 (Figure 9.4). In the case of Ireland, a period of fairly stable prices and slightly fluctuating alcohol consumption (1953-9) was followed by sharp and continual increases in the price and consumption of alcoholic beverages. A possible econometric explanation for this is provided by Walsh (1980). Walsh points out that a number of studies (Walsh and Walsh, 1970; Kennedy *et al.*, 1973; McCarthy, 1977; and Pratschke, 1969) show that price elasticity of demand for alcohol in Ireland is less than unity and that income elasticity of demand for alcohol in Ireland is above unity. Thus, whereas drinkers in Ireland are not easily persuaded by price rises to reduce their consumption they are prepared to allocate a substantial amount of any increases in their incomes to buying alcohol. This is substantiated by the fact that both the proportion of personal disposable incomes and of personal expenditure on goods and services devoted to purchasing alcohol increased continually in Ireland between 1960 and 1970 (Walsh, 1980). Walsh also points out that there is a tendency in Ireland for lower income groups to devote a higher proportion of their income to purchasing alcohol than do other income groups. Hence, any increase in taxation on alcoholic beverages in Ireland, which is already amongst the highest in Europe, would be regressive. However, the lowest price elasticity in Ireland is associated with beer (and within the beer group with stout, traditionally the workingman's drink), while spirits appear to be more price sensitive. Under these circumstances, Walsh maintains that 'increases in the price of spirits would have a greater deterrent effect on consumption, and run less risk of pushing up the proportion of income devoted to buying drink, than similar increases in beer prices' (Walsh, 1980).

Figure 9.4: The Relationship Between the Price of Alcoholic Beverages and Alcohol Consumption in Ireland and in France

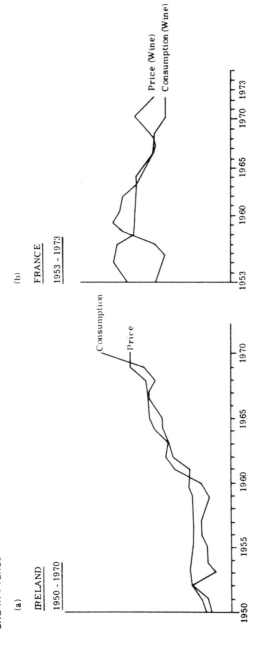

The trends in Figure 9.4(b) are for the real price and consumption of wine in France between 1953 and 1973. Beer consumption has tended to increase in France during this period while spirits consumption decreased between 1950 and 1960 and then increased again. Since wine consumption accounts for in excess of 70 per cent of all alcohol consumption in France, the trend in overall alcohol consumption since 1950 has closely mirrored that of wine consumption. Brown (1978) attributes the decline in wine and overall alcohol consumption in France to the health education and the information work of the Haut Comité d'Etude et d'Information sur l'Alcoolisme, and to restrictive legislation. The latter includes a complicated differential licensing system for the on-premises consumption of different beverage types and strengths, a restriction on the issue of new licences on the basis of number of inhabitants, both for on- and off-premises consumption, and some controls on the advertising of alcoholic beverages. However, in the absence of any evaluation data on these measures and data on price and income elasticities for the different beverage types, it must remain speculative as to why the consumption of wine and all alcohol has declined as price has fallen in France.

More recent data on the relationship between price and alcohol consumption are available for Ireland and the United Kingdom. In the case of Ireland (Figure 9.5) the relationship between price and alcohol consumption between 1970 and 1979 is much different than that between 1960 and 1970 (Figure 9.4(a)). A clear and strong inverse relationship is observed. The decline in the real price of alcoholic beverages in Ireland post-1970 is consistent with Walsh's observation that the taxes on alcohol during this period failed to keep up with overall inflation in Ireland. It is also worth noting that in the two years during the 1970s when the real price of alcohol did increase, 1974–6, the real value of taxation on alcoholic beverages and the proportion of income allocated to alcohol both increased. The latter is consistent with the high income elasticity of demand for alcohol in Ireland noted earlier.

For the United Kingdom between 1970 and 1979 (Figure 9.6) it is possible to express developments in the real price of alcoholic beverages in three ways. First, the price of 'alcoholic drink' is expressed in relation to the price of 'all items' in the consumer price index. This shows an inverse relationship with per capita consumption between 1970 and 1974, and 1977-9. Between 1974 and 1977, according to this method of measuring price, the real price of

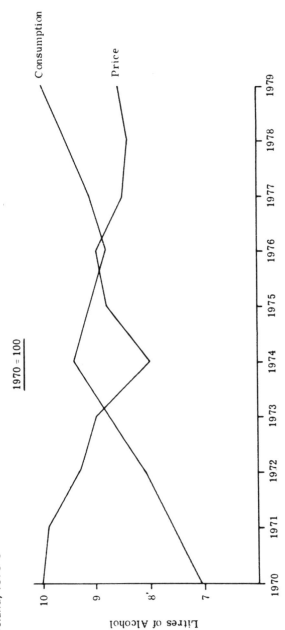

Figure 9.5: Trends in Per Capita Alcohol Consumption and the Real Price of Alcoholic Beverages in the Republic of Ireland, 1970-9

Source: Walsh (1980).

Figure 9.6: Trends in Per Capita Alcohol Consumption and the Price of Alcoholic Beverages in the United Kingdom 1970-9

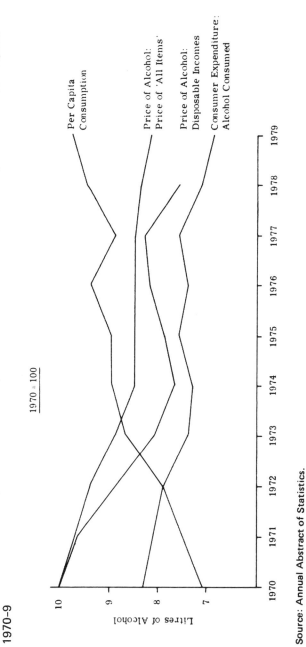

Source: **Annual Abstract of Statistics.**

alcoholic beverages remained constant while consumption was stable, then increased and then decreased. Second, the price of alcohol is expressed in relation to the level of real disposable incomes. Again, an inverse relationship with consumption is observed in all years between 1970 and 1978, except 1974-6. Finally, price is expressed in terms of the indirect method mentioned earlier, that is, the proportion of expenditure on alcohol by households divided by total annual consumption of alcohol. This provides the most consistent data showing an inverse relationship between price and consumption over the entire nine-year period.

Summary and Discussion

Discussions of alcohol control often deteriorate to absolute positions *vis-à-vis* the role of alcohol taxation and price manipulation. On the one hand tax and price manipulation is sometimes suggested as a panacea for the growth of alcohol consumption and alcohol problems. Alternatively, price and taxation are sometimes held to have nothing to do with alcohol consumption and alcohol-related harm.

This chapter has examined the relationship between alcohol taxation, prices and consumption in two ways. First, a rather static view was presented of these variables in the countries of the EEC. This shows that there is considerable variation amongst these countries in the level of taxes on alcohol, in the proportion of taxation in the retail prices of alcoholic beverages, and in the frequency and magnitude with which alcohol taxation is adjusted. It also shows that in general those countries which have higher taxes and prices on alcoholic beverages tend to have lower alcohol consumption and liver cirrhosis deaths. From this perspective, price and taxation appear to have some effect on the level of alcohol consumption and liver cirrhosis mortality in different countries.

Second, the relationship between the price of alcoholic beverages and alcohol consumption over time in the countries of the EEC has been examined. This indicates that a variety of relationships between these two variables are observable within and between these countries over time, and that alcohol consumption can and does develop independently of price. From this perspective, alcohol taxation and price seem to have a limited and mixed effectiveness in controlling alcohol consumption, varying, it would seem, from time to time and according to beverage type.

In those countries where alcohol consumption has at times developed independently of price, e.g. Ireland and France, other economic and non-economic factors appear to have played an important role. Differentials in price and income elasticities were seen to be important in the apparent ineffectiveness of price increases to reduce or control alcohol consumption in Ireland between 1960 and 1970. In France, other economic controls on the availability and promotion of alcoholic beverages, as well as health education and information work, have been invoked in order to explain falling consumption along with declining real prices of alcohol. Price and income elasticities, however, are descriptive terms used by economists and other social scientists to indicate patterns of consumer behaviour under certain circumstances. Like the willingness of governments to pursue alcohol control policies, these have to be seen in a wider context of cultural, religious, historical and sociological factors. The notorious 'workingman's pint', and the environment in which it is consumed in the United Kingdom and in Ireland, is something that would probably not enter the determination of price and income elasticities of demand for beer in Italy or France. Brown (1978) points out that the most extensive government monopoly systems exist in those countries where strong temperance movements developed in the late nineteenth and early twentieth centuries. She notes that in Italy, where the temperance movements has never been very strong, there is a relaxed, unconcerned attitude surrounding alcoholic beverages and their availability. Moreover, Italy is often cited as a country in which intoxication and public drunkenness is much less frequent than in other European countries, and is apparently frowned upon if not negatively sanctioned.

This, however, cuts both ways. On the one hand non-economic factors may well combine, as in the case of Italy and France, to produce a pattern of alcohol consumption and some alcohol problems which is apparently unrelated to economic control measures. On the other hand, as has been indicated in this chapter, Italy and France have the highest rates of death from liver cirrhosis in the European Community. Given that neither of these countries has experienced economic control measures which would bring about long-term stable or rising alcohol prices, it remains a matter of conjecture as to whether, over time, such measures would combine with non-economic factors to produce falling consumption, lower levels of intoxication and drunkenness, and fewer deaths from liver cirrhosis. What is much more certain, from an international comparative perspective, is that a deterministic model of the effectiveness of alcohol taxation and price manipulation is untenable. As with many economic arguments, those factors which make up the *ceteris paribus* condition are the ones which may determine the effectiveness of economic control measures, in particular jurisdictions, at particular points in time.

10 AN EVALUATION OF THE CONTROL OF CONSUMPTION POLICY

David J. Pittman

Introduction

... most policies directed at decreasing consumption of alcohol through legal strictures have been aggregate policies, falling like sober rain from heaven upon the problem and problem-free drinkers alike. (Gusfield, 1976)

The above quotation from Gusfield is one which succinctly states the major defect of the control of consumption model as a primary prevention measure to reduce alcoholism and alcohol problems. This model, global in its conceptualisation, singles out the total society as the key variable through which amelioration of alcohol-related problems will occur, with its concomitant heavy reliance on governmental intervention through legal and administrative rules and regulations pressing on all people regardless of their drinking status.

Historically, the control of consumption model is based on the original work of Ledermann (1956, 1964) to provide a mathematical model of estimating the distribution of alcohol use in an homogeneous population.

However, the control of consumption model is only one of several schemes which have been discussed by social policy-makers to reduce the cost of alcohol abuse to society. The various models of social controls to minimise alcohol problems have been presented in detailed form by Lemert (1962) in a provocative essay and further refined by Pittman (1980a). These other models may be briefly noted as:
(i) prohibition on the manufacture, distribution, sale, and in some cases even the consumption of alcoholic beverages; (ii) the educational model with its emphasis on informational campaigns to inform the public about the consequences of the misuse of alcohol to the individual and the society as a whole, with the goal that such educational programmes will lead either to abstinence or to drinking appropriate to the situation; (iii) the functional equivalent model by which the costs of intoxication and drinking can be reduced by the substitution of behaviours which would take the place of drinking in the society;

160   *An Evaluation of the Control of Consumption Policy*

(iv) the social structural model which posits that many alcohol-abuse problems are partially the result of individual and group deprivations which are a consequence of inequities in American social structure; and (v) the neo-prohibitionistic model which is most comparable to the control of consumption one with its emphasis that the costs of intoxication can be reduced by governmental controls on the manufacture, distribution and sale of alcoholic beverages which regulate the price, the method of distribution, the availability by age, place, time, etc., and the advertising of alcoholic beverages.

The Ledermann Model

The statistical basis of the control of consumption model has as its basic foundation the seminal work of Ledermann. No understanding of control theory can be obtained without a careful examination of Ledermann's work. First, the control model developed from his studies of alcohol problems, but he is clear that it is an attempt to describe and predict in *homogeneous populations* (never defined in his work) the distribution of consumption of alcoholic beverages. It should be noted that homogeneous populations do not exist in complex industrial societies such as the United States, the Soviet Union, the United Kingdom and many other Western societies (except as subcultural groups). Thus his disciples such as Schmidt, de Lint, Bruun and others have violated this assumption in their studies which apply his statistical principles.

As Miller and Agnew (1974) have noted correctly in their critique of Ledermann's works, the implications in the model are concerned with 'number of heavy drinkers, the amount of alcohol consumed by heavy drinkers and the population of alcoholics'.

But first consider an abbreviated version of Ledermann's model on the distribution of alcohol consumption. This model assumes that a normal curve does not adequately predict the distribution of alcohol consumption. In the normal curve the left-hand side or portion encompasses negative sums. Because there cannot be negative consumption of alcohol, the left-hand portion must be bounded by zero to obtain a normal curve.

This theory asserts that the frequency distribution of alcohol consumption in an homogeneous population could be estimated with a lognormal rather than a normal curve. This suggests that natural logarithms of consumption rather than raw consumption frequencies

An Evaluation of the Control of Consumption Policy   161

are normally distributed. This implies that the vast majority of consumers drink small amounts while a very few drink large amounts. Two parameters of the distribution of consumption are needed to define a lognormal distribution in a population. They are: (i) mean consumption and (ii) dispersion of consumption as measured by the standard deviation. When dealing with a lognormal distribution, each level of mean consumption implies a family of lognormal distributions.

Ledermann assumed that very few, if any, people would consume more than 1 litre of absolute alcohol per day (365 litres per year) because such consumption would be fatal; and further, that the number of drinkers who would consume this extreme amount would be independent of the mean consumption of the population. He used these assumptions to establish the right-hand tail of the distribution of consumption. Thus, the Ledermann model is a one-parameter case of the lognormal distribution in which the mean consumption of alcoholic beverages determines their distribution.

The Ledermann curve can thus be presented in graphic form where the abscissa is the annual amount of beverage alcohol consumed in any population and the ordinate is either the number or the percentage of drinkers (Figure 10.1).

The major assertion of the model is: 'Knowledge of the mean consumption, one parameter of the distribution of consumption, is sufficient to predict the other parameter, the disperson [of consumption] as measured by the standard deviation' (Parker and Harman, 1978). Bruun *et al*. (1975) claim that 'differences as to dispersion between populations with similar levels of consumptions are quite small'. Thus it is claimed by advocates of this model 'that knowledge of the magnitude of increases and decreases in mean consumption is sufficient to predict the proportionate increases or decreases in the prevalence of heavy consumption' (Parker and Harman, 1978). Therefore it is assumed that one has to know only one parameter of the distribution, the mean consumption, to predict the other parameter of the curve, the percentage of drinkers in the heavy consumption category. That mean consumption predicts the actual dispersion of consumption is not fully supported by the research in this area.

Another major assertion of the model is that if mean consumption is lowered, the Ledermann curve will be shifted to the left, and the number of persons at the right-hand end of the distribution would be reduced (i.e. a decrease in the number of heavy drinkers). Conversely, if the mean consumption in a population increases, Ledermann and

Figure 10.1: The 'Ledermann Curve'

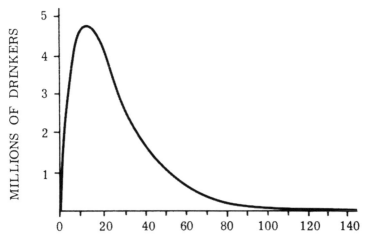

Source: Miller and Agnew (1974).

his disciples assert that the curve will shift to the right and there will be an increase in the number of heavy consumers. Thus it is from these questionable statistical assumptions that the emphasis on the control of consumption model to reduce alcohol use in any society emerged.

Ledermann's Sample Populations

In constructing his model on which the lognormal distribution of consumption was derived, Ledermann used nine sample populations, including, for example, samples of the purchases of alcoholic beverages by individuals, the annual consumption of alcoholic beverages by a population hospitalised for carcinomas, blood alcohol concentrations of drivers stopped at random in an American city as part of a traffic accident study, etc.

Ledermann's samples, from which he constructed and tested his lognormal distribution of consumption, are inadequate and

An Evaluation of the Control of Consumption Policy   163

questionable for a number of reasons. First, purchase of alcoholic beverages by a population is not identical to consumption behaviour in the same population. The same error is repeated by de Lint and Schmidt (1968) in their study of the purchase distribution of distilled beverages and wine for a sample of regions in Ontario in March 1962 and March 1964. J. de Lint and Schmidt statistically demonstrate that those individuals who purchased large quantities of alcoholic beverages commonly did so over several transactions. From this they assume that the distribution of purchases is representative of the distribution of consumption. Despite this assumption, the authors overlooked the fact that a household may have more than one consumer of alcoholic beverages, that their use of one month's records (March) ignored seasonal variations in purchases, and that beer purchases are excluded, as well as those at outlets other than stores (restaurants, taverns, cocktail lounges and illicit sources). Also they ignore that some individuals may buy large quantities at one time to 'stockpile' their beverage alcohol supply for subsequent months. In short, de Lint and Schmidt's study of purchases has serious methodological flaws. Second, at least three of Ledermann's samples use clinical populations who had physical illnesses or occupational problems. In no sense do these populations represent normal population samples. Third, the samples are characterised by inadequate measures of total annual consumption of alcoholic beverages with their emphasis on wine drinking, and even for this beverage, annual consumption is rarely given. Fourth, the samples, outside of those who purchased beverages, are extremely small and all of them are non-random; thus it is impossible to generalise to a total population from them. Finally, measurements of blood alcohol concentrations (BAC) in two samples are only one-time occurrences, and no evidence is presented that such BACs are either lognormally distributed or are representative of the annual consumption of beverage alcohol in these groups (Ekholm, 1972).

From a critical appraisal of Ledermann's samples, on which he based his assumption that the natural logarithms of consumption are normally distributed, the conclusion which must be drawn is that his premise is fallacious. Central to this criticism is the comment by the statisticians, Duffy and Cohen, that Ledermann's assumptions contain

> ... two mistaken beliefs: (a) that skew data are always rendered normal by a logarithmic transformation, and (b) that a fitted distribution applied equally well in the tail as in the centre. Misunderstanding (a) is probably the reason for the unfortunate

insistence that the distribution of alcohol consumption does not change with time or population being studied and (b) is the reason for use of the distribution to estimate the proportion of excessive drinkers. (Duffy and Cohen, 1978)

In summary, there is probably little doubt that the consumption of alcoholic beverages is skewed; i.e. a small number of drinkers (2 per cent to 12 per cent) contribute to a disproportionate share of the alcoholic beverages consumed in a society. These disproportionate consumers of alcoholic beverages are those who are classified as addicted drinkers or heavy drinkers in sample surveys such as those of Cahalan *et al.* (1969) and Paula Johnson *et al.* (1977) in the United States. But there is the serious question as to whether the distribution of consumption which is skewed will be rendered normally distributed by logarithmic transformation.

The Constant Relationship Between Mean Consumption and Prevalence of Heavy Consumers in the Ledermann Model

Ledermann's disciples who have pursued his line of inquiry have continued to assert the basic proposition of the model — that knowledge of the mean consumption of alcoholic beverages in any population, which is only one parameter of the distribution of consumption, is adequate to determine the other parameter; namely, the dispersion of consumption as measured by the standard deviation (Parker and Harman, 1978). This is questionable.

As Duffy and Cohen (1978) have noted, there has been relatively little scientific discussion of a major fallacy in the Ledermann model that alcohol consumption in a population has a constant pattern of distribution from those who abstain to those who are heavy imbibers of beverage alcohol. This assumption means that the researcher must accept as an article of faith that the distribution of alcohol consumption does not either change over time for a population or with the group being studied. This assumption is contradicted by longitudinal survey data of the drinking behaviour of college students originally studied by Straus and Bacon (1953) in 1949-51, who were resurveyed by Bacon (1979) approximately 25 years later, which found significant changes in individual drinking patterns at follow-up.

Thus it is essential to know the dispersion of consumption or the variance from the mean consumption, as drinking patterns, including amounts consumed, do vary by age, sex, race, religion, ethnicity and other sociocultural variables within a national population as well as between national populations. The Ledermann model, while providing data on the mean consumption of alcoholic beverages in a population, does not confront the problem of the dispersion of consumption. For example, it is quite possible for two populations to have the same mean consumption but to have radically different (high and low) dispersions in their distributions. Inferences derived from drinking surveys of subpopulations would dictate the assumption that the amount of absolute alcohol consumed by a total population can be distributed among consumers in quite different amounts.

Brunn *et al.* (1975) confront this question of whether significant dispersion or variance exists among different population samples by providing dispersion data from 14 samples (six adult and eight youth populations). Bruun *et al.* state, 'the data have been derived from natural populations, rather than special ones such as groups of alcoholics, and includes cultures as varied as Italian urban dwellers on one hand and Norwegian youth on the other'. Are these samples really as culturally diverse and natural samples as Bruun *et al.* would like us to believe? The answer is provided in the critique of Bruun *et al.* and by J. de Lint who is himself identified with control theorists. He states that

> ... [several samples] represent assorted segments of a larger sample (e.g. Norwegian boys aged 16-17 and 18-19, and girls aged 16-17 and 18-19) whereas ... [others] ... represent groups of respondents who reported some consumption during the 24 hours or during the week immediately preceding the interview (e.g. French adults, Italian residents in Rome, Dutch adults). The former selections are given too much weight, the latter are clearly biased in direction of regular heavy use. (de Lint, 1976)

Unfortunately the 14 samples chosen by Bruun *et al.* are inadequate to test the variance or dispersion of consumption in populations, not only for the reasons de Lint cited but also because 9 of the 14 are from Sweden and Norway, both relatively small homogeneous societies; in addition, 13 of the 14 samples are derived from Western Europe with only one from the United States. These samples lack significant cultural diversity (no Eastern European or non-Western societies are included) and are not representative of even Western societies.

Despite this deficiency in the selected samples, Bruun *et al.* claim, after their statistical analysis of these data, that 'the apparent stability in dispersion [derived from the 14 samples] seems to indicate a certain invariance in the distribution pattern'. But Bruun *et al.* further weaken their argument by boldly generalising from their inadequate samples that

> The *prima facie* possibility of substantial differences [in this dispersion] between different cultures does not, according to the available evidence, manifest itself in real life.

But when the same evidence from the 14 samples used by Bruun *et al.* is subjected to statistical analysis by Duffy and Cohen they reach the conclusion that

> ... [the data] represent highly statistical significant differences in dispersion since many of the samples are based on large numbers of drinkers and that in addition ... there are important substantive differences in their effect on the estimation of the proportion of excessive drinkers in lognormal assumptions. (Duffy and Cohen, 1978)

Therefore, statements by Bruun *et al.* about the invariance in the distribution of consumption have been disputed by some statisticians, and the assumption of invariance in dispersion of consumption through time and between cultures remains controversial.

A recent study by Singh (1979) of a random household sample's drinking and drug usage patterns in an agricultural village in the state of Punjab in India questions the validity of the Ledermann curve when applied to non-Western cultures. In the sample of 108 households, composed of 701 persons, of whom 423 were 15 years of age and over, none of the adult females (173) was a user of alcohol, but 124 of the 250 males were users of alcohol. It should be noted that India is a culture with a strong abstinent tradition. For the whole adult population, only 29.3 per cent are users of alcohol, which is significantly lower than the percentage of users in Western societies.

For those who drank in this sample, the per capita consumption was 10 litres yearly, which is a relatively high level of consumption for the drinkers. When Singh compared the expected percentages of drinkers, estimated by lognormal distribution, at various levels of consumption

An Evaluation of the Control of Consumption Policy 167

using the Ledermann equation, he found that the Ledermann model significantly underestimates the number of moderate and heavy drinkers. Singh states his major findings as follows:

> Our findings therefore suggest that the distribution of alcohol consumption is not the same in all populations. In a population in which alcohol use is limited to a minority, the distribution roughly approximates a lognormal curve, but the differences in dispersion and the estimates of the expected number of heavy users obtained by this method when compared with actual survey findings are fairly large and cannot be dismissed as 'small and probably of little practical relevance'. (Singh, 1979)

Thus the control of consumption advocates should not only more closely examine the role of social and cultural factors affecting the distribution of alcohol consumption, but should also test their model on more geographically diverse populations, e.g. non-Western and Eastern European societies.

In spite of the lack of convincing evidence to support the assumption that the distribution of consumption is invariate through time for different cultures, why do control theorists still maintain that they do not need to know the dispersion of consumption, only the per capita consumption of beverage alcohol, to predict the number of heavy drinkers in the society? Parker and Harman offer perhaps the best explanation in their statement:

> ... the variance is most difficult to obtain since production or sales data do not usually yield it, and that accounts for the appeal of Ledermann's 'special case' in which the mean alone gives the curve. (Parker and Harman, 1978)

In summary, the original Ledermann model of lognormal distribution of alcohol consumption and the attempts by control theorists empirically to justify it still require two parameters to be known to construct the distribution — namely the mean and variance of consumption — despite protestations otherwise. Attempts by Bruun *et al.* (1975) to assume invariance in dispersion must still be scientifically verified. Likewise, no study has shown that lowering the mean consumption has the same consequences at all levels of consumption; e.g. do moderation messages and control measures on availability of alcohol beverages have the same impact on heavy, moderate and light drinkers?

Summary

The underlying assumptions of the control of consumption model based on Ledermann's works are distributional: that for any population alcohol consumption is lognormally distributed and there is an invariant relationship between mean or per capita consumption and heavy ingestion of alcohol by alcohol-abusing individuals. Thus, policies aimed at reducing mean or per capita consumption will, *ceteris paribus*, reduce the prevalence of heavy consumption and alcohol abuse. Criticisms of the distributional assumptions of the Ledermann model have been presented by Miller and Agnew, Duffy and Cohen, and Singh among others. Sampling inadequacy, error in measurement of total consumption and, most importantly, the lack of generalised invariance in the relationship between mean consumption and dispersion undermine the statistical foundations of the control of consumption model.

Social Policy Implications of the Control of Consumption Model

The control of consumption model based on the Ledermann assumptions implies a number of governmental strategies for the prevention of alcohol-related problems in any society. As Schmidt and Popham (1978) have recently stated, the major propositions of the control of consumption model are:

1. A change in the average consumption of alcohol in a population is likely to be accompanied by a change in the same direction in proportion of heavy consumers.
2. Since heavy use of alcohol generally increases the probability of physical and social damage, the average consumption should be closely related to the prevalence of damage in any population.
3. Any measures, such as those regulating the availability of alcohol, which may be expected to affect overall consumption are also likely to affect the prevalence of alcohol problems; and hence should be a central consideration in any programme of prevention.

Per Capita Consumption

Thus, the central goal of preventive policies in the area of alcohol

An Evaluation of the Control of Consumption Policy 169

problems, according to control theorists, is either to stabilise and/or to reduce the current levels of per capita consumption of alcoholic beverages. Specifically, Ernest Noble, former Director of the National Institute on Alcohol Abuse and Alcoholism (NIAAA), stated at a meeting of the National Advisory Council on Alcoholism in 1977, that one of the long-range objectives of his organisation was to maintain 'the present level of per capita alcohol consumption (The Alcoholism Report, 1977). There is no indication that this goal of NIAAA has changed (Beauchamp, 1980). Since per capita consumption statistics derived from production and sales data are the foundation of NIAAA's policy pronouncements, it is germane to note that these data have limitations as to their accuracy on an international, national and local basis. Furthermore, per capita consumption of alcohol beverages statistics are crude measures which ignore differences in the age-sex distribution as well as differences in the classification of individual drinking patterns from abstinence to heavy drinking in different populations.

Alcohol researchers who work with production, sales and consumption statistics can derive significant benefits from *a close examination of the studies in the field of demography*, especially those concerned with the age-sex distribution of the population at one point in time and projections of this distribution over time. Demographic studies of fertility offer an excellent model for the analysis of consumption statistics of alcohol beverages. Briefly stated, demographers rarely use the crude birth rate, i.e. the number of children born to females in a one-year period, to establish the birth rate for a population. The population experts have established that the more precise the measurement of any phenomenon, the more accurate and meaningful it becomes for understanding current trends in fertility and for making future projections. Thus the birth rate for females becomes more precisely defined, i.e. the number of births per 1,000 women in the child-bearing period of 15 through 44 years of age, with refinements such as the *age-specific birth rate* for age categories, such as 15-19, 20-4, 25-9, 30-4, 35-9 and 40-4. The age-specific birth rate is essential, for births are not randomly distributed through the female's child-bearing years. Numerous other refinements of the birth rate can be presented, such as by age and race, age and state, age and country, etc.

The same procedures for refining measures of consumption need to be developed by alcohol studies researchers. Sample population surveys of drinking patterns, despite their inadequacies, need to be used more extensively by those who are now engaged in massive global studies (generally neither very reliable nor valid) of international and intranational rates of per capita consumption. These macroscopic studies, simplistic in nature, generally reach the conclusion that the per capita consumption of beverage alcohol has increased worldwide since the end of the Second World War (1945) and that alcohol problems have reached the proportion of a worldwide epidemic. This evidence is flawed by the lack of rigorous supporting data which can be obtained only by miscroscopic studies of the age-sex distribution of the population; the ordering of populations into comparable drinking groups by the conventional, rigorously defined categories of drinkers, i.e. abstainers, light, moderate and heavy drinkers; and the specific rates of consumption by such crucial variables as age, sex, race, ethnicity, economic status, religious affiliation and participation, etc. The field of alcohol research would profit from studies which chart the per capita levels of consumption through time for specific age groups, refined to include distinct rates for males, females, racial and ethnic groups, etc.

There is nothing startling about these suggestions for focusing less on global studies of consumption; researchers have known for decades that consumption of beverage alcohol is not randomly distributed throughout the world, any nation, or a section within a nation. The proposed studies of per capita consumption in specified groups using rigorous measures through time would allow the scientist more precisely to address group differences in drinking patterns which are reflected in different levels of consumption.

Reducing Per Capita Consumption

Despite the lack of precision in the measure, per capita consumption, those who are advocates of a control of alcohol consumption policy have proposed a number of social policy initiatives not only in the United States but also in European countries on both sides of the Iron Curtain to reduce the consumption of alcoholic beverages. In the United States these measures may be catalogued as follows:

1. Advertising restrictions on beverage alcohol, including ads being banned in both print and electronic media.
2. Disallowing alcoholic beverage advertising as a business tax deduction.

An Evaluation of the Control of Consumption Policy   171

3. Mandatory health warning labels emphasising the effect of alcohol on the fetus on alcoholic beverage containers.
4. Raising the minimum age for purchasing alcoholic beverage to 21 years of age.
5. Increased taxes at the local, state and federal level on beverage alcohol.
6. Earmarked taxes on beverage alcohol to help defray the cost of rehabilitation programmes for alcoholics.
7. Restrictions on the availability of alcoholic beverages:
    (a) restrict the number of commercial outlets (both on- and off-premise sales locations);
    (b) limiting the hours and days of sales;
    (c) limiting the number of sales outlets in lower income neighbourhoods.
8. Mandatory increases in the cost of alcoholic beverages to match the increase in the consumer price index (CPI).
9. Mandatory public information messages by the alcohol beverage industry to point out the potential health and social damage to individuals who use these products.

Although it is beyond the scope of this chapter to evaluate the empirical evidence (where present) of the effectiveness of each of these proposed measures to reduce per capita consumption and to prevent alcohol problems in a society, it can safely be stated that the common themes are to limit the availability and the demand for alcoholic beverages to the exclusion of other preventive techniques (Room, 1981). Unfortunately, a number of these proposals are based on opinion, not on empirical evidence that would support the contention that they either lower per capita consumption or reduce alcohol problems; e.g. health warning labels on containers of alcoholic beverages (Pittman, 1980b), advertising restrictions (Pittman and Lambert, 1978), raising the legal drinking age to 21 years, etc. For other measures the evidence is either equivocal or negative. For example, in reference to the availability of alcoholic beverages, Smart (1977), reviewing the relationship between the availability of beverage alcohol and per capita consumption and alcoholism rates in the United States, indicated that consumption and alcoholism rates in the United States are more closely related to urbanism and income than to availability. Strickland (1981), in a study of teenage alcohol consumption patterns and advertising exposure, has reported virtually no associations between advertising exposure and alcohol abuse. In short, it would be difficult for a national government such as the United States to adopt such controls on availability and demand of alcoholic beverages when the scientific evidence is neither available nor fully supports the contentions of the control of consumption advocates.

11 THE ECONOMICS OF ALCOHOL TAXATION
Brendan M. Walsh

The economic considerations that should be taken into account in formulating policy towards alcohol taxation are discussed in this chapter. The aim pursued is to summarise in non-technical language the standard theory of consumer behaviour and taxation as it applies in the case of a commodity such as alcohol whose consumption is widely believed to play a part in numerous social problems. This entails spelling out in detail some of the points summarised by Leu in Chapter 1.

The economist is concerned with trying to alter tax structures, so that they approach more closely to what would be optimum according to a set of well-defined economic criteria. In practice, however, there may not exist a reservoir of insights whose neglect has led to the adoption of seriously deficient policies. In fact, a review of the question of alcohol taxation suggests that there are few concrete recommendations that can with any confidence be derived from the application of standard economic theory in this area. In particular, it would be a presumptious economist who would undertake to pass judgement on whether a particularly country's alcohol taxes were 'too high' or 'too low'.

To some extent this reflects the fact that alcohol taxation has received relatively little attention from economists and hence there is a dearth of well-grounded empirical research in the area. This is in contrast with the burgeoning literature on the health economics of smoking. There are some issues relating to the consumption of alcohol on which further research will undoubtedly shed light and permit firmer policy inferences to be drawn. These are discussed later in this chapter. But even if we possessed all the research findings that are relevant to the problem, the contribution that could be made by economic analysis in an area that has far-reaching social and even religious ramifications would remain relatively modest.

The Economist's Perspective

Some of the assumptions about human behaviour and social welfare generally accepted in mainstream contemporary economics contrast starkly with those implicit in much of the medical and public health literature on alcohol. Before turning to the details of alcohol tax policy it may be helpful to summarise these differences.

An important feature of the way economists approach the analysis of consumer behaviour is the presumption that individuals' valuations of the consumption options open to them are the best index of their well-being or welfare. Although the cruder version of 'economic man' as a calculating automaton, motivated only by a desire for material gain, is not an accurate view of the way economists analyse consumer behaviour, even the most sophisticated analysis retains the following assumptions: (i) individuals are the best judges of what contributes to their own welfare; (ii) they make reasonably systematic evaluations of the available alternatives; and (iii) in the long run they obtain and act on accurate information concerning the prices and other characteristics of the commodities they consume, and are not unduly influenced by persuasive advertising. The status of these and related propositions concerning economic rationality has varied in the history of economics between axiom and working hypothesis, but there is no doubting their central importance to mainstream economic theory (Blaug, 1980).

The medical and public health literature in general but particularly in the area of alcohol policy seems to be based on a very different view of human behaviour. In contrast with the economist's acceptance of the sovereignty of consumers' preferences, there is a presumption that in many important instances individuals do not know what is really for their own good. This ignorance may be due to the baneful influence of advertising or to the difficulty the ordinary person is said to have in acquiring accurate information about complicated issues, but whatever its origins it is believed to be pervasive, and to provide ample justification for large-scale intervention with the normal functioning of a market economy.

There is also a marked contrast between the tendency of public health experts to regard almost any gain in longevity as worthwhile and the insistence of economists on the fact that measures which prolong life usually entail significant costs, either in medical resources or lifestyle or both, and hence the optimal allocation of resources to the promotion of longevity will stop far short of the limits set by medical technology or an impeccable life-style. Economists tend to the view that we can obtain some idea of how much people value an increment to life expectancy by observing their behaviour in pursuing risky pastimes or purchasing safety equipment. By way of contrast, the implicit cost-benefit analysis adopted by some public health experts implies an almost infinite value for any gain in life expectancy. While it is easy to caricature the extremes of either approach, it is fair to say that much of the difficulty economists and alcohol education experts experience in communicating derives from these contrasts in basic philosophical assumptions.

General Tax Maxims

Textbooks on public finance typically approach the question of excise taxation in two stages.[1] First there is a discussion of the relative merits of specific excise taxes compared with an income tax or a general tax on all commodities. This is followed by a discussion of which commodities are appropriate targets for specific taxation.

Economists in general take the view that if a government wishes to raise a certain amount of revenue, the loss of welfare to consumers is less if the money is raised through an income tax or a general tax on all commodities rather than through selective taxes on specific commodities. This proposition is the complement of the equally widespread view that cash transfers are preferable from an economic point of view to subsidies on specific commodities.

Specific excise taxes are regarded as inefficient because they cause the price ratios facing consumers to alter even though there has been no change in costs of production. The consumer adjusts his consumption pattern in response to the change in prices, and thus not only is his total consumption reduced in order to transfer resources to the government, but the *mix* of goods consumed is changed because the tax has distorted the structure of prices. The change in the mix of consumption attributable to the impact of the tax on relative prices is as a 'deadweight' loss because it represents a reduction in the consumer's welfare not matched by an increase in government revenue. The magnitude of this loss depends on how sensitive the consumption of the taxed good is to price changes.

Before the introduction of significant income taxes and general sales taxes in the present century most government revenue was raised through high excise taxes on a narrow range of commodities. These commodities were selected partly on the grounds of administrative convenience but also because their consumption was relatively insensitive to price increases. Thus there is some overlap between the attributes that recommend an item to an administrator trying to raise tax revenue at a minimum cost and those that economists believe will minimise the deadweight loss of the tax.

A further consideration that should be taken into account in connection with any significant changes in tax is the effect on the income of the owners of resources used to produce the taxed commodity. If these resources are highly specific to the industry whose product is taxed, the resultant reduction in consumption will cause a loss of income to all owners of these resources. In as much as this income exceeded the amount required to ensure that the resources in question were not transferred to some other activity, it contained an element of pure profit or economic rent. The abolition of this rent entails no costs to society, whatever its political significance. This is a point that should be kept in mind when vineyard owners or similar groups seek to deprive consumers of access to cheap sources of supply. It is not the government's role to preserve the artificially high income of any group in the economy. However, this argument assumes that resources can be switched from one line of production to another without serious adjustment costs, and in an era of persistently high unemployment this assumption has become increasingly unrealistic.

These general considerations imply that the deadweight loss or economic cost of a tax is likely to be minimised when the taxed commodity is price inelastic in demand and/or supply. A high excise tax on a country's staple alcoholic beverage (such as beer in northern Europe or wine in southern Europe) would therefore seem to entail little economic loss and serve the goal of raising a given amount of revenue efficiently. This rationale for specific alcohol taxes is hardly the full story, however, and in recent years there have been calls for a policy of high alcohol taxation motivated by public health considerations. The next section is devoted to a review of the economic merits of this approach to alcohol tax policy.

External Effects

The ideas concerning taxation outlined above implicitly assume that an individual's consumption decisions affect only himself. The possibility that these decisions affect others was ignored, as was the question of how consumption decisions are made within the household. In fact these topics have received considerable attention from economists and this literature is relevant to alcohol tax policy.

Economists refer to the direct repercussions of one person's decisions on others as externalities. The early literature on this topic was mainly concerned with the effects of production processes on unpriced amenities such as the environment, but more recently the analysis has been extended to the situation where the externality arises in any production or consumption activity. An example of an externality due to a consumption activity is the way the level of traffic congestion in a city rises as a result of individual decisions to drive downtown, taken on the basis of private cost-benefit calculations that ignore the cost imposed on other motorists by each individual motorist. The standard analysis of these cases calls for a tax on the activity that generates the externality so as to bring its private cost more closely into line with its social cost. In contrast with the maxims of taxation derived from analysis that ignores externalities, the conclusion is now reached that a good tax is one which reduces the amount of the taxed commodity purchased sufficiently to bring the value of an additional unit of consumption to the consumer into line with its social cost.

Recently economists have pointed out that the need for a corrective tax derives not so much from the existence of the external effect *per se* as from the difficulty of operating a market where those who are adversely affected could pay the consumer to reduce his consumption in line with their valuation of the damage being caused. An example of such an arrangement would be if the residents of a neighbourhood could bribe the local music fan not to play his stereo too loudly or, alternatively, if the music fan had to bribe his neighbours for permission to intrude on their peace and quiet.[2] If such arrangements could be reached, there would be no need for the government to levy a special 'decibel tax' to counter the externality. In practice negotiated solutions to externality problems are highly improbable due to the enormous costs of organising them and hence even the died-in-the-wool *laissez-faire* economist concedes that there is a case for specific taxes to correct externalities. As a consequence of this it is recognised that the appropriate tax structure will entail some deadweight loss, but economists argue that this loss will be less than that involved in attempts to regulate the problem through administrative restrictions or controls.

The validity of the assumption that the consumer is always the best judge of his own welfare was questioned by Pigou in the 1920s in the context of how people allocate their income between present consumption and savings. He believed that consumers place too low a valuation on future income with the consequence of a less than optimal level of capital formation. The appropriate remedy was, in his view, a subsidy to savings (Pigou, 1960).

The same line of reasoning could be used to justify a tax on alcohol if it is believed that consumers are ill-informed about the damage its consumption inflicts on them. Alternatively, the taxation of alcohol could be justified in terms of the damage its consumption inflicts on others. A straightforward exposition on this argument is provided by Scitovsky:

> ... if [a consumer's] consumption affects other people's welfare, it should be restrained in the interests of these other people. One person's consumption of alcohol affects the health of his family and descendants and may, in addition, be a nuisance to his neighbours. Hence, while an excise tax on alcoholic drinks lowers the drinker's welfare, it is likely at the same time to raise the welfare of his family and neighbours and may thus, on balance, cause more gain than less ... (Scitovsky, 1951)

There are thus several roles that a tax on alcohol could be designed to play. Among these are:

1. to correct for the fact that drinkers decide on how much to drink in ignorance of the adverse health implications of (excessive) drinking;
2. to help drinkers overcome the addiction caused by past levels of consumption, which makes it difficult for them to adjust their present consumption to the level they now feel is appropriate;
3. to correct for the effects of the fact that, although aware of the damage to health caused by the level of his drinking, the consumer does not take the costs of treating this damage into account because they are borne by free public health services or private insurance schemes that do not structure their premia so as to reflect the health risks of heavy drinking;
4. to raise the price of drinking to drinkers so that it reflects the cost of externalities such as killing others through drunk driving, assault and violence due to drunkenness, etc.

Undoubtedly significant problems arise under all four headings and their existence can be invoked to justify high excise taxes on alcohol. However, we know relatively little about the magnitude of several of these problems. Even in the case of cigarette smoking, pleas for further research to clarify similar issues do not seem to have borne fruit (Atkinson, 1974; Harris, 1980). In the literature on alcohol-related problems, it is striking that few if any attempts have been made to judge whether actual levels of excise taxation are appropriate in the light of the magnitudes of the externalities which it is hoped they will redress.

It should be understood that the goal of a tax levied on an externality-generating activity is not to reduce the level of that activity to zero. Such a goal is probably impractical and would entail wasteful enforcement costs. A tax on alcohol forces the drinker to pay a premium over and above the costs of producing the commodity to reflect the damage imposed on others by his drinking. Even when the price to the consumer reflects the social costs of drinking, he is prepared to pay this premium to continue drinking, albeit at a reduced rate. From a strictly economic viewpoint, the social costs imposed by the amount he is willing to drink at the higher price have been paid for through the excise tax, and further reductions in consumption beyond this point represent a loss of welfare even if they result in further reductions in alcohol-related problems.

Economists have to recognise, however, that many commentators may find this type of reasoning repugnant if, for example, the costs in question include the death of innocent persons. Although some would argue that even these costs can in principle be measured in cash and have been reflected in the optimal tax structure, most would probably agree with Mishan (1981) when he writes:

> Whenever propositions raised on a utilitarian calculus clash with ethical norms, such propositions cannot be sustained by economists who aspire to fashion a body of prescriptive doctrines acceptable to society . . .

But even this does not imply that economists should accept analyses that implicitly assume that the value of a human life is infinite and that unlimited resources should be placed behind attempts to avert all loss of innocent lives. In several areas — road engineering, safety legislation, court awards — society reveals its valuations of human life, and these should be used as a guide to the resources that ought to be devoted to enforcing laws designed to protect the innocent from the threat posed by alcohol abuse.

Problems of Taxing the External Effects of Drinking

In order to design a tax structure that is appropriate to the problems associated with excessive drinking it would be necessary to have fairly accurate information about the link between consumption and ensuing damage. Unfortunately, we lack reliable results about the nature of this link. It seems plausible, however, that the probability of damage increases non-linearly with increasing consumption. The ideal tax structure would take this into account and would rise steeply as the total amount drunk increased. It might also be differentiated between different population groups, bearing more heavily on those (e.g. the young) who are most likely to cause damage by their drinking patterns.

A complicated tax structure of this type would, of course, be completely impracticable and most countries charge a uniform tax on all units of a particular beverage sold. The tax rate can, however, be varied between beverages, but this is at best a crude approximation to the goal of differentiating the tax rate by risk of damage. (The issue of a flat rate versus graduated tax is discussed again later in this chapter.)

It can be argued that the imposition of a high excise tax indiscriminately on all drinkers is not an appropriate response to the externalities that are generated by excessive drinking. A parallel could be drawn with petrol taxation: a high excise tax on petrol is a very inefficient way of trying to alleviate the severe congestion caused by driving in crowded cities at peak hours. In this instance an alternative to the excise tax exists (namely, supplementary licences for cars entering the congested areas) and has been used in some countries (e.g. Singapore). It is regrettably difficult to conceive of a counterpart to the supplementary licence system in the area of alcohol policy!

This objection to the use of across-the-board excise taxes to reduce alcohol-related damage loses much of its force if it can be shown that a significant proportion of problems arises among relatively light drinkers, so that any reduction in consumption leads to a roughly equal proportionate reduction in problems. For this reason, the type of investigation reported by Cook in Chapter 12 of this volume is of particular importance from the viewpoint of formulating an appropriate alcohol tax policy. It is particularly interesting that his findings appear to support the view that increased taxation results in a reduction in drinking among chronic heavy drinkers, and that this leads to a reduction in deaths from liver cirrhosis, as well as among a broader group of drinkers, with a resultant fall in traffic fatalities. Findings of this type could be used in conjunction with estimates of the value of these reductions in alcohol-related damage and of the loss of consumer surplus due to the higher rates of taxation to try to estimate the optimal tax structure.

Another objection to the use of excise taxation to adjust for the externalities associated with drinking can be based on the idea that it may be more efficient to tackle the externality directly rather than indirectly through an activity with which it is associated (Green and Sheskinski, 1976). It may, for example, be more efficient to try to curb drunk driving directly through increased enforcement of traffic regulations rather than indirectly through measures to reduce the level of drinking.

The relative efficiency of these two approaches is an empirical issue revolving around the ease with which a reduction in the externality can be achieved through alternative measures. If enforcement of strict traffic laws is in fact the less costly way of attaining the desired result, this would provide an illustration of an exception to the general rule that taxation is to be preferred to regulation in dealing with externalities.

Taxation and Addiction

Most textbooks on consumer theory have nothing to say about addictive patterns of behaviour. It is not clear whether this reflects a belief that such patterns are unimportant or simply that the analytical issues at stake are too intractable to be readily incorporated into the basic economic model of consumer behaviour. An exception to the essentially static view of demand found in most expositions is the Houthakker and Taylor model of consumption (Houthakker and Taylor, 1970), in which consumption in the present period depends not only on prices and incomes but also on the (unobservable) psychological stock built up by past consumption and representing, in the case of non-durable goods, the effects of habit formation, or inertia, on consumption. Studies using the Houthakker-Taylor formulation generally conclude that, for commodities such as alcoholic beverages, the evidence is consistent with the hypothesis of habit formation or addiction (Kennedy, Ebrill and Walsh, 1971).

The implications of habit formation for government intervention have been explored in the smoking context by Atkinson, who treats the problem of overcoming habit as a cost of adjustment associated with changing consumption between periods (Atkinson, 1974). The effect of the cost is to reduce the net gain to society from any reduction in the level of smoking achieved through health education or increased taxation.

In a similar vein, Stigler and Becker have elaborated a theory of demand that incorporates the effects of past levels of consumption on the utility derived from current consumption. In their model, a commodity is 'beneficially addictive' if the enjoyment associated with a given amount of current consumption is higher the more of the commodity that has been consumed in the past. An example might be 'good' music whose current enjoyment is enhanced by the stock of music appreciation built up through listening to similar music in the past. In the case of harmful addiction, past consumption diminishes present enjoyment. They give the example of the consumption of alcohol with a view to generating a desired level of 'euphoria': the more alcohol has been consumed in the past, the larger the amount that must be consumed in the present to attain any level of euphoria. But if the demand for 'euphoria' is inelastic, alcoholics are willing to pay a higher price in terms of consuming more and more alcohol to attain the desired level of euphoria. According to this view, the demand for alcohol is derived from a deeper desire for euphoria, and it is the inelasticity of the demand for euphoria that causes the consumption of alcohol to grow even as its effectiveness in delivering euphoria falls. Thus addiction to alcohol is viewed as the *result* of an inelastic demand (for euphoria) rather than as its *cause*.

This view of consumer behaviour has important implications for taxation of harmfully addictive goods. Taxes that raise the price of harmfully addictive, and hence price-inelastic, commodities will, according to this view, mainly result in a transfer of income away from addicts, and cause little reduction in the consumption of the harmful substance.

These considerations are primarily theoretical and not backed by empirical testing. But they give no grounds for believing that a policy of heavy taxation is an appropriate response to the problems associated with harmfully addictive patterns of consumption.

Effects on Income Distribution

It is often regretted that high alcohol taxes, even if justifiable as a corrective of externalities, tend to result in a less acceptable

Table 11.1: Reported Expenditure on Alcoholic Beverages as Percentage of Total Household Expenditure (Urban Areas), 1977

Social group	Beer	Spirits	Wine	Drink undefined	Total alcohol
Professional	1.6	0.8	0.6	0.7	3.7
Salaried employers	2.8	0.7	0.3	0.9	4.7
Other non-manual	5.1	0.7	0.1	0.7	6.6
Skilled manual	5.6	0.7	0.1	0.5	6.9
Semi- and unskilled manual	6.1	0.6	0.0	0.6	7.4
Other	3.3	0.4	0.2	0.5	4.4
All households	3.8	0.7	0.3	0.7	5.5

Gross weekly household income	Total alcohol*
Under £20	2.7
£20–£29	4.9
£30–£39	4.8
£40–£49	5.3
£50–£59	6.1
£60–£69	4.9
£70–£79	5.2
£80–£89	5.2
£90–£99	4.7
£100–£119	5.7
£120–£149	5.7
£150–£179	5.2
£180+	6.2
All households	5.5

* Data for individual beverages not published.
Note: These reported figures seriously understate the proportion of income devoted to alcohol as shown in national accounts data.
Source: Centrral Statistical Office (1977).

distribution of after-tax income. This point is made by referring to alcohol excise taxes as 'regressive'. By this is generally understood that because the poor spend a higher proportion of their income on alcohol than the rich, they also pay a disproportionate share of the tax on alcohol.

The empirical basis for this assertion is not strong. In the first place, there are major differences between alcoholic beverages in regard to consumption patterns. In Britain and Ireland beer figures more prominently in the budgets of lower than higher income groups, but spirits and wine are 'luxuries' in the sense that high income groups spend relatively more on them than low income groups, and a more than proportionate share of any increase in income is devoted to their purchase. The cross-sectional evidence for Ireland is shown in Table 11.1 which is strikingly similar to data for the UK (Jones and Nobes, 1978).

Even when all alcoholic beverages are grouped together (see Walsh, 1982), the income elasticity of demand for 'alcoholic beverages' is high when one controls for family size. The impression to the contrary conveyed by the zero or negative correlation between expenditure on alcohol (as a proportion of total expenditure) and total expenditure derives from the relatively small outlay on alcohol in larger households which also have relatively high incomes (Pratschke, 1969). When the influence of household size is allowed for, a strong tendency emerges for higher income groups to spend larger shares of their income on alcohol. Time series econometric analyses also reveal that expenditure on alcohol rises at least proportionately with income (Walsh, 1980). Thus the conventional view of the adverse effects of alcohol taxation on the distribution of income seems to be less than well founded at least as far as the evidence for Ireland is concerned.

Revenue Effects of Tax Increases

An increase in an excise tax increases the price paid by consumers by somewhat less than the full amount of the tax (depending on the supply and demand schedules for the commodity). The higher retail price is associated with a lower quantity consumed. The reduction in the consumption of the good may or may not result in a fall in total outlay on it. If the demand schedule is inelastic ($\eta < 1$) over the relevant range, outlay on the commodity will increase. But the effect on tax revenue depends on a different criterion, namely, whether the elasticity of demand *times* the share of the tax in the retail price is less or greater than unity

$$(\eta \cdot \frac{t}{p} < 1)$$

(Geary, 1973). Since even in Ireland alcohol taxes generally represent no more than 50 per cent of the retail price (see Table 11.2), as long as the elasticity of demand with respect to the retail price does not exceed 2, higher excise taxes on alcohol will increase the total tax yield. In view of the relatively low price elasticities found in econometric studies

Table 11.2: Share of Taxes in Retail Prices of Beer and Spirits in Ireland (%)

	1975		1981 (September)	
	Beer	Spirits	Beer	Spirits
Base price*	54.4	51.1	51.9	47.8
Excise taxes	39.3	42.5	35.1	39.2
VAT	6.3	6.4	13.1	13.0
Retail price	100.0	100.0	100.0	100.0

* This is the retail price less taxes.
Source: Department of Finance data.

of the demand for beer, there is every reason to believe that higher tax rates would continue to yield higher revenue, even in periods of slow income growth.

The revenue perspective is a narrow one and fails to take account of either the economic or public health arguments for higher taxation. The dependence of the exchequer on alcohol and tobacco taxes in Ireland and Britain in the past reflected administrative and political convenience rather than a calculated use of the tax system to influence consumption patterns. The growth of revenue from new and buoyant taxes during the twentieth century has greatly reduced the pre-eminence of the old excise duties as sources of revenue. None the less, in Ireland the revenue from the excise tax on alcohol still accounts for 10 per cent of total tax revenue (compared with 18 per cent in the early 1950s).

The continued importance of the revenue from alcohol taxation in a country such as Ireland illustrates the success from the exchequer's point of view of pursuing a policy of heavy taxation of a group of commodities for which the demand is price inelastic. But there is another, less attractive, consequence of this policy. A price increase on a commodity which is price inelastic leads to increased expenditure on this item from a given level of income. Thus, a high tax rate on alcohol tends to create a situation where households devote a large proportion of their total expenditure to alcohol. This is illustrated by the fact that Ireland is remarkable for the pre-eminence of alcohol in the expenditure of households, even though the quantity of alcohol consumed per capita is not exceptional. Moreover, in periods of static living standards and rising levels of alcohol taxation, the proportion of income devoted to alcohol tends to rise, as for example in 1976 when it reached a peak of 13 per cent of household expenditure. This dominance of alcohol in the expenditure pattern of consumers, and the tendency for heavier taxation to aggravate it, undoubtedly generates social costs by diverting purchasing power from other items of expenditure, and these costs must be set against any gain attributable to the reduction of alcohol consumption.

Ad Valorem or Excise Taxes?

The traditional British and Irish tax on alcoholic beverages is an excise tax that is stipulated as so many £ per proof gallon of spirits, standard barrel of beer or gallon of wine. During inflationary periods governments tend to encounter resistance to adjusting these taxes so as to maintain their real value. From this point of view, there would be administrative advantages in shifting to an *ad valorem* tax such as VAT, a change that is already underway due to EEC regulations in the case of tobacco products.

There are subtle differences between the effects of the two types of taxes. As Barzel points out (Barzel, 1976), an excise tax must be levied on specific characteristics of a product but not on others. Usually it is so much per *unit* regardless of price. For example, the excise tax on petrol is so much a litre regardless of octane rating. This may induce consumers to increase their consumption of untaxed, and now relatively cheaper, attributes such as octane in this example. The clearest example of this incentive in the area of alcoholic beverages is the way in which the British and Irish excise tax on wine bears heaviest on the cheaper varieties, thereby encouraging a switch to higher quality wine, but it is more important to ask about the effects of the excise tax on beer and spirits. In these instances, the excise tax is on the alcohol (i.e. standard barrel or proof gallon) but all other components of the final product escape it. The untaxed elements include the other components of the beverages (mainly water!) and the drinking ambience. The excise tax on beer and spirits may therefore have played a part in the well-documented trend in Ireland and Britain towards the consumption of lighter but more expensive beers and weaker spirits in increasingly elaborate drinking locales. In the United States, on the other hand, excise taxes on alcoholic beverages have fallen sharply in real terms and this may have hastened the trend towards off-premise consumption. This possible effect of the continued reliance on excise as opposed to *ad valorem* taxes on alcohol has received very little attention.

Flat Rate or Graduated Taxes?

The appropriate tax structure for alcoholic beverages depends on the manner in which drinking generates externalities. Arguments of the type 'beer is the drink of moderation' seem to imply that the damage caused by a given alcohol intake is less the weaker the beverage in which it is drunk. This belief would provide a public health rationale for the policy of taxing the alcohol in stronger beverages more heavily than that in weaker beverages. In Ireland, for example, the tax per litre 100 per cent alcohol is IR£21.60 for spirits and IR£14.10 for beer (July 1981). In fact the reason for this structure of taxation is probably the knowledge that spirits constitute more of an economic luxury than does beer.

It is relevant to note that Harris argues that even if the health damage caused by smoking depends only on total intake of tar and nicotine, regardless of the average tar and nicotine content of the cigarettes smoked, it would still be more advantageous to have a graduated tax, with higher rates on stronger cigarettes, rather than the flat rate tax imposed in most countries (Harris, 1980). By analogy the tradition of taxing the alcohol in spirits more than that in beer may be soundly based.

Conclusion

This chapter has reviewed some general considerations concerning taxation and their application to alcoholic beverages. Several dilemmas emerge from the analysis. From one point of view, the best excise tax is one that is imposed on a commodity that is price inelastic in demand. The deadweight cost of such a tax is less, and the buoyancy of revenue as a result of tax increases is greater, than in the case of a tax imposed on a price-sensitive commodity. But from a public health point of view, it is desired to use taxes to alter consumption patterns and reduce externalities, which will only occur if the taxed commodity is price sensitive.

The key ingredient in an evaluation of alcohol tax policy is, therefore, the price elasticity of demand for alcoholic beverages. Here the evidence seems to be unfavourable to the use of higher excise taxes as a means of curbing the social costs associated with heavy drinking. The relatively low price elasticities reported in many countries for alcoholic beverages suggests that higher rates of tax will not reduce consumption dramatically. Moreover, any curb on consumption achieved in this way will lead to more money and a higher share of total expenditure being devoted to alcohol.

Finally, price elasticities should not be considered in isolation from other influences on consumption over time. The evidence of relatively high income elasticities especially for new beverages implies that any curb on the growth of consumption achieved by heavier taxation could be rapidly eroded by the effects of income growth.

The Irish experience in relation to alcohol taxation is not encouraging. The excise tax on all alcoholic beverages, but on beer in particular, is extremely high. The Irish retail prices of these beverages are exceeded only in Denmark, which implies that alcohol is probably more expensive in relation to income in Ireland than anywhere else in the Western world (Sulkunen, 1978). Although the real value of the excise taxes fell during the initial years of the current inflation, the real tax on beer is now close to its historic peak, and that on spirits is not far below it. Despite these rigorous fiscal policies, there has been a steady increase in per capita alcohol consumption during the 1960s and into the 1970s, with an attendant rise in at least some of the indices of alcohol-related problems. Of course, if alcohol tax policy had been more lenient, it is likely that the increase in problems would have been more rapid, but the available econometric evidence suggests the effect would not have been dramatic. Moreover, one consequence of the policy of high alcohol taxes has been a marked rise in the proportion of income devoted to purchasing alcoholic beverages to the point where Ireland is now ahead of all other countries on this statistic.

There is an understandable temptation for medical or social researchers to seek elements of a solution to the problem of alcohol abuse in a tougher fiscal policy. Undoubtedly many countries have neglected this possibility and taken an unduly lenient approach to the taxation of alcoholic drink. The Irish experience, however, suggests that only limited inroads on the problems associated with excessive drinking can be expected from a policy of high alcohol taxes.

Notes

1. The term 'excise tax' is used to refer to any *lump sum* tax levied on a commodity, regardless of who is legally obliged to pay over the tax. A tax of so

much per £ of sales or turnover is an *ad valorem* tax.

2. These alternative solutions would not result in the same outcome. As is shown by E.J. Mishan (1981), the question of who has the right to do what makes a difference to the equilibrium level of the offensive activity.

12 ALCOHOL TAXES AS A PUBLIC HEALTH MEASURE

Philip J. Cook

The US federal excise taxes on alcoholic beverages have not been raised since 1951. These tax rates − $10.50 per proof gallon for liquor,[1] $0.29 per gallon of beer, and between $0.17 and $3.40 per gallon of wine depending on alcohol content and type − were quite steep at the time they were first enacted, but inflation has reduced their real value to less than one-third of their value in 1951. Partly as a result, the real price of alcoholic beverages has declined sharply. Between 1960 and 1980, the real price of liquor declined 48 per cent, of beer 27 per cent, and of wine 20 per cent (Moore and Gerstein, 1981).

There appears to be renewed interest in raising federal alcohol taxes to help compensate for the recently enacted and perhaps overly generous reductions in other taxes. Besides reducing the federal budget deficit, there is another argument in favour of raising the federal alcohol tax at this time − it will reduce drinking, and thereby perhaps reduce some of the adverse consequences of drinking. Indeed, alcohol taxation is increasingly being touted as an effective public health measure. While there is not yet any consensus among experts on this issue, my own research lends support to the public health claim for alcohol taxation. My results indicate that alcohol taxation is both effective and surprisingly well targeted on heavy drinkers − they pay most of the tax bill, and their drinking is quite responsive to tax changes. In this chapter some of the important arguments concerning alcohol taxation are reviewed and some of the author's recent statistical work is summarised.

Two Perspectives for Evaluating Alcohol Taxes

Gusfield has suggested that alcohol control policies fall 'like sober rain from heaven upon the problem and problem-free drinkers alike' (Gusfield, 1976). Taxation and other control policies are criticised as overly blunt instruments, reducing the enjoyment of the many for the sake of curtailing the alcohol-related problems suffered by the relatively few. There are two important comments to be made in response to this critique.

First, much of the social costs of excess drinking also fall upon 'the problem and problem-free drinkers alike' as well as the abstainers. The US government social insurance tax rates and private auto and health insurance premiums reflect in part the costly consequences of drinking. The drunk driver puts everyone at increased risk of an injury or death on the highway. Thus it can be argued that an *effective* alcohol control measure will indirectly benefit the 'non-problem' drinkers (as well as those who abstain) by reducing the collective costs generated by problem drinking.

Second, the incidence of the direct costs of alcohol control measures such as taxation is more or less proportional to the amount of alcohol an individual consumes — the 'sober rain' falls on all drinkers, but with much greater intensity on the chronic heavy drinkers than on others. In the US, it is estimated that the top 10 per cent of all drinkers consume about 40-50 per cent of all beverage alcohol sold each year (Moore and Gerstein, 1981). To the extent that alcohol taxes are proportional to ethanol content, then this top group of drinkers will also pay 40-50 per cent of the taxes. Thus the relatively small group of drinkers who have the highest incidence of alcohol-related problems also pay the bulk of the alcohol taxes.

To summarise, alcohol taxes, if effective in reducing the costly consequences of excess consumption, reduce the burden alcohol imposes on society at large. Furthermore, *whether or not* alcohol taxes are effective in reducing the costly consequences of excess consumption, they have the characteristic of exacting payment in proportion to consumption and hence (very roughly) in proportion to social costs engendered by drinking. Taxes are more discriminating than rain.

Both of these points lend themselves to empirical documentation and refinement. Unfortunately, the precise relationship between the incidence of alcohol taxes and the incidence of socially costly alcohol-related problems has not been studied in any detail. The first point, relating to the effectiveness of alcohol taxation in reducing alcohol-related problems, has been studied. The next two sections summarise some recent findings on this issue.

Alcohol Taxes and Alcohol Consumption

An increase in taxes on liquor or beer results in an increase in the average prices of these commodities and a reduction in alcohol consumption from these sources. (More precisely, consumption is less as a result of the tax increase than it would have been without the increase.) This result has been established beyond reasonable scientific doubt for data from the US and Canada (Johnson and Oksanen, 1977; Cook and Tauchen, 1981; Ornstein and Hanssens, 1981). More important and controversial is the question of how taxes and prices influence consumption levels of the heaviest drinkers. It is logically possible that average consumption would fall as a result of a tax increase solely due to its effect on moderate drinkers; that the heaviest drinkers are immune to economic incentives. An argument supporting this possibility can be stated by the following chain of propositions: (i) A large portion of the heaviest drinkers are alcoholics, in the sense that they are addicted to alcohol; (ii) Alcohol addicts will drink something like the biological maximum every day, pratically regardless of the cost of obtaining their drinks; (iii) Therefore it must be the more moderate drinkers who adapt their drinking practices to the price of alcohol beverages, because the heaviest drinkers will not respond.

This sort of argument may seem plausible to many. In reply, an economist would want to point out that a price increase has a greater economic impact on an alcoholic (who may already be spending one-third or more of his income on alcohol) than on a moderate drinker, and that ordinarily this greater impact would be expected to yield, if anything, a *greater* response in consumption behaviour. In any event, this issue is better resolved through careful empirical analysis than through unsupported generalisations about the behaviour in question.

The Effect of Alcohol Taxes on Cirrhosis Mortality

Statistics on the prevalence of chronic heavy drinking are not routinely available. However, there is a widely accepted proxy measure — the mortality rate due to cirrhosis of the liver. Liver cirrhosis death rates have provided the basis upon which nearly all alcoholism prevalence rates have been estimated (Seeley, 1960).

Most people who die of liver cirrhosis, especially after the age of 30, exhibit a history of chronic intense drinking. Schmidt, for example, found that about 80 per cent of all cirrhosis deaths in Ontario in 1974 were alcohol-related (Schmidt, 1977). The typical victim of alcohol-related cirrhosis has consumed an enormous amount of alcohol; Lelbach estimates that drinking roughly 21 oz of 86 proof liquor every day for about 20 years yields a 50 per cent chance of contracting liver cirrhosis in a primarily healthy subject weighing 150 pounds (Lelbach, 1974). Thus for any one individual there tends to be a long lag between the onset of heavy drinking and death (if he lives long enough) from liver cirrhosis. The cirrhosis mortality rate thus is not a direct indicator of the current fraction of alcoholics in a population, but does give a good indication of the fraction who have been drinking heavily for a decade or two (Skog, 1980a). It must be kept in mind that the cirrhosis mortality rate is of interest in its own right, as well as being a proxy for the prevalence of alcoholism — cirrhosis is one of the leading causes of death in the US, Canada and most European nations.

Using this statistical indicator of the prevalence of chronic excess consumption, it is possible to explore the relationship between alcohol taxes and excess drinking. The author's first study of this relationship (Cook, 1981) was based on annual observations on 30 states for the 15-year period 1960-74. During this period there were 38 instances in which one of these states increased its liquor tax by a substantial amount.[2] I viewed each of these tax increases as a test case in a sort of 'natural experiment'. For each of these test cases, the percentage change in the state's cirrhosis mortality rate was calculated; the test statistic was defined as the mortality rate during the three years before the tax increase, minus the mortality rate during the three years following the tax increase, divided by the mortality rate during the three-year-period centred on the year of the tax increase. The control groups for each of these test cases were the other states in the corresponding years. The result was that states that raised their liquor tax typically had a greater reduction (or smaller increase) in cirrhosis mortality than other states in the corresponding year (see Table 12.1). Indeed, 63 per cent of all test cases fell into the bottom half of the distribution with respect to the test statistic — a result that would occur by chance alone with probability 0.072. This result is fairly strong evidence that the tax increase reduced the cirrhosis mortality rate, at least in the short run.

Why did some (38 per cent) of the tax increase states experience a relative *increase* in cirrhosis mortality? The author's interpretation of this result is that cirrhosis mortality fluctuates from year to year for a variety of reasons in addition to changes in liquor prices. In some of the test cases these chance fluctuations happened to be positive and large enough to more than compensate for the consumption-suppressing effect of the tax increase. The fact that in most cases (62 per cent) the state exhibited a relative reduction in cirrhosis mortality suggests

194 Alcohol Taxes as a Public Health Measure

Table 12.1: Effect of State Liquor Tax Increases, 1960-74, on Cirrhosis Mortality Rates

Rank order	Number of test cases	Percent of test cases
1-5	9	
6-10	9	63.2%
11-15	6	
16-20	3	
21-25	9	36.8%
26-30	2	

Interpretation: Each year during the sample period the 30 states are rank ordered with respect to percentage change in cirrhosis mortality. The state with the largest increase is ranked 30th, the state with the largest reduction is ranked first. This table shows that states that raised their taxes were usually at the low end of this distribution in the year of the tax increase.
Source: Cook (1981), p. 277.

that this consumption effect does exist (or, in the language of classical statistics, 'the hypothesis that cirrhosis mortality is not affected by liquor tax increases can be rejected at the 0.072 confidence level').[3]

This quasi-experimental approach to studying the effect of liquor taxes on heavy drinkers has the virtue of simplicity and ease of interpretation (Simon, 1966). It does not generate a usable estimate of the *magnitude* of the effect in question, however. Primarily for this reason the author undertook a second study (together with George Tauchen) which applied a parametric estimation technique (analysis of covariance estimated by generalised least squares regression) to annual data from the same 30 states for the period 1962-77. Before undertaking this estimation task, the annual state level cirrhosis mortality data were refined. The dependent variable was the age-adjusted mortality rate for state residents aged 30 and over.

The principal result can be stated this way: other things being equal, a one dollar per proof gallon increase in a state's liquor tax will reduce the state's cirrhosis mortality rate by 1.9 per cent in the short run.[4] The 95 per cent confidence interval for this estimated reduction is (0.4 per cent, 3.5 per cent); thus the parameter estimate is statistically significant by the usual standards of social science. The parameter estimate suggests further that the tax effect is far from trivial — according to this estimate, a doubling of the US federal liquor tax would reduce the nation's cirrhosis mortality rate by 20 per cent.

Given the normally long lag between the onset of heavy drinking and death from cirrhosis, it may not be obvious how an increase in the liquor tax could cause an immediate reduction in cirrhosis mortality. The reason is that the cirrhotic process is interruptible — if at any time an alcoholic should stop drinking, his liver will cease to deteriorate. (This cessation may not apply to females.) If his rate of consumption slows, then the deterioration process also slows. At any one time there is a 'reservoir' of people who are within one year of death from cirrhosis at their current rate of consumption.[5] If some of them reduce their consumption in response to a tax increase, then not all of them will die in that year — i.e. the mortality rate will decline the first year. How about the trend in mortality in the long run? The mortality rate will gradually decline after the initial drop, as the size of the 'reservoir' gradually shrinks. The total effect of the tax increase will not be realised for many years. The ultimate reduction in mortality rates due to a tax increase will exceed the initial reduction. Thus estimates understate the full effect (Cook and Tauchen, 1981).

In conclusion, there is considerable statistical evidence that a liquor tax increase causes an immediate and substantial reduction in cirrhosis mortality. If cirrhosis mortality rates are a reliable indicator of the prevalence of alcoholism, then it can be inferred that alcoholics' drinking habits are quite sensitive to the price of liquor. Alcohol taxation is an effective public health policy instrument.

The enormous decline in the real value of the US federal excise taxes on alcoholic beverages has benefited heavy drinkers in financial terms, but has had the effect of increasing the prevalence of alcoholism and its attendant costs. Increasing the excise tax would be a rather well-targeted response to the social burden which heavy drinkers as a group impose on the rest of society. There are a number of alternatives for reducing the US budget deficit. Few of them have the substantial beneficial side-effects that would result from raising the alcohol excise tax rates.

Notes

1. A 'proof gallon' is the amount of beverage that contains 64 oz of ethanol.
2. Greater than $0.24 per proof gallon.
3. The principal challenge to the validity of this interpretation is that a state legislature's decision to raise the tax is influenced, directly or indirectly, by cirrhosis trends in the state. If this were true, then tax changes would not have the important statistical property of being exogenous to the system being studied. For example, if a sudden increase in cirrhosis mortality led to a tax increase and was followed by a natural regression to the cirrhosis mortality trend, then the tax increase would be followed by a reduction in mortality but not cause it. This

possibility is tested in both Cook (1981), and Cook and Tauchen (1981). There is no evidence from these tests to support this perverse interpretation of the author's results — tax increases apparently *are* largely exogenous.

4. The tax variable in the regression was adjusted for inflation, as measured by the consumer price index. The statement of results given here is converted to current dollars (October 1981).

5. The use of the term 'reservoir' in this context is due to Schmidt and Popham (1980).

13 GOVERNMENT POLICIES CONCERNING ALCOHOL TAXATION: BEYOND THE EXCISE TAX DEBATE

James F. Mosher

This chapter attempts to provide a somewhat novel view of the perspectives offered in Chapters 11 and 12, a tactic that is particularly appropriate since the author (an attorney) is not qualified to give a technical analysis. There has been considerable debate in the literature concerning the relationship of price, consumption and problems — a central aspect of the taxation question — and it is therefore appropriate to examine some of the policy and legal implications that stem from those debates.

The conclusions found in Walsh's and Cook's chapters provide a good starting point for this examination. Professor Cook conducts a complicated economic analysis to determine the price elasticities of alcohol consumption, liver cirrhosis and auto fatalities. He finds that the elasticities do indeed exist and are quite high. This suggests that government initiatives to raise retail alcohol prices (either through excise taxes or, in monopoly jurisdictions, through direct pricing policies) constitute an effective policy for preventing alcohol-related problems. Cook does not conclude that price increases are desirable in all cases. He instead introduces a cost-benefit framework for determining the advisability of price increases in particular situations and for setting future research agendas. His analysis does suggest, however, at least implicitly, that pricing policies should be given a high priority for future prevention policy.

The Cook analysis is extremely difficult to follow, at least to this non-economist. None the less, his findings appear to have been made on a sound basis. The issues raised in his conclusion, however, still remain. When is an excise tax increase an appropriate policy measure and to what level should it be raised? The responsiveness of consumption and certain alcohol problem indicators are interesting, but clearly other variables not examined may have equal or greater effects — such variables as minimum drinking ages, income, occupation, industry structure, availability by other control means, to name a few.

Walsh's chapter addresses these crucial questions, and several of his points are relevant here. First, he appears to voice a fundamental disagreement with Cook. Walsh concludes, based primarily on an analysis of Irish data, that alcoholic beverages show relatively low price elasticities, which suggests that higher taxes will not reduce consumption dramatically. Second, an additional variable is introduced — the percentage of alcohol expenditure to total consumer expenditure. Walsh argues that a high ratio of alcohol expenditures to total expenditures may result in consumers forgoing essential purchases, an unintended negative result of raising taxes. Finally, Walsh discusses Irish tax policies and shows that consumption has been rising steadily despite high prices, particularly when analysed in conjunction with income, concluding that tax policy initiatives have severe limitations.

Walsh's and Cook's apparent disagreements constitute a difficult puzzle to solve. At one level, a rather simple observation can be made — Cook concludes that the tax policy lever should not be ignored and may be a very attractive component of an alcohol prevention policy, while Walsh concludes that the Irish experience has demonstrated its limitations. This may well be an unfair oversimplification of their views. Rather than attempting to reconcile the apparent contradictions, two important policy areas are discussed, which are suggested by Cook's emphasis on price and Walsh's cautions regarding excise tax policies. First, what other aspects of tax policy beyond excise taxation *per se* influence rates of consumption and rates of alcohol-related problems? Second, what other economic factors beyond taxation influence price, and do they provide viable policy alternatives?

Instead of beginning at a theoretical level, drawing assumptions concerning consumer behaviour, the lawyer goes to the tax laws and regulations themselves and tries to make sense of the actual mechanisms employed. Regarding alcohol, there is a strikingly wide variety of tax provisions beyond excise taxes that appear to have a profound impact on the supply and consumption of alcohol beverages.

Most tax provisions fall outside tax's revenue collection function and bear no relationship to 'rational' consumer behaviour and current cost-benefit analyses. Rather, they are explicit policy formulations (termed 'tax incentives' or 'tax expenditures') designed to alter taxpayers' behaviour, usually at the corporate or wealthy individual level (Mosher, 1982a). They represent the expenditure of governmental resources through the tax system rather than through the ordinary budgetary process. The Reagan Administration has relied on tax incentives in its economic recovery programme and many economists now view them as one of the key mechanisms for setting social policies today.

How has alcohol policy been affected? In several ways. At the consumption level, virtually all corporate alcohol expenditures are considered business expenses in the United States (and most Western European countries as well), which means they provide a direct means for lowering corporate tax liabilities. These purchases are estimated to amount to 12 per cent of all alcohol expenditures in the US in a given year — $5.6 billion in 1979 or a $2 billion to $3 billion tax loss to the federal government. This form of tax expenditure has been reviewed elsewhere (Mosher, 1982b). Suffice it to note that it provides a tremendous inducement to drink in a wide variety of settings and creates numerous health risks that corporations themselves have identified as extremely serious.

Tax expenditures have a more profound impact at the level of production than at the level of consumption. Tax policy is a primary means for setting the supply structure for production, making some products more profitable than others. In the US, tax policies provide very powerful incentives to the large alcohol manufacturers, which have contributed substantially to the monopolisation of alcohol production. Some of these provisions, such as the tax investment credit and special depreciation allowances are common to other product lines (which have also tended to become monopolised). Others are alcohol-specific. For example, between 1969 and 1973, $1 billion was invested in vineyard expansion in the US, fuelled by a special tax shelter which substantially reduced tax liabilities for participating wealthy taxpayers (Bunce, forthcoming). This increase in supply (its impact on price can only be speculated) was created without any regard to consumer demand, and was a government response to certain economic pressures without regard to any of its health implications.

There are several other examples. The US government has recently moved greatly to increase incentives for capital investments, which has surely benefited beer and spirit industries in particular because they are so capital-intensive. The price implications have not been researched, but one can reasonably speculate that lower prices will result. The US also has a special tax rebate policy regarding alcoholic beverages produced in the US island territories of Puerto Rico and the Virgin Islands (Mosher, 1982b). All taxes collected on such beverages sold on the US mainland are rebated to the islands, making rum sales a key aspect of the island governments' revenue collection. This tax policy, which again has no relationship to rational consumer demand, has led to numerous island initiatives to promote consumption, including ambitious promotional campaigns and very low prices. Although adequate research has not been conducted concerning the impact on alcohol-related problems, it should be noted that liver cirrhosis rates are extremely high in both territories.

The second question, which considered other economic factors beyond taxation which influence price, stems from this broadened discussion of tax policies. As these special tax provisions suggest, alcohol availability is not passively responding to consumer demand. According to Walsh and others in this volume, welfare economics assume that consumers make rational purchase decisions based on available choices. Leaving the issue of rationality alone for the moment, economist colleagues are urged to take a more careful look at the dynamics of 'available choices'. Diverse economic forces (including tax), carefully manipulated by government and industry forces, have major impacts on consumer options and prices. The extent of monopolisation, marketing practices, price fixing, governmental priorities regarding agricultural production and international trade, to name only a few such factors, set the stage for consumer choice. Alcoholic beverages are now treated substantially as ordinary consumer commodities, and their availability has been greatly expanded. They have been granted extremely favourable governmental treatment as a positive consumer option in the allocation of consumer resources. Governmental economic policies which are continuing these trends need to be examined by economists and non-economists alike from a public health standpoint.

Once price has been found to be an important variable for regulating consumption and problems, these additional economic variables cannot be ignored. Walsh and Cook, then, have opened the door to these broader issues in their discussion and analyses of excise tax policies.

14 ADVERTISING EXPOSURE, ALCOHOL CONSUMPTION AND MISUSE OF ALCOHOL

Donald E. Strickland

The impact of mass media, especially television, on social problems in the United States has been debated for almost three decades. The relationship between television programming and juvenile delinquency was the subject of the Kefauver congressional subcommittee hearings in 1954-5, the effects of advertising on drug use and abuse was the focus of the Moss congressional subcommittee hearings in 1971, and, more recently, the Hathaway congressional subcommittee hearings in 1976 examined the issue of television's effects on drinking behaviour.[1] As recently as December 1980, the issues of the content and impact of alcohol beverage advertising had again reached the federal policy arena: the Bureau of Alcohol, Tobacco and Firearms (BATF) issued proposed changes to the regulations governing the content of beverage alcohol advertising.[2] The intensity of the debates has, unfortunately, been little informed by scientific studies of even the content of alcohol beverage advertising, let alone findings on the impact of advertising. Nevertheless, recent strategies for the primary prevention of alcohol abuse have included two policies focusing on the regulation of alcoholic beverage advertising: limitations on the extent and nature of alcoholic beverage advertising and disallowance of alcoholic beverage advertising as a business tax deduction.

Unfortunately, the concern of scholars and policy-makers with the impact of advertising on alcohol use and misuse has failed to generate a research framework which distinguishes clearly among the issues involved. Yet these distinctions are necessary to disentangle the complexity of the issues surrounding advertising and alcohol abuse. Too often these distinctions become blurred in the intensity of the discussions. As a result, specific research programmes which usefully inform the debates have not developed. In addition, global policy recommendations are often linked to desired outcomes with little consideration of the dynamics of the process involved.

Four analytically separate sets of research concerns form the substance of the current debates over the role of alcohol beverage advertising in the creation and maintenance of alcohol problems. These concerns are presented here to situate more clearly the present research within the logical framework hidden by much previous discussion and to delineate complementary, albeit empirically related, research agendas:

... *the content of alcohol beverage advertising*: the crucial issues here revolve around the nature of the themes and appeals used and the portrayal of human models;

... *the targeting of alcohol advertising to supposedly susceptible population subgroups*: the issues here involve differential targeting, disproportionate exposure, and the relative susceptibility of such groups (i.e. youth, women, blacks) to mass media influence;

... *the ubiquity of portrayals of consumption as normative*: the critical issues here, involving programme content and media portrayals of drinking, encompass far broader concerns than advertising, although advertising is one of the major vehicles for portrayals of alcohol use;

... *the effects of alcohol advertising*: the linkages among advertising exposure, alcohol consumption and alcohol abuse remain the central, and most complex, issue.

The research reported in this chapter is intended to inform this last, but vitally important, component of the advertising-alcohol abuse debate. It is our contention that the confusion of these analytic components of the debates and the primacy of the last component are largely responsible for the abundance of assertions concerning the effects of alcohol beverage advertising and the dearth of empirical evidence. The present research, focusing on the effects of exposure to television alcohol beverage advertising, reports initial baseline results from a large-scale, systematic survey of some 1,000 teenagers and their families of orientation. Following a brief review of the previous research literature on advertising and alcohol consumption, an outline is presented of the theoretical framework guiding the study and the methodology used.

The findings and policy implications of this research are then presented and discussed.

Previous Research and the Present Analytic Framework (Strickland, 1981)

Research on the specific topic of alcohol beverage advertising and alcohol use is virtually non-existent at the individual level. As indicated in several recent reviews, there have been few systematic studies of the effects of alcohol advertising on the consumption and abuse of this drug (Pittman and Lambert, 1978; Waterson, 1981; Comstock, 1976; Kinder, 1975; National Academy of Science, 1981). In fact the absence of scientific research results on which to anchor present policy discussions and the failure to distinguish between consumption *per se* and abusive consumption underlie much of the confusion in the regulatory arena.

What few macro-level efforts exist to examine the relationship of alcohol advertising to consumption generally consist of (i) econometric analyses of aggregate consumption and advertising expenditure levels and (ii) assessment of the impact of advertising bans on aggregate consumption levels. Along with inconsistent findings, each strand of research has omitted consideration of the behavioural mechanisms by which exposure to beverage alcohol advertising influences individual drinking behaviours.

The econometric demand models have found conflicting advertising effects on alcohol beverage consumption, yet the magnitudes of those effects have been uniformly small. Most reliably established are market share influences of advertising; overall aggregate demand effects have ranged from moderately positive to modestly negative, with many studies finding virtually no relationship between advertising and aggregate or per capita consumption (i.e. sales volume). Much criticism of the econometric analyses has focused on: (i) the measurement of advertising using expenditure data; (ii) the problem of causal reciprocity between advertising expenditures and sales of beverage alcohol; (iii) the *ceteris paribus* assumption of policy recommendations of such studies; and (iv) the tendency, in some cases, to project estimated effects far beyond the range of the data employed. Nevertheless, it is this area in which the effects of advertising have been most closely examined (Simon, 1969; Ackoff and Emshoff, 1975a,b; Barnes and Bourgeois, 1977).

Another set of relevant macro-level findings comes from studies of partial bans on advertising in two Canadian provinces. Smart and Cutler found no effect on per capita consumption from a fourteen-month ban on advertising alcoholic beverages in print media and on electronic media in British Columbia (Smart and Cutler, 1976). In a more recent study, Ogborne and Smart reported no effects of a regulation in Manitoba which removed beer advertising from print and electronic media. A time-series analysis of monthly per capita beer sales for four years prior to the ban and four years after the ban concluded that there was little evidence that the cessation of beer advertising had affected per capita consumption in any way (Ogborne and Smart, 1980). None the less, since neither ban involved prohibitions on all forms of marketing efforts nor controlled access to media originating outside the provinces, the lack of effects must be interpreted cautiously.

The present study focuses on the micro-level linkages among advertising exposure, alcohol consumption and alcohol problems. The theoretical framework guiding the present investigation is that of social learning theory (Bandura, 1977; Akers, 1977; Akers *et al.*, 1979; Weissbach and Vogler, 1977; Strickland, 1982). Drinking, like most other behaviours, is learned and, more particularly, is learned in the socialisation process attendant to the transition from childhood to adulthood. The learning mechanisms by which this transition is accomplished are specified by the principles of social learning theory, as are the effects of the personal and impersonal environments which impinge on the socialisation process. In the case of advertising and alcohol consumption, social learning theory is especially appropriate both because of its emphasis on the interaction of the person and his or her environment in regulating behaviour and because of its emphasis on learning via observation of the behaviour of others. This latter process, often imprecisely called modelling or imitation, is a major explanation for the presumed effects of alcohol beverage advertising on drinking behaviour.

Three core principles of social learning theory guide the present research: (i) behaviour, including drinking, is regulated by its consequences, that is, by the balance of reinforcement associated with it; (ii) behaviour can be learned observationally through a variety of vicarious reinforcement mechanisms; and (iii) behaviour can be cognitively represented, enabling symbolic enactment of behaviour and anticipation of consequences. The importance of behavioural consequences, learning through observation, and symbolic representation of behaviour consequence routines suggests three congeries of potential influences on the adoption and maintenance of teenage drinking patterns: (i) family and peer groups which control individuals' sources of reinforcement and expose them to behavioural models and normative definitions; (ii) mass media and especially advertising portrayals of alcohol use which provide the symbolic modelling of drinking behaviour and activate the processes of vicarious reinforcement and shape definitions of normative social practice; and (iii) proximity to adult status, with the cognitive development processes and adult-behaviour definitions attendant to the stages of the transition to adulthood. These three conceptual sets, unified by the social learning model, provide an integrated framework for our analysis of the effects of exposure to alcohol beverage advertising on alcohol consumption patterns.

The focal relationships of this research express the simple mechanism by which exposure to alcohol beverage advertising is purported to increase drinking problems among adolescents: Advertising Exposure → Consumption → Alcohol Abuse. This is a two-step process in which advertising exposure is hypothesised to increase consumption and an increase in consumption leads to increased problem drinking. The latter mechanism has received substantial empirical support in previous studies of alcohol consumption and problem drinking; the former has emerged as a supposition in recent debates over the control of advertising as one of the 'control of consumption' policies aimed at the prevention of alcohol abuse (US Senate Subcommittee, 1976). The present research is intended to explore not only the proposed link between advertising and consumption but the effects of advertising, both direct and indirect, on alcohol problems.

Methods

Sample and Procedure

Data were collected by administering a self-report questionnaire to a sample of seventh, ninth and eleventh grade students in the Saint Louis metropolitan area and by mail self-administered questionnaires to members of the students' families. A multistage probability sample approach was used to select the participating students. From schools containing seventh, ninth and eleventh grades in public, parochial and private schools, the primary sampling frame of homerooms was enumerated. The 2,238 homerooms (or equivalent groupings) were stratified by grade (7, 9, 11) and school type (city public, county public, Archdiocesan and private/non-affiliated religious); homerooms were randomly selected with probabilities proportional to enrolments in each grade and school-type stratum. A final sample of 109 homerooms was selected and each member of the selected homerooms was requested to participate in the survey.

The questionnaire was administered to all students in the selected homeroom who were present on the day of the survey and who had obtained written parental permission. The attrition from the parental permission procedure and absenteeism resulted in 65 per cent of the students enrolled in the respective homerooms completing the survey.[3] The total number of students participating in the study was 1,650.

From the student questionnaire, data on the composition of each student's family were obtained. Since the intent of the study was to obtain data from each parent or guardian and one older sibling of the target students, categories of family composition were developed with randomised procedures used to select participating siblings in multiple older-sibling households. Thus appropriate family-member questionnaires and return envelopes were mailed to each family within three days after the child's class had been administered the questionnaire. These procedures resulted in 988 families in which at least one parent returned the questionnaire, including 817 families in which all eligible parents in the family participated in the survey and 740 families in which all eligible parents and the designated older sibling completed questionnaires. The 988 families provide the data for this analysis.

Measurement of Variables

The questionnaires used for each family member were parallel in content, with differences largely reflecting the fact that the student questionnaire was constructed for group administration by professional interviewers,[4] while the parent and sibling instruments were designed for self-administration. The extensive questionnaires were approximately 30 pages in length and were structured into four sections: mass media involvement; personality system and social-psychological states; alcohol use behaviours and attitudes; and family structure, communication and decision-making patterns. All questionnaires included appropriate demographic measures. The purpose of this analysis is to explore the baseline relationships between advertising exposure, alcohol consumption, and alcohol abuse and to compare these effects with some of the major, non-advertising determinants of adolescent alcohol use/abuse suggested by the social learning framework, namely peer and family influences. The particular measures used in this analysis are described herein.[5]

Advertising Exposure. Following the methodology used in recent research on advertising and proprietary drugs, we have constructed a programme-based measure of exposure to televised alcohol beverage advertising (Milavsky *et al.*, 1975; Robertson *et al.*, 1979). Respondents reported the number of times they had watched some 70 randomly selected programmes during the previous month for weekly shows and during the previous week for daily shows. The seconds of alcohol advertising appearing during specific broadcasts of each show were obtained from local station logs and Broadcast Advertisers Reports. The general algorithm used to develop the primary advertising exposure measure is as follows:

$$TE = \sum_i (F_i * C_i * N_i * W_i) * A_p$$

where TE = total seconds of alcohol advertising exposure during the specified recall period
F_i = frequency viewing programme i during recall period
C_i = average number of seconds of alcohol advertising appearing in programme i in different recall periods
N_i = adjustment for differential number of airings of shows of programme i in different recall periods
W_i = adjustment for non-proportional sampling of programme i across channels and viewing times
A_p = adjustment for differential number of programmes airing during different recall periods

Total advertising exposure scores, expressed in seconds per week, are adjusted to reflect the exigencies of television schedules during the specific recall periods since questionnaires were completed on different days. Nevertheless, the correlation of our adjusted scale with the unadjusted scale based only on frequency of viewing and advertising aired is extremely high (0.86), as is the correlation between the programme-based measures of advertising exposure and television viewing (0.78).

Alcohol Consumption. The measure of consumption used is the standard *quantity-frequency index of consumption*, expressed in ounces of alcohol per day, constructed by combining responses to a pair of quantity-frequency questions for liquor, wine and beer separately into a summary index of average total or usual consumption. Details of the components and assumptions used in the present analysis are available from the author. For the present analysis we have chosen consumption level as the measure of alcohol use for two reasons. First, one of the major concerns in the alcohol policy field is the supposed impact of advertising on alcohol misuse, which is thought to be largely a function of excessive consumption. Secondly, while the factors influencing an individual to drink or not to drink are equally important, much substance abuse and social learning research suggests different causal processes for the acquisition of behaviour than for the maintenance of a behaviour pattern; emphasis is focused on the latter processes in this analysis.

Problem Drinking. The approach taken in developing measures of problem drinking is a youth-specific adaptation of previous measures used in alcohol abuse research (Cahalan and Room, 1974; Straus and Bacon, 1953; Mulford and Miller, 1960; Cisin and Crossley, 1969). In this study three problem-drinking domains are delineated: (i) symptomatic consumption behaviour: (ii) negative consequences of drinking; and (iii) psychological involvement with the use of alcohol. Two symptomatic consumption measures are used in this report: *frequency of intoxication* and a summated scale of eight items felt to be of clinical relevance in identifying problem drinkers, called the *symptomatic consumption* scale. The eight items include such behaviours as drinking alone, sneaking drinks, drinking before a party to get a head start, skipping meals while drinking, gulping drinks for quicker effect, etc.; the frequency of occurrence of each item was measured on a five-point scale from never to very often.

Negative consequences of drinking were measured by summing frequency of occurrence responses to some 18 items designed to indicate problems in several domain-specific areas: problems with family, friends, task performance, legal authorities, schoolwork or job, and belligerence. This measure is a standard non-clinical measure of negative behavioural outcomes due to drinking. The measure of *psychological involvement* used here is intended to measure psychological relief or the degree to which alcohol is used to relieve tension, anxiety and pain or to overcome feelings of inadequacy. Responses from eleven items imbedded within a list of some twenty-nine putative reasons for drinking were summed to form the scale. The responses to each item ranged from (1) Not Important at All to (4) Very Important. As a final measure of problem drinking, we use the respondent's self-report of the degree to which drinking has been a problem within the past year. *Self-reported problem* scores range from one (no problem) to four (serious problem).

Reliabilities for the multiple-item problem-drinking scales for the total student sample, measured by omega coefficients (Heise and Bohrnstedt, 1970) are: psychological involvement (0.91), symptomatic consumption (0.81), and negative behavioural consequences (0.90). The magnitudes of these coefficients are well above the level of acceptability.

Interpersonal Influences. Social learning theory posits a variety of interpersonal context variables as primary influences on teenage drinking behaviour. For the present analysis three social learning variables were selected. These were used in previous research on adolescent and teenage alcohol use: (i) *peer drinking norm qualities*, measured by the respondents' perception of the approving-disapproving attitudes towards drinking held by their friends (a five-point scale from strongly disapproving to strongly approving); (ii) *differential peer association*, measured here by the proportion of the respondent's close friends who drink, constructed from the respondent's report of the number of close friends and the number who drink; and (iii) *Parental drinking norm qualities*, measured by the respondent's perception of the attitude of his or her father (or mother in households where father is not present) towards drinking by children of the respondent's age (scaled from [5] strongly approve to [1] strongly disapprove).

Presentation of Findings

Table 14.1 presents the zero-order correlation matrix for the variables used in the analysis, along with their means and standard deviations. Since the focus of this analysis is on consumption and alcohol abuse, we have used only those students classified as current drinkers in this report (N = 772); the classification is based on the response to an item asking whether or not the individual has had more than three drinks in his or her lifetime and on his or her present consumption level (zero or non-zero). This is a fairly standard distinction in the alcohol literature and resulted in 78.1 per cent of the sample classified as drinkers.

The variables consist of three groups of measures: the focal variables (advertising exposure, total alcohol consumption and five measures of alcohol abuse), control variables (age, sex, race and total television viewing), and the interpersonal influence variables (differential peer association, parent drinking norms and peer drinking norms). While

Table 14.1: Means, Standard Deviations, and Correlations*: Focal Variables, Control Variables, and Alternate Social Learning Variables (Drinkers Only) (N = 772)

	Correlations													Mean	Standard deviation
	1	2	3	4	5	6	7	8	9	10	11	12	13		
1. Age														14.94	1.68
2. Sex (0 = Female, 1 = Male)	-02													0.47	0.50
3. Race (0 = White, 1 = Black)	02	-04												0.09	0.32
4. Television viewing	-24	11	22											26.14	16.54
5. Advertising exposure	-18	15	11	78										432.27	291.50
6. Total consumption	26	13	-12	-05	05									0.49	0.88
7. Frequency intoxicated	23	14	-07	-07	-03	66								1.06	2.22
8. Psychological involvement	15	-07	-12	-01	03	37	32							16.32	6.44
9. Symptomatic consumption	26	09	-13	-04	01	62	60	58						10.26	4.00
10. Negative consequences	26	15	-11	-08	00	62	64	43	72					21.97	7.00
11. Self-reported problems	07	03	-09	-07	-03	25	23	26	32	42				1.14	0.40
12. Peer association	42	08	-11	-18	-11	40	37	31	46	39	15			0.63	0.38
13. Parent drinking norms	11	16	01	00	09	19	12	09	10	09	-01	11		1.99	0.89
14. Peer drinking norms	28	10	-09	-08	-01	31	22	26	32	29	11	35	18	3.51	0.91

* Decimals omitted; correlations ≥ 0.07 are significant with p ≤ 0.05.

the focal relationships among advertising, consumption and alcohol abuse are of primary interest, the control variables enable us to explore more 'pure' effects of exposure and the interpersonal influence variables provide for the analysis of theoretically justified alternative explanations for consumption behaviour.

The most striking aspect of Table 14.1 is the uniformly small magnitudes of the correlations between advertising exposure and each of the alcohol use/abuse measures. On the surface, the correlations indicate virtually no relationship between alcohol advertising exposure and alcohol use and problem outcomes! This situation is partly explained by the confounding effects of the control variables which, on balance, tend to suppress the 'true' relationship between exposure and alcohol behaviours in the zero-order case. Looking first at age, we find a moderate positive correlation (0.26) with total consumption and a negative relationship (-0.18) with advertising exposure. Consistent with prior research on adolescent and teenage development, television viewing, and thus advertising exposure, is greater for younger teens while consumption levels are higher for older teenagers. As a result, the relatively low correlation between exposure and consumption could be a function of the effects of age on this relationship.

Similar arguments can be made for the potentially distorting effects of race. The correlation between race and advertising exposure (0.11), indicating higher exposure levels for blacks, is in the opposite direction from that between race and consumption (-0.12), indicating lower consumption levels for blacks. Thus, race may operate to suppress the true relationship of advertising exposure to consumption. While sex is positively related to both consumption (0.13) and advertising exposure (0.15), indicating predictably higher levels for males, it has been included as a control variable to complement the other demographic controls of age and race.

Finally, total television viewing is included as a control variable for conceptually different reasons. While one may argue that the potential suppressors of age, sex and race operate primarily through the different levels of television exposure manifest in each group, television viewing, net of these variables, may operate to suppress the true relationship between exposure and alcohol use through two mechanisms: (i) the conventionality hypothesis: as the literature review showed, recent research has suggested that increased television viewing is associated with increased conventionality, both in terms of behaviours and attitudes; (ii) the opportunity-structure hypothesis: we would also argue that the negative relationship between television viewing and consumption may reflect the family or home-centred location of such viewing, with its attendant constraints on the opportunity for engaging in alcohol-related behaviours. In either case, the level of television viewing *per se* may confound the true relationship between exposure and consumption behaviours.

Table 14.1 also shows the expected positive relationships between consumption and measures of alcohol abuse, ranging from 0.66 for negative behavioural consequences to 0.25 in the case of degree of self-reported perception of problems. Note, in general, that the smallest associations with consumption level are for the more psychologically-oriented problem measures. While the translation of consumption into problem behaviour is imperfect at best (explaining approximately 40 per cent of the variance in each behavioural outcome measure), it is even more problematic as an explanation for psychological involvement and perception of alcohol problems.

The relationships between the set of interpersonal influence variables and the consumption behaviour set are in stark contrast with the zero-order correlations between advertising exposure and consumption behaviour. The correlation between differential peer association and consumption is 0.40; the relationship between peer association and the measures of alcohol abuse are substantial, ranging from 0.46 for symptomatic consumption to 0.15 for self-reports of alcohol problems. The influence of the control variables on the relationships between the interpersonal influences and consumption behaviour, given the zero-order correlations, is likely to be less than in the case of advertising and consumption behaviour.

The remainder of the analyses in this section present estimates of effects based on a set of structural equations congruent with the causal structure suggested by the Advertising Exposure → Alcohol Consumption → Alcohol Abuse mechanisms, as well as the proposed causal structure suggested by aspects of general social learning theory. Since the focal relationships and social learning theory propose specific linkages or behavioural mechanisms through which exposure to advertising and more interpersonal influences affect alcohol abuse, the author has represented these theoretical structures as a set of causal models and estimated the effect coefficients. The analyses of effects in the following tables are net of the confounding effects of control variables, thus reducing the likelihood of biased estimates of the structural coefficients because of specification error. In addition, while first are presented separate parallel models for the causal structure relating advertising to consumption behaviours and differential peer association to consumption behaviours, the social learning framework suggests a multicausal model incorporating both explanatory mechanisms. Consequently, a model is presented which includes both explanatory factors, enabling one to assess the relative impact of each process on drinking behaviour, and the relative orthogonality of the processes involved.

Table 14.2 depicts a path model of the focal relationships among advertising exposure, alcohol consumption and several measures of problem drinking. The effects coefficients are standardised path coefficients resulting from OLS-estimates in the model shown. While elaboration of this basic model within the larger context of family, peer and environmental influences is the ultimate goal of the larger study from which these data are derived, such complex analysis is beyond the scope of this chapter. The more modest goal of this presentation is to examine the major effects hypothesised by outlining the preliminary, baseline results.[6]

Each of the endogenous variables in the model is shown as a separate dependent variable in Table 14.2, which is divided into two panels. The first presents the path diagram modelling the causal structure; the second presents correlations showing the influence of the control variables on the focal relationships, as well as estimates of total causal effects, which can be decomposed into direct and indirect effects implied by the model. The core relationship between advertising exposure and consumption level, net of the control variables, is significant and positive (partial correlation = 0.117). Thus, as expected, the effects of the control variables acted to suppress the true relationship (compare the total correlation of 0.048). The partial correlation indicates that just over 1 per cent (1.4 per cent) of the variance in alcohol consumption is uniquely associated with advertising exposure, a statistically significant but substantively trivial finding. The reduced-form effect, or the total causal effect implied by the model, of advertising on alcohol consumption is 0.182; thus, *ceteris paribus*, a change of one standard deviation in advertising exposure (4.86 minutes per week) is associated with a change of 0.18 standard deviation units of alcohol consumed (0.16 ounces of alcohol per day).

As might be expected from social learning theory, even this small effect of advertising exposure on consumption is not consistently translated into an effect on problem-drinking outcomes. As Table 14.2 shows, for only one of the five alcohol abuse measures is there a

Table 14.2: Effects of Advertising Exposure on Alcohol Use/Abuse: Total Effect and Decomposition of Direct and Indirect Causal Effects

MODEL

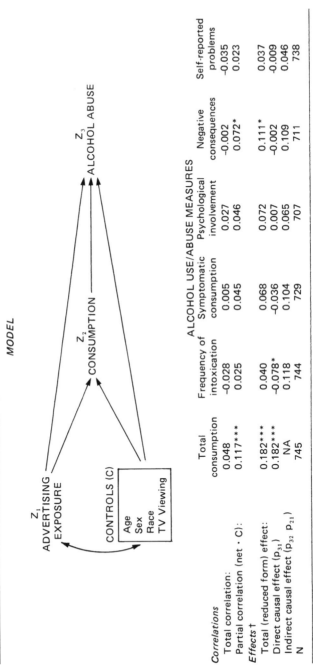

	Total consumption	Frequency of intoxication	ALCOHOL USE/ABUSE MEASURES Symptomatic consumption	Psychological involvement	Negative consequences	Self-reported problems
Correlations						
Total correlation:	0.048	-0.028	0.005	0.027	-0.002	-0.035
Partial correlation (net · C):	0.117***	0.025	0.045	0.046	0.072*	0.023
Effects †						
Total (reduced form) effect:	0.182***	0.040	0.068	0.072	0.111*	0.037
Direct causal effect (p_{31})	0.182***	-0.078*	-0.036	0.007	-0.002	-0.009
Indirect causal effect (p_{32} p_{21})	NA	0.118	0.104	0.065	0.109	0.046
N	745	744	729	707	711	738

† All effects are standardised coefficients *net* of the control variables (C): age, sex, race and total TV viewing.
  * $0.05 < p \leq 0.10$.
 ** $0.01 < p \leq 0.05$.
*** $p \leq 0.01$.

Advertising Exposure, Alcohol Consumption and Misuse 215

significant relationship between exposure and the problem measure, even controlling for the confounding effects of the control variables.[7] For only the measure of negative behavioural consequences, comprised of problems in several life domains (family, tasks, friendships, etc.), is the partial correlation significant; even then, only one-half of 1 per cent of the net variance in behavioural problems is associated with advertising exposure. The decomposition of the reduced form effect (0.111) shows that virtually all of that effect is a function of advertising's effect on consumption, the indirect effect (0.109).

Aside from the general lack of effect of exposure on the alcohol abuse measures and the relatively small magnitudes of those few significant effects, two aspects of Table 14.2 warrant comment. First, although no significant reduced-form effect of advertising on frequency of intoxication was found, the decomposition indicates that a positive indirect effect through consumption was offset by a significant *negative* direct effect of exposure on frequency of intoxication (-0.078). Secondly, a number of the direct causal effects from advertising exposure to particular alcohol abuse measures, while not statistically significant, are negative effects: net of the effect through consumption, higher exposure to advertising is inversely related to several problem-drinking measures. Although controlling for total television viewing effectively obviates a viewing-conventionality explanation for this effect, Leventhal (1964) has suggested that the content of advertising may inhibit the abuse of alcohol by portrayals which identify cultural standards for drinking and which imply sanctions for the misuse of alcohol. Certainly, the negative direct effects reported, especially in the case of frequency of intoxication, are suggestive at this point in the research.

In Table 14.3, a parallel model to that presented in Table 14.2 is presented, but using one of the interpersonal influence sources suggested by a social learning theory of alcohol consumption behaviours as the primary explanatory mechanism. Within the social learning framework, differential association with drinking peers has been posited to influence consumption behaviour through the reward structure controlled by such individuals, by the modelling and imitation processes attendant to the association, and by the development of evaluative definitions/rationalisations formed in interaction with drinking peers. While social learning theory postulates the vicarious reinforcement and modelling processes which explain mass media (advertising) effects on consumption behaviour, its emphasis on the behaviour-reward contingencies and the experiential learning occurring in interaction with others has received substantial empirical support (Akers *et al.*, 1979; Strickland and Wilson, 1980). The control variables, less likely to result in specification error if omitted from the model in Table 14.3, are included to make the results parallel with those presented in Table 14.2.

The most striking feature of Table 14.3 is the significance of the effects of differential peer association on virtually every measure of consumption and alcohol abuse. In addition, the magnitudes of all of these effects (total, direct causal and indirect causal), in every case, are larger than the effects of advertising exposure presented in Table 14.2. The top two rows of the table show some effect of the control variables on the peer association and alcohol behaviour relationships: in each case, the partial correlation is smaller than the total correlation between peer association and consumption, due primarily to their common association with age. Older teens associate with more drinking peers and have higher consumption levels than younger teens; thus, part of the observed total covariation is due to age effects. Nevertheless, the magnitudes of the partial correlations indicate that substantially more variation in drinking behaviours is associated with the processes of differential peer association than with the processes of mass media exposure.

Table 14.3 also presents the decomposition of the causal effects of differential peer association into direct and indirect causal components. The differences with the results presented in Table 14.2 are clear. For each alcohol use/abuse measure, there is a significant reduced-form effect from differential peer association. In addition, for all of the alcohol problem measures except self-reported problems, not only is there a substantial indirect effect of differential association through consumption but there is also a significant direct effect, net of the consumption mechanism! This means that differential peer association has an impact on alcohol problems through other interpersonal processes than those associated with influencing consumption. For two of the four alcohol problem measures for which the direct effect is significant, the direct effect is greater than the effect due to increased consumption, not an altogether unexpected result given the character and functions of much teenage drinking.

Table 14.4 presents a causal model that includes the suggested peer association influence and the advertising exposure influence as exogenous variables. As in the previous tables, the effects presented in this table are net effects, controlling for the confounding effects of age, sex, race and total television viewing. In this model a direct

Table 14.3: Effects of Differential Peer Association on Alcohol Use/Abuse: Total Effect and Decomposition of Direct and Indirect Causal Effects

MODEL

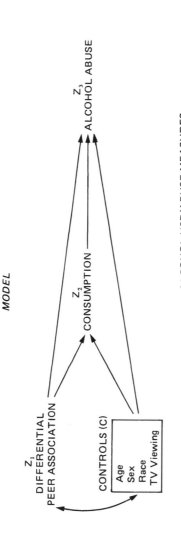

	Total consumption	Frequency of intoxication	Symptomatic consumption	Psychological involvement	Negative consequences	Self-reported problems
Correlations						
Total correlation:	0.396***	0.374***	0.453***	0.299***	0.393***	0.146***
Partial correlation (net C):	0.316***	0.303***	0.383***	0.266***	0.312***	0.114***
*Effects**						
Total (reduced form) effect:	0.339***	0.327***	0.410***	0.291***	0.332***	0.127***
Direct causal effect (p_{31})	0.339***	0.131***	0.238***	0.190***	0.149***	0.045
Indirect causal effect ($p_{32}\ p_{21}$)	NA	0.196	0.172	0.101	0.183	0.082
N	706	705	691	670	677	702

* All effects are standardised coefficients *net* of the control variables (C): age, sex, race and total TV viewing.

* $0.05 < p \leqslant 0.10$.
** $0.01 < p \leqslant 0.05$.
*** $p \leqslant 0.01$.

comparison is made of these theoretically complementary explanations for alcohol consumption and related behaviours. One general observation from Table 14.4 is that, net of the control variables, the effects of advertising exposure and differential peer association in the combined model are little different from their effects separately, as presented in Tables 14.2 and 14.3 respectively. The relative orthogonality of these principal explanatory mechanisms means that at least one alternative causal structure to that shown in Table 14.4, namely that differential peer association is simply one more intervening mechanism through which exposure to alcohol advertising affects consumption and problem behaviours is unlikely adequately to fit the data.

Table 14.4 shows that both advertising exposure and differential peer association have significant effects on consumption, with reduced-form effects of 0.179 and 0.335 respectively. Thus the total effect of the interpersonal influence measure used here is almost twice that of the mass media effect. Frequency of intoxication shows no significant effect from advertising exposure but a moderately strong total differential association effect (0.327). The decompositions indicate that, in the case of advertising, the positive indirect effect through increased consumption is largely balanced by the negative direct impact, whereas differential peer association has both positive direct and indirect effects on this measure of alcohol misuse. Since frequency of intoxication fairly directly indexes excessive consumption, it is little surprise that the effects of the exogenous variables are largely indirect through their effect on consumption.

Symptomatic consumption, which measures that complex of behaviours that has previously been identified with undue dependence on alcohol and forms that component of Jellinek's *alpha* alcoholism concerned with the contravening of social rules governing drinking, is little affected by television advertising exposure. On the other hand, we see not only the direct and indirect effects of differential peer association, but that the direct effect is larger than the indirect effect operating through increased consumption (0.238 v. 0.170). Likewise, the same pattern exists in the case of psychological involvement with alcohol, which is a measure of the extent to which alcohol is used as a coping mechanism or a mechanism for escape from the problems of everyday life. The absence of a significant advertising effect and the magnitude of the direct effect of differential association (almost twice the indirect effect) are the important findings. These two alcohol misuse measures, both involving dependence and psychosocial

Table 14.4: Comparison of Advertising Exposure and Differential Peer Association on Alcohol Use/Abuse: Total Effects and Decomposition of Direct and Indirect Causal Effects

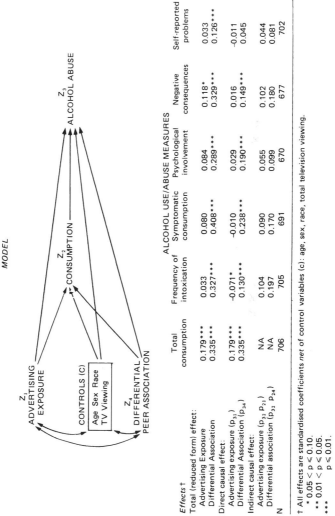

MODEL

Effects†	Total consumption	Frequency of intoxication	ALCOHOL USE/ABUSE MEASURES Symptomatic consumption	Psychological involvement	Negative consequences	Self-reported problems
Total (reduced form) effect:						
Advertising Exposure	0.179***	0.033	0.080	0.084	0.118*	0.033
Differential Association	0.335***	0.327***	0.408***	0.289***	0.329***	0.126***
Direct causal effect:						
Advertising exposure (p_{31})	0.179***	-0.071*	-0.010	0.029	0.016	-0.011
Differential Association (p_{34})	0.335***	0.130***	0.238***	0.190***	0.149***	0.045
Indirect causal effect:						
Advertising exposure ($p_{32} p_{21}$)	NA	0.104	0.090	0.055	0.102	0.044
Differential association ($p_{32} p_{24}$)	NA	0.197	0.170	0.099	0.180	0.081
N	706	705	691	670	677	702

† All effects are standardised coefficients *net* of control variables (c): age, sex, race, total television viewing.
* $0.05 < p \leq 0.10$.
** $0.01 < p \leq 0.05$.
*** $p \leq 0.01$.

involvement with alcohol are as much a function of direct interpersonal processes as they are of the result of the effects of such processes on increased consumption levels.

The measure of negative behavioural consequences, consisting of undesirable outcomes due to drinking in a number of life-domains, is the only problem drinking measure for which a significant advertising exposure effect appears. This total effect is, however, roughly one-third the size of the effect of differential peer association, and is almost exclusively an indirect effect through the consumption mechanism. Further analysis of the individual domain-specific problems indicates this relationship is largely a function of the effect of such advertising on the belligerence dimension, which included measures of hostile feelings and aggressive behaviour, indirectly through the impact on consumption. The effect of differential peer association, almost three times the advertising effect, is both direct and indirect, again suggesting that the role of differential association in problem drinking behaviours is far more than simply that of affecting the level of consumption.

The other two interpersonal influence variables used in this analysis, peer-drinking norm qualities and parent-drinking norm qualities, were also analysed in a manner parallel to the preceding analysis. For brevity, we report here only the patterns of effects and omit the comparable tables. Peer norm qualities (attitudes), one component of differential association, was found to have statistically significant effects on all of the drinking outcome measures, although slightly smaller than differential association, with reduced-form effects ranging from 0.24 for psychological involvement to 0.08 for self-reported problems. These findings are consistent with the social learning explanations which posit both modelling of actual behaviour and the acquisition of evaluative definitions of that behaviour as components of social learning.

In the case of parent norm qualities, perception of father's attitude had a significant impact on consumption and frequency of intoxication (reduced form effected of 0.14 and 0.07, respectively); parent norm qualities were unrelated to the four remaining alcohol abuse outcomes. These findings are consistent with our previous research on the differential modes of interpersonal influence attributed to parents and peers which suggests that parents are definers of drinking behaviour and peers are both models and definers of such behaviour (Strickland and Wilson, 1980).

Conclusion: Social Learning, Advertising and Social Policy

This chapter has presented the results of an analysis of the effects of televised beverage alcohol advertising on the alcohol consumption behaviour of teenagers. The role of advertising was explicated within the framework of social learning theory, which posits both observational influences and experiential influences as factors leading to the acquisition and maintenance of drinking behaviour. In general, advertising was shown to have meagre effects on the level of consumption, and these effects rarely translated into effects on alcohol problems. While suggesting that the role of advertising may be less powerful than often suggested, these results also confirm the importance of distinguishing consumption from alcohol abuse for policy purposes.

In contrast to the advertising effects, a set of interpersonal influences, especially differential peer association, was shown to have significant impact on both consumption levels and alcohol abuse behaviour. Moreover, these effects on alcohol abuse or problem drinking behaviours were both indirect through effects on consumption *and* direct, implying that other interpersonal processes substantially impact alcohol abuse behaviours among teenagers. Clearly, these results indicate that social processes are as important in determining the level of problem drinking as is the simple mechanism of the amount of alcohol consumed, which is itself inadequately explained by advertising exposure.

The strength of the empirical evidence presented here rests not only on the theoretical imbeddedness of the relationships examined but also on the methodological adequacy of the research. It is acknowledged that arguments about cumulative advertising exposure and the temporal-ordering of the variables in causal structures are more adequately examined using longitudinal data. The results presented here represent cross-sectional analyses. At this point one may only add that these initial results are consistent with the aggregate analyses of advertising effects on per capita alcohol consumption and, more importantly, with the recent studies of television advertising of proprietary drugs, both cross-sectional and longitudinal.

The minimal impact of advertising exposure on alcohol abuse does not articulate well with a strategy of increased control of advertising as a policy for the prevention of alcohol abuse and alcohol problems among youth. Reducing the amount of advertising or eliminating advertising of alcoholic beverages is likely to have minimal impact on consumption and virtually no impact on the prevalence or severity of alcohol problems among youth. Given the supposed susceptibility of youth to mass media influences, the findings of this study suggest that advertising restrictions would be even less likely to influence drinking behaviours in the general population, an implication consistent with aggregate consumption analyses.

Notes

1. US Sub-Committee to Investigate Juvenile Delinquency (1955); US Sub-Committee on Commerce (1971); US Sub-Committee on Alcoholism and Narcotics (1976).

2. The proposed changes concern the use of the terms 'natural', 'pure' and 'light' in alcohol beverage commercials, the portrayal of athletes and athletic events, comparative advertising, curative or therapeutic claims, and the use of subliminal techniques. The scheduled dismantlement of BATF and the uncertainties regarding the transfer of regulatory functions have delayed implementation of proposed regulations.

3. The response rate is comparable to that obtained in recent national surveys of adolescent and teenage alcohol use. In the present study, parental permission was solicited for the participation of the student and other family members, thus complicating the permission process. In spite of this, a satisfactory response rate was obtained. Finally, due to an outdated and inflated district-wide homeroom roster supplied by the city public schools, the actual 'true' response rate is probably much higher than that reported.

4. Two administrators were used in each classroom to administer and supervise the completion of the questionnaire. Because of the varied levels of reading proficiency among the students, one member of the survey team read the directions and each question, while the other member monitored the students' progress, giving special attention to those who could not keep up with the administration pace. In addition, models of beverage containers, along with the volumes associated with each container, were displayed during the administrations to assist in the estimation of quantities of alcohol consumed. This technique has been used successfully in similar retrospective recall studies of food intake and nutrition to increase the accuracy of respondent judgements.

5. For purposes of control, described in the following section, the authors also use straightforward measures of age, sex and race, as well as a measure of television viewing. The television viewing scale is a weighted sum of frequency of viewing specific programmes by the length of each programme and is expressed in hours of viewing per week. The algorithm used is parallel to that described in the text for advertising exposure.

6. In order to test the appropriateness of the strictly additive model estimated in this analysis, the authors examined the second-order and third-order interactions between advertising exposure and the control variables; none of the interactions was significant. Thus, the effects reported are similar over levels of the control variables.

7. Convention has it that 0.05 is the usual level of probability for rejecting the null hypothesis. In this chapter a more liberal critical region is used (< 0.10) since this work is largely exploratory and not a strictly formal test of hypotheses.

15 ADVERTISING, ALCOHOL CONSUMPTION AND POLICY ALTERNATIVES

Theo van Iwaarden

Advertising of products and services is an almost fully accepted phenomenon in the Western hemisphere. The promotion of beverage alcohol however, especially on radio and television, is a controversial issue in most countries. Brewers, distillers and wine-sellers discern their ambivalent position, and self-imposed limitations regarding the content of advertisements are by no means an exception.

If there is a positive relationship between the overall alcohol consumption in a population and the prevalence of alcohol-related problems, the crucial question becomes whether an increased total amount of publicity creates an increased aggregate demand for alcoholic beverages. In short: does advertising result in a higher consumption and therefore in more alcohol problems? Answering the first part of this question is the main purpose of this chapter. The answer to the second part falls beyond the scope of this chapter; we assume by and large that there is some kind of a positive relation. As Bruun *et al.* (1975) put it: 'Changes in the overall consumption of alcoholic beverages have a bearing on the health of the people in any society.'

Now, if the answer to the problem posed is in the affirmative, then alcohol advertising can be considered as socially harmful and could well be prohibited on that ground. A negative or inconclusive outcome will leave us with the question of the social wastefulness of this type of message.

But before delving into the theories and empirical evidence concerning the impact of advertising on drinking, it is necessary to discuss briefly the functions of commercial publicity in a mixed economy. Next, some data on the situation in the Netherlands are presented. The chapter ends with a discussion on the policy alternatives and the pros and cons of a ban on radio and TV advertising for beer, wines and distilled beverages. In view of the growing importance of broadcasting in everyday life and the concomitant discussion on this topic, throughout the chapter special reference will be made to commercials.

Advertising in a Mixed Economy

In his classic study Borden (1942) concludes that advertising contributes to the welfare and well-being of the consumer by stimulating a dynamic and expansive economy. Alcohol advertising, arguably, does not deserve this credit as it can do nothing but give 'information' about current and new brands and types of alcoholic beverage. If advertising of a certain brand or beverage were successful, and accepting the addition-hypothesis, the overall consumption would be raised (Sulkunen, 1976). In the section on the theory of the market shares we shall go into this matter more thoroughly. Here the conclusion is warranted that advertising of alcoholic beverages does not fulfil any specific socially useful function.

Opposing this so-called social perspective we find the commercial point of view: advertising is just another element of the marketing mix, that further consists of the price, the quality, the assortment and the distribution. To what extent publicity is applied in this marketing mix depends, among other things, on the phase of the product life-cycle, the degree of price competition and the market structure (Simon, 1967). By this the researcher is confronted with almost insurmountable problems in isolating the effects of advertising.

By brand advertisements using selective appeals, the individual firm emphasises the product differentiation and in this manner attempts to 'cultivate' consumers' preferences for its product. Since competitors advertise too, the essential question is now whether total demand for a class of products expands as a result of brand advertisements. In this respect Borden (1942) concluded: '. . . that advertising by competing sellers, even when they employ selective appeals, under certain conditions has a primary effect. It may increase total demand for any class of products, provided this demand is *expansible*.' As all producers compete for the consumers' budgets, this requirement is quite logical. In view of the drastically increased alcohol consumption during the past thirty years, one can in restrospect certainly speak of an expansive alcoholic beverages market in an international perspective.

Protection and promotion of public health is a priority in most government policies. However, *to what extent and by which method* should the government curtail the purchase and use of a product of which excessive consumption conflicts with this public health aim? Fundamentally, this is a philosophical problem: the political solution strongly depends on the structure of a particular society and therefore will change in time.

Theories and Empirical Evidence Concerning the Effects of Advertising on Alcohol Consumption

Brewers, wine-sellers and distillers consequently take the view that brand advertising does not raise total demand. On the contrary, it would exclusively be aimed at and bring about nothing but shifts in the distribution of market shares. It should be noted here that in other branches this viewpoint is not so easily taken for granted.

Impact of Advertising

Regarding the influence of advertising on purchasing behaviour, theories as well as empirical findings are strongly conflicting. Essentially, the hypothesis: '. . . that because advertising influences the formation of consumers' tastes, it can influence spending decisions in major and undesirable ways' (Galbraith, 1958), is opposed by one of the most sophisticated scholars in the field of advertising: 'After surveying the work of others and extending it in various directions, the study still reaches negative conclusions: there is barely a molehill of hard evidence behind the mountain of prose on the subject of advertising' (Schmalensee, 1972).

Although the null-hypothesis that advertising has no impact at all finds little support, no one seems to know why, let alone how, it has effect. In this respect three problems face the researcher. The first one relates to the supposed psychological influence on the consumer. This process has been labelled 'learning without involvement' (Krugman, 1971). It runs as follows: after a perceptual impact the consumer alters his behaviour by way of a purchase and finally a gradual change of his attitude to the product would take place. Marketing insiders too express growing doubts with respect to the classic advertising-attitude-purchasing behaviour model (Public Affairs Consultants, 1977). At the moment the opinion prevails that attitudes and behaviour — both in some way influenced by advertisements — mutually influence one another.

Measurement of advertising effects is the second major research problem. Leaving aside the methodological problem of neutralising the various intervening factors, one is confronted with the fact that in a fairly stable market the advertising budget of a certain product in general is a fixed percentage of the sales volume (Schmalensee, 1972). The differential effectiveness of the various mass media, the targeting of advertisements on certain consumer groups, and the possible cumulative long-term effects of publicity bring about even more research difficulties (Bass, 1969; Palda, 1964; Simon, 1969; Walsh, 1979).

The most complicating problem, however, results from the reciprocity of the relationship between advertising volume and consumption level. In the mid-sixties the Dutch Economic Foundation, for example, estimated a mean advertising elasticity value of +0.07: a 1 per cent rise of the total amount of publicity would increase alcohol consumption by 0.07 per cent (Nederlands Economisch Instituut, 1966). But the same study revealed that a 1 per cent increase in the overall alcohol consumption in the Netherlands resulted in 2.23 per cent higher advertising budgets on the average. The high disparity between the two elasticity values justifies the conclusion that consumers hardly react to more advertising, while producers on the other hand respond very elastically to a rising overall use of alcohol. The bulk of studies into the impact of advertising supports these findings (Lambin, 1975; Schmalensee, 1972).

Determining (the directionality of) the causal relationship — if any — in this research area remains very complicated, although the appliance of econometric techniques has made things easier.

Theory of the Market Share

Though alcohol publicity is an obvious target for those advocating restrictive measures, it should be noted that the theory of market shares does have empirical support (Comanor and Wilson, 1974; Lambin, 1975; Schmalensee, 1972). As regards alcohol advertising the most outstanding example is the Budweiser-study of the Anheuser-Bush company (Ackoff and Emshoff, 1975a and 1975b). Research in several marketing areas sought to elucidate the feasible causal relation between advertising (stimulus) and sales volume (response). The main purpose of the research project was to determine the optimum level and distribution in time of the advertising budget and the relative and absolute effectiveness of the various mass media.

Holding other marketing variables constant, some remarkable results were obtained: the publicity budget was much too high; TV advertising was most effective and after a total abolition of Budweiser messages in some marketing areas, the demand for Budweiser beer did not decline until after eighteen months. After the reintroduction of advertisements it took only six months until the initial percentages of growth of the beer sales were attained (Ackoff and Emshoff, 1975a).

Next, Anheuser-Bush Inc. applied these research findings on a national base. This led to the following results during the 1963-8 period:

the sales volume of Budweiser beer doubled;
the market share increased from an initial 8.14 per cent to 12.94 per cent;
and the advertising expenditures per barrel beer were cut down from $1.89 to $0.80 (Ackoff and Emshoff, 1975a).

Pittman and Lambert (1979) give another example: in 1978 the total beer production in the United States increased 3.4 per cent, while the two biggest brewers — Anheuser-Bush Inc. and Miller Brewing Company — accomplished a growth of their production of 13.6 per cent and 29.1 per cent respectively.

These findings appear to support the hypothesis of shifting market shares, partly as a consequence of advertising. This however by no means excludes the feasibility of aggregate demand effects, resulting from brand advertising.

Aggregate Demand Effects of Advertising

Good empirical research into the overall impact of advertising is scarce. Lambin's (1976) study is the most extensive one. After an econometric analysis of the data of 108 brands in 16 classes of products in 25 product markets, the author concludes that advertising seldom increases the primary demand for a class of products. This is in line with the conclusion reached by Schmalensee (1972). Research by Leeflang and Reuijl (1980), however, points out that the possibility of a total demand effect — even in a satiated market — should not be precluded.

With respect to alcohol advertising, the authors of the most detailed and sophisticated study found that for beer, wines and distilled beverages separately, the press, radio and TV advertising volumes were significantly related to the consumption per head of these beverages during the period 1951-74 in Canada (Bourgeois and Barnes, 1979). 'But the directionality of these relationships were different across models', they further remark. Regarding the relation between the total amount of publicity and overall alcohol use, their findings forcefully led to the following conclusion: 'The effect of this difference in directionality is that no significant relationship is observed between the advertising variables and the level of per capita consumption of total absolute alcohol' (Bourgeois and Barnes, 1979).

By and large the estimated *short*-run elasticities of advertising are negligible and/or statistically not significant (Hamilton, 1972; Simon, 1967). Even the long-run elasticity values seldom surpass +0.15, that is to say: a 10 per cent rise of the spendings on publicity by the beverage industry would in the long run result in an overall demand increase of not more than 1.5 per cent (Johnston, 1980; McGuinness, 1982).

Notwithstanding the advanced statistical techniques and the many data corrections in econometric studies, such as those mentioned above, it appears that the identification problem, resulting from the reciprocity of the advertising-consumption relationship, is not completely solved. Here we may conclude that the empirical evidence is rather weak, controversial and sometimes contradictory. In fact, one can only state that the theory of the shifting market shares finds as much support as the aggregate demand effects-hypothesis.

Another scholar, for example, found a fairly high brand loyalty (0.75) as a consequence of advertising distilled beverages in the United States (Simon, 1969). This outcome was not influenced by price variation, sales volume or amount of publicity. Measuring the short-run advertising effect in such circumstances becomes almost impossible. The study revealed also that at every level of advertisement spending, decreasing returns (of extra advertising) instead of economies of scale came into being. This might partially account for the success story of Budweiser beer (Ligthart, 1981).

In conclusion, it seems that, without a substantial amount of publicity, a successful sales campaign is hardly feasible, but therefore not yet assured. Advertising is a necessary, but not a sufficient condition.

The Marginal Impact of TV Advertising

The growing importance of TV broadcasting in everyday life stimulates the discussion about the desirability of a ban on commercials for high-risk substances such as alcohol, medicines and tobacco. A second argument in favour of a prohibition is the well-known fact among marketing insiders, that for most mass products the marginal impact of TV advertising is highest. Because the optimum level of the advertisement budget depends upon the mean marginal effectiveness of an extra dollar spent on publicity, the aggregate advertising volume of the beverage industry might well decrease in case of a ban. This happened in the United Kingdom after the prohibition of tobacco commercials (Hamilton, 1972). Total spending on tobacco advertising decreased substantially, as only a partial substitution by other mass media took place.

Concerning the specific impact of commercials on purchasing behaviour, the empirical evidence is again strongly contradictory. In general one may conclude that this influence should not be overestimated (Ackoff and Emshoff, 1975a and 1975b; Krugman, 1971; Simon, 1969; Strickland in Chapter 14).

On the other hand there is the study by Blizzard (1976) who found a strong relationship between the number of commercials and per capita alcohol consumption in Australia. The brand commercials would neutralise each other, but together they would nevertheless have an overall impact. In California too a very significant correlation has been shown between the rising wine consumption in recent years and the number of wine commercials (Katzper, Ryback and Hertzman, 1978).

However, the existence and especially the directionality of a causal relationship remains not proven in this kind of study.

Some Data on Alcoholic Beverage Advertising in the Netherlands

Television advertising was introduced in 1968 in the Netherlands. Within a few years TV advertising for alcohol amounted to about one third of total expenditures on alcohol publicity (excluding spending on bill boards, promotion at point of sale, etc.; see Table 15.1). Three remarks should be made about these figures. There is a striking resemblance between the degree in which alcohol consumption and real spendings on advertising increased, respectively 79 per cent (1968-78) and 75 per cent (1968-79). Instead of this being an argument in favour of the aggregate demand hypothesis, it appears that it once again illustrates the policy of the alcohol producers: namely, setting next year's advertising budgets as a percentage of the projected sales volume.

Secondly, it is surprising to note that in 1976 the share of commercials in total spending stabilised. In recent years even a substantial decline can be observed (Table 15.1). The growing fear of the Dutch alcoholic beverage producers of a ban on commercials might account for this phenomenon (van Iwaarden, 1981).

Finally and most remarkable is the fact that throughout the period surveyed the share of spending on alcohol promotion in the total of advertising expenditures for all products and services remained fairly constant. In spite of the doubling of alcohol consumption, advertisement budgets apparently were not raised as much as those for other products, the use of which in most cases did increase much less.

Last but not least it should be mentioned that if the overall use of alcohol during some specific year shows a sudden increase, then

Table 15.1: Alcohol Consumption (per Drinker*) and Advertising Expenditures on Alcoholic Beverages in the Netherlands (1968-80)

Year	Mean consumption per drinker (ltrs ad 100% alcohol)	Total of press, radio and TV advertising expenditures (deflated; x 1 mnlf)	Share of radio and TV advertising expenditures (in %)	Share of alcoholic beverages advertising expenditures (in %)
1968	7.42	12.6	22.0	4.8
1969	8.30	11.0	26.3	4.2
1970	9.05	11.0	27.1	4.2
1971	9.62	13.2	29.7	5.1
1972	10.45	16.0	35.5	6.4
1973	11.66	18.5	34.5	4.9
1974	12.36	18.5	37.9	5.1
1975*	12.78**	17.9	38.5	4.9
1976	12.85	17.9	38.0	4.7
1977	13.13	20.3	35.1	4.7
1978	13.27	21.3	36.4	4.5
1979*	13.17**	22.0	33.9	4.4
1980	13.01	20.6	29.0	4.2

* Estimated percentages of drinkers: 1968-70 (84%); 1971-4 (85%); 1975-8 (86%); 1979-80 (87%).
** Corrected for stock purchases anticipating the tax increases on distilled beverages per 1 January 1976 and 1980.
Sources: Based on data in Produktschap voor Gedistilleede Dranken (1981); Bureau voor Budgetten Controle (1968 through 1981); Zwart (1981).

advertising budgets will be raised. This is necessary to maintain or even enlarge their own market share. Secondly, the increased sales volume will normally result in higher profits which would lead to higher business tax payments. To prevent this and at the same time to invest in future goodwill for the specific brand, it is profitable to spend more on advertising in that same year. In the Netherlands, for instance, the business tax levy on the net profits amounts to 48 per cent, so in fact the government — that is, the tax-paying citizen — 'pays' half of the higher advertising expenditures.

Considerations such as these raise the question of the fruitfulness of present research in this field. It might be that research focusing on the relationship between gross profits in the alcohol industry and advertising spending would turn out to be more realistic.

Policy Alternatives

If restrictive measures on alcohol publicity are advocated, one should consider two things: (i) does it have any moderating effect on the overall level of alcohol consumption?; (ii) are there any repercussions associated with a particular restriction?

When the moderating effect is negligible, the only justification for such a measure is the government's wish to express its concern about rising alcohol use. Several authors note that there is no relation between the extent of advertising regulation and alcohol consumption (Bourgeois and Barnes, 1979; Ogborne and Smart, 1980).

Moreover, even if a substantial impact did occur, introducing a partial or total ban may not be preferable because of possible adverse effects. One should realise that brewers, distillers and wine-sellers have at their disposal several other marketing instruments to increase sales. Greater price competition, for example, might result. Normally, this will lead to a lowering of the average price of alcoholic beverages and thereby stimulate consumption (Walsh, 1979). The overall effect could well be an enlarged aggregate demand.

But before discussing the pros and cons of a ban on alcohol promotion, we will consider four basic policy alternatives with respect to advertising of products, the use of which is generally thought of as hazardous to one's health and conflicting with the public health aim. First, the government can persuade or force the alcohol industry to implement limitations, for example: stabilisation of the present advertising volume; application of a code of behaviour (no reference to sports or youth); regulations regarding the contents of the advertisements or the requirement that the commercials include a certain amount of information about the health aspects of drinking. It appears that in most countries the industry will eagerly take advantage of such a proposal, as the possible introduction of far-reaching measures is at least postponed. In the Netherlands, for example, alcohol manufacturers quickly implemented a code of behaviour after a speech by the Minister of Public Health and Environmental Protection about a forthcoming alcohol control policy, which might include a ban on alcoholic beverage commercials (van Iwaarden, 1981). The industry in its publicity now refrains from linking the use of alcohol with youthfulness, health or sportiveness and the public at large are no longer addressed collectively ('Drink more wine'). Lack of effective sanctions on the side of the government — except the threat of a ban — and the almost unavoidable concomitant bureaucracy, however, are serious disadvantages of this kind of approach.

The second alternative is based upon the premise that alcohol advertising is socially wasteful (not harmful) and therefore should be taxed or disallowed as a business tax deduction. McLure and Thirsk (1978) note that such a tax: 'might, of course, be shifted in part to consumers', and therefore: 'might have the ultimate effect of reducing consumption', assuming of course a negative price elasticity. As most governments are preoccupied with their revenue sources, this alternative seems appealing. Especially because the low demand elasticities make the source of revenue reliable and easy to predict. From a health-oriented point of view the advertising tax rate should be calculated on a pure alcohol base. However, if one takes into consideration the income distribution, it is preferable to base such a rate upon the wholesale prices of the various brands. The most important aspect of an advertising tax is arguably that the government really intends and clearly presents it as an instrument to curb alcohol consumption. Otherwise it looks like, and in fact is, just another new revenue source.

Thirdly, the government might promote health education. Public health messages, warning of the potentially harmful effects of a certain pattern of consumption, might have some (temporary) impact, as the econometric studies by Atkinson and Skegg (1973), Hamilton (1972), Sumner (1971) and Warner (1977) suggest. In this respect Sumner (1971) points out that 'while the effect of anti-smoking propaganda is measurable and statistically significant, and appears to be increasing over time, it remains small'. The crux, however, is that all of the above-mentioned studies pertain to the impact of anti-smoking publicity, in which a firm statement can be made about the risks of even moderate use. As regards alcohol, such a claim is not warranted (Walsh, 1979). Thus, what message — other than that of moderation — should an anti-drinking publicity campaign convey to the drinking population? The few studies into the moderating effects of anti-drinking propaganda on a national base are too seriously flawed methodologically to discuss here. Blane (1974) is especially critical and holds a very pessimistic view concerning the feasibility of health education through the mass media. Still, if such an approach is considered, in the case of commercials, for example, the amount of anti-propaganda could easily be linked to the level of total spending on radio and TV advertising of beverage alcohol. This might (partially) offset the possible existing overall demand effects of commercial publicity (Hamilton, 1972; Sumner, 1971).

The fourth and most drastic approach comprises three sub-alternatives: limitation, partial prohibition or a total ban of all alcohol publicity. A limitation might be implemented through a quota system. The total physical amount of advertising per producer and for the whole industry could be limited to present levels. This might result in quota-induced advertising price increases. Profit-maximising firms will react by reducing their level of advertising, but 'it cannot be claimed with certainty that the results of this will be a reduction in the total consumption of the advertised product', and 'Neither can it be asserted that such advertising reductions would necessarily result in decreased product prices', as Baye (1981) recently pointed out. Exceeding individual or collective quotas should result in a proportionally diminished deduction from the business tax. Again, from a pragmatic point of view, this is a complicated and bureaucratic alternative, while it might also result in a stabilisation of market shares. On the other hand, the advertising volumes will be stabilised, should consumption keep rising and it does not create a 'forbidden fruit' climate. For the researcher an almost unique situation would evolve to conduct experimental research into the effects of alcoholic beverage advertising.

Probably due to the higher marginal impact of radio and TV advertising and the presumed harmfulness of distilled as opposed to fermented beverages, the discussion about a partial prohibition always focuses on banning all commercials, or only those for liquor. Economic theory suggests that such a ban would not be *fully* neutralised by more press advertisements or promotion at points of sale. Because of the intensifying discussion on this topic, the pros and cons of this policy approach will be discussed at length in the next section.

A total ban on all alcohol publicity — if it could be enacted and enforced — does not comply with the principles of a mixed economy and almost certainly would have adverse consequences, such as a more severe price competition. It therefore seems less desirable. This holds even more strongly if such a ban is not part of an integrated set of alcohol control policy measures.

Advantages and Disadvantages of a Ban on Alcoholic Beverage Commercials

Three studies must be mentioned: Smart and Cutler (1976) found no significant effects on monthly or yearly per capita consumption as a result of the 14 months ban on radio and TV advertising in British Columbia; in Manitoba, too, no impact was revealed following the prohibition of beer commercials: overall beer consumption increased just as much as in the control province Alberta during the period 1974-8 (Ogborne and Smart, 1980); finally there is the study by Lynn (1981) who states that it is difficult to demonstrate any effect of advertising on alcohol use in either Ireland (liquor commercials prohibited) or the United Kingdom (no ban).

It will be evident that these findings do not give rise to much hope. However, many governments are prone to give priority to this instrument when control measures are considered. It is easy to implement, does not antagonise consumers and, most of all, it temporarily takes a lot of wind out of the sails of those who lobby in favour of harsh alcohol control policy measures.

Merits of a Ban on Commercials

Whatever may be the specific political context in a country, the following arguments can be listed as supporting this type of legal action.

- The *possibility* that commercials after all do increase overall consumption is eliminated.
- In general the industry may be expected to advertise somewhat less: therefore, and because two important mass media are excluded, the consumers' psychological exposure to alcohol publicity lessens.
- It expresses the government's concern and its will to do something about the increasing prevalence of alcohol-related problems. Besides, if the background of this legislative measure is seriously documented and profoundly conveyed, it should bring home to the drinking population the magnitude and gravity of the alcohol problem.
- The overall impact on employment in the advertising industry will be small, owing to the partial substitution through other mass media.
- The most important merit of a ban could turn out to be the fact that a firm can not launch a new brand or sort of beverage anymore by way of an all-embracing mass media sales campaign. At the moment, if a new drink is introduced in the Netherlands, one is confronted with this 'event' several times a day: through heavy promotion and discount pricing at the many points of sale, during daytime on the radio and at night by way of TV commercials. This lasts a couple of months. Furthermore, the producer offers opportunities to taste his

'delightful beverage' at special events such as street fairs and exhibitions or sometimes even in supermarkets and liquor stores. A ban on commercials would seriously diminish the coverage and intensity of such a psychological bombardment. It is exactly such an integrated media coverage that is lacking in most alcohol education programmes (Blane, 1974).

Disadvantages

The effectiveness of a certain control measure would be enhanced by considerable public support (Goodstadt, Smart and Gillies, 1978; Smart and Cutler, 1976). In addition, if there is no conclusive evidence as to the harmful impact of the activity to be forbidden, one must indeed query the feasibility of such a control measure in moderating the overall alcohol use and especially in decreasing the prevalence of alcohol-related problems. It is certainly naive to expect that heavy drinkers are influenced by a ban on commercials. As regards the overall impact of advertising, the diffusion of the cannabis habit and the heavily increased use of alcohol in the countries behind the Iron Curtain — both without any commercial publicity — are obvious and examples often referred to (Walsh, 1979).

The arguments below should be considered as disadvantages of this type of prohibition, if it is not part of the implementation of a comprehensive alcohol control policy.

- A subtle sort of 'forbidden fruit' climate might come into being. This would conflict with the often propagated 'responsible drinking' approach (Plaut, 1967).
- Such a ban would discriminate against those firms which until then strongly relied on commercials. The necessary change of their marketing approach would benefit competitors for several years.
- The internationalisation of the mass media makes a ban in one country a marginal affair, while international legislative bodies operate in a slow and bureaucratic way.
- The showing of alcohol consumption and especially insidious advertisements will normally continue or even be augmented.
- The introduction of a new brand or beverage would be severely hampered. If a new brand is involved, economists argue this could lead to a stabilisation of market shares. In case of a new beverage, for example light beer containing 3.5 per cent volume of alcohol, the argument holds only if we reject the addition-hypothesis and assume that substitution of stronger drink by such a beverage

would take place and would be preferable from a public health point of view (Sulkunen, 1976). Only then would a ban not be preferred, as the chances that the beer brand hits the market would be very much diminished owing to the vital importance of commercials in successfully introducing a new mass product.
- The industry might campaign against a prohibition, as happened in British Columbia (Smart and Cutler, 1976). Should public opinion turn to their side, or just because of the free publicity for alcoholic beverages, adverse repercussions would be expected.
- If the heavy promotion of alcoholic beverages is directed at consolidation of the oligopolistic structure of the beer and spirits industries in many countries, and besides is targeting certain brands at high-profit consumers — thus inducing firms to restrict sales to low-profit buyers — the consequences of a ban could well be more competition and higher sales (Ackoff and Emshoff, 1975b; Simon, 1967; Walsh, 1979).
- The national brewers and distillers would resist a ban on the ground that their present market shares might fall. The smaller countries especially are in a disadvantageous position as imported brands have a vested reputation and 'continue to benefit from their worldwide publicity' (Walsh, 1979).

In conclusion, a ban on commercials will not have any direct impact on the overall use of alcohol. Even in the long run the effects probably would be hardly substantial.

It should be noted, however, that advertising itself will never stabilise or diminish the consumption per head and thereby, it is to be hoped, the prevalence of alcohol-related problems. In this context it would be very interesting to observe what happens to the total amount of alcohol advertising, should the overall use decline.

We should ask ourselves whether from a welfare-economic point of view a prohibition is preferable on balance. Walsh (1979) appears correct in stating that 'those who advocate this measure would need to be able to document real benefits in terms of a reduction in consumption and in alcohol-related problems'.

The whole research area into the functions and effects of alcoholic beverage advertising is dominated by blurred 'scientific' polemics. Prejudices and vested interests often over-rule a sound scholarly judgement. Certainly the econometric research of the past decennia offers some insight, but much remains unsolved. Here the stereotype at the end of a chapter, that much research is still needed, is indeed warranted.

Ethical and moralistic arguments prevail in the controversial discussion on the relationship between advertising and consumption of alcohol. One thing is evident: it is a mutual one. Furthermore, it should be mentioned that the social policy discussion about regulating alcoholic beverage advertising is occasionally very hypocritical. The state alcohol monopolies of Finland and Poland, for instance, advertise their vodkas abroad; France applies different regulations for advertising foreign and national distilled beverages and international brewers refrain from some types of advertisements in the Western countries, while at the same time targeting heavy promotion campaigns at teenagers in the Third World.

This chapter has tried to arrange some research evidence and to exclude prejudices as much as possible. On purely scientific grounds, and with the present state of the art, no definite policy recommendations regarding radio and TV advertising of alcoholic beverages are warranted. As always with issues like these, the final decision will have to be a political one.

16 THE DEMAND FOR BEER, SPIRITS AND WINE IN THE UK, 1956-79

Tony McGuinness

Introduction

In the light of comments made by Walsh (1981) and Duffy (1981) on the article by McGuinness (1980), this chapter presents estimates of the separate demand functions for beer, spirits and wine in the UK. The opportunity has been taken to extend the period of analysis, estimation now being based on annual observations over the period 1956-79. The implications of the results for any policy designed to control alcohol consumption are discussed at the end of this chapter.

Specification and Estimation of the Demand Equations

The specification and method of estimation follow McGuinness (1980), except that separate demand functions for beer, spirits and wine are estimated. In each case the dependent variable is the volume consumed per adult. In each equation the explanatory variables are: a time trend (T), the real price of beer (RPB), the real price of spirits (RPS), the real price of wine (RPW), real disposable income per person (RYN), the number of licensed premises per adult (PUBSN), real advertising of beer per adult (BRAN), real advertising of spirits per adult (SRAN), real advertising of wine per adult (WRAN), and real advertising of cider per adult (CRAN).[1] Each demand equation is assumed to have a linear functional form, so that the mathematical form of the typical demand equation is

$$\text{Volume Consumed per Adult} = \alpha_0 + \alpha_1 T + \alpha_2 RPB + \alpha_3 RPS + \alpha_4 RPW$$
$$+ \alpha_5 RYN + \alpha_6 PUBSN + \alpha_7 BRAN$$
$$+ \alpha_8 SRAN + \alpha_9 WRAN + \alpha_{10} CRAN$$

Ordinary Least Squares (OLS) regression is used to estimate each demand equation. The equations are estimated with variables measured in first-difference form, to overcome the high multicollinearity that exists amongst the levels of variables.

Results of the Estimation

The estimated demand equations are reported in Table 16.1. As Walsh (1981) found, a different picture of the effect of real income on consumption emerges than when all types of alcoholic drinks are aggregated. In particular, it has a significant[2] effect on spirits and wine consumption, but not on beer consumption. The number of licensed premises is significant only in the beer equation. Beer and spirits consumption are significantly related to real changes in their own prices. The real price of spirits also has a significant effect on beer consumption and (virtually) on wine consumption, though in opposite directions. Changing the real price of alcoholic drinks would also have a significant indirect effect on the consumption of spirits and wines, by way of changing the value of real income. Of the three types of drink, only beer consumption is significantly related to real changes in its own advertising. Cider and wine advertising are estimated to have significant effects on consumption of beer and spirits, respectively.

Policy Implications of the Estimated Results

The results are less supportive than those of Walsh (1981) and Duffy (1981) to the use of price as a means of controlling alcohol consumption. This is because the statistical significance of the complementarity between spirits and wine is more in doubt than in Walsh (1981), whilst beer would seem to be a substitute for spirits. Moreover, the magnitude of the estimated elasticities of demand for wine and spirits with respect to their own prices is much smaller (in absolute terms) than those in Duffy (1981). Table 16.2 gives estimates, based on the results in Table 16.1, of the per cent by which volumes consumed in 1979 would have been lower if the real price of all types of alcohol had been 1 per cent higher in that year. The 'compensated' figures are based on the assumption that the increase in alcohol prices is offset by reductions in other prices (e.g. via cuts in taxation on other goods) so that the real income of the personal sector is left unchanged; the 'uncompensated' figures assume that no such offsetting takes place.[3]

The figures suggest that a price policy could be used to reduce consumption, but that consumption is not so responsive as Duffy (1981) suggests. Moreover, the elasticities are so low in (absolute) magnitude that the fall in consumption would be accompanied by an

Table 16.1: OLS Estimates of the Volume of Alcohol Consumed per Adult, 1956-79 Variables Measured in First-Difference Form

Dependent variable	Time trend	Explanatory variables								$\bar{R}^2$	DW
		PRB	RPS	RPW	RYN	PUBSN	BRAN	SRAN	WRAN	CRAN		
Beer	0.181 (1.65)	-9.624** (-3.43) -0.30	4.689** (2.43) 0.12	1.298 (0.77) 0.03	0.003 (0.88) 0.13	6.897** (4.94) 0.78	0.034** (5.13) 0.16	-0.002 (-0.15) -0.01	-0.012 (-1.39) -0.03	-0.050** (-2.73) -0.02	0.99	2.18
Spirits	-0.014 (-1.16)	-0.132 (-0.42) -0.15	-0.388* (-1.80) -0.38	-0.149 (-0.79) -0.15	0.001** (2.61) 1.54	0.103 (0.66) 0.43	0.0005 (0.67) 0.09	0.001 (0.85) 0.13	-0.002* (-1.79) -0.15	0.0005 (0.23) 0.01	0.77	2.67
Wine	0.001 (0.05)	-0.394 (-0.63) -0.18	-0.746 (-1.73) -0.30	-0.431 (-1.14) -0.17	0.002** (2.30) 1.11	0.275 (0.88) 0.47	-0.001 (-0.43) -0.05	0.004 (1.26) 0.16	-0.002 (-0.92) 0.01	0.002 (0.42)	0.69	2.40

Notes: The t-value of each coefficient is recorded in brackets.
** Denotes statistical significance at the 5% level. (2-tail test)
* Denotes statistical significance at the 10% level. (2-tail test)
Elasticities (at 1979 values of the levels of variables) are reported beneath t-values.

Table 16.2: Estimated % Change in Volume following a 1% increase in the Real Prices of all Types of Alcohol (% based on 1979 levels)

	Beer	Spirits	Wine
Compensated	−0.18	−0.38	−0.30
Uncompensated	−0.18	−0.48	−0.37

increase in expenditure on alcoholic drinks, a consequence which itself might impose financial hardship on other members of the drinker's household. Though perhaps attractive politically, the economic case for a fiscal control policy does not appear to be as strong as some people have recently suggested.[4]

The results suggest that consumption of spirits and wine would rise during periods of rising real incomes. The important question, which economists usually ignore, is why this response exists. In other words, what things influence consumers' tastes, which are reflected by the nature of their response to relaxation of their budgetary constraint (e.g. Duffy, 1981)?

One possibility is that tastes are influenced by advertising. The results of this study, and also of Walsh (1981) and Duffy (1981), do not suggest that small changes in the levels of real advertising of alcohol will have much of an effect on consumption levels. But perhaps one would not expect this to happen, given the high level of the advertising and social acceptability of alcohol over the last twenty years. Economists are used to considering the effects of marginal changes, but control of alcohol consumption may be something that cannot be achieved by marginal changes. In this context, it must be emphasised that no study of the kind presented here, necessarily based on data from a period of high consumption and advertising, can provide a good prediction of the consequences of policies that are, by historical standards, drastic in magnitude.

Finally, the magnitude and statistical significance of the number of licensed premises in the beer equation deserves comment. As discussed in McGuinness (1980), there is a question, still unanswered, about whether the estimated relationship reflects only the causal effect of the number of licensed premises on consumption, or at least partly reflects a causal connection in the reverse direction. Duffy (1981) deals with the issue by assuming that the causal connection is *entirely* in the reverse direction, but this is clearly unsatisfactory given the existence of plausible reasons why an increase in the number of licensed premises might stimulate consumption. For example, easier access and an increase in point-of-sale marketing efforts (window stickers, displays inside supermarkets, etc.) are two such reasons. The present study reveals that the estimated relationship is strongest for beer. This remains true for the most popular type of alcoholic beverage in the United Kingdom. Accordingly, this would seem to make it more important, for any one interested in designing policies to control alcohol consumption, to give high priority to further investigation of the nature of the relationship between consumption and the number of licensed premises.

Notes

1. For the sources and further discussion of the data see McGuinness (1980).
2. In this section of the paper the word 'significant' is confined to its use in a statistical sense, i.e. to denote a conventionally high level of confidence that the effect of a variable on consumption is not zero.
3. In calculating the elasticities in Table 16.2, coefficients which are not statistically significant at the 10 per cent level are assigned a value of zero. (An exception was made for the cross effect of spirits price on wine consumption, since this is almost significant at the 10 per cent level.) The 'uncompensated' elasticity is the compensated elasticity (if significant) plus the income elasticity (if significant) multiplied by the 1979 share of alcohol expenditure in personal disposable income (0.066).
4. The ethics of such a means of controlling consumption are, in the author's opinion, dubious.

17 ALCOHOL ADVERTISING REASSESSED: THE PUBLIC HEALTH PERSPECTIVE

Larry Wallack

Increasing attention to widespread social and health problems commonly associated with the consumption of alcohol has led to growing interest and concern regarding the role of alcoholic beverage advertising. Such advertising is a massive enterprise in many countries and probably contributes to a significant, but technically unknown, extent to the cultural imperatives concerning drinking times, places and meanings.

In the United States over 1 billion dollars worth of alcoholic beverage advertising time and space was purchased in 1981. It is heard on radio, and seen on billboards, television, magazines, buses, subways, calendars, sports schedules and almost any other place where space is available. In 1979, beer producers alone purchased $369 million worth of print and broadcasting space. In 1980, $903 million was spent by alcoholic beverage advertisers on 'measured' media – magazines, radio, television, newspapers and outdoor placements. This includes over $316 million in advertising space purchased for distilled spirits and $134 million worth of wine advertising placements. Numerous other types of advertising such as sponsorship of various athletic and cultural events and on-site, point-of-sale promotions are not included in the advertising figures. Also these estimates do not include the production costs for these creative and technically sophisticated advertisements.

Although such advertising is usually justified on the basis of providing useful consumer information, so that an informed choice can be made, few such advertisements actually offer such consumer information. Such messages often misleadingly link the attainment of valued ends with product use. Alcoholic beverage advertisers rely heavily on persuasive messages that have little to do with the product. In a study of US national magazines, wealth, prestige and success were found to be an 'indirect promise' made in 28 per cent of alcoholic beverage ads. Another 23 per cent of the appeals focused on social approval or peer acceptance as a consequence of product use. In general, the researchers found, 'little logical relationship between the product and the advertised message'. Content relevant to public health concerns such as cautions regarding the negative effects of excessive drinking were 'seldom mentioned' (Breed and DeFoe, 1979).

It is clear, at least in the United States, that the advertising of alcoholic beverages is ubiquitous and very often misleading. Given the serious public health consequences of alcohol consumption, the current permissive orientation towards advertising is out of touch with a broader reality.

In trying to understand the impact of advertising, three paths have been pursued. In the first path, studies have assigned an arbitrary value to such ads (based on amount of money spent or no ads allowed versus ads allowed) and plugged this variable into econometric models. Chapter 7 by Schweitzer *et al.* is a relevant example here, as is the one by McGuinness. Second, we have tried to understand advertising by assessing the effects of such efforts on individuals. Survey research and small focus group-type studies are methods used in this area. Two recent studies have made considerable efforts to attend to traditional notions of scientific rigor and have contributed to knowledge on this level (Atkin and Block, 1981; Strickland, Chapter 14). Strickland's chapter will be discussed below. Third, there are content analyses of advertising that try to understand such ads by counting different representations in each ad (Breed and DeFoe, 1979; Atkin and Block, 1981). Because these types of studies try to focus on the question of meaning, they are severely criticised as subjective and methodologically flawed. Even when the issue of meaning is addressed, it is seldom tied to the larger social structure that mediates and validates such images. There are, however, some cases in the general advertising area where these issues are addressed (Ewen, 1976; Williamson, 1978).

The problem with the above approaches to understanding is that they are extremely reductionist. None of the approaches addresses the critical issue of the meaning and values that are established, reinforced, transmitted and absorbed into 'popular' culture as a result of massive levels of advertising. These approaches, by attempting to scientifically control for these intangibles, either statistically or by assumptions that deem them unimportant, fail to provide a true representation of advertising issues. What is needed is to look at advertising issues not in isolation but as they relate to a much larger public health and social policy context.

The fundamental issue to be addressed here is whether such messages are consistent with the goals of a society concerned with minimising the social, economic and personal hardship associated with current levels of alcohol-related problems. The promotion of alcoholic beverages is an issue of social policy. As Martin Rein notes, 'Social policy is, above all, concerned with choices among competing values, and hence questions of what is morally or culturally desirable can never be excluded from the discussion' (Rein, 1976). Facts play less of a role in determining policy than the values we hold which colour the way we interpret these facts. Empirical studies, whether analysing content in alcoholic beverage ads or assessing impact on consumption or problems, are based on sets of values. The numerous decisions that researchers make as they frame their research questions, construct their categories for content analysis, and elect what to look at, analyse and ignore, all involve subjective judgements.

There have been and will continue to be studies on advertising content and effects. All these studies will be subject to criticism on methodological or ideological points and will always be inconclusive from a scientific and policy perspective. The question what kind of alcoholic beverage advertising we should have can only be answered by considering the role that such promotions serve on the broader social agenda. Do these advertisements facilitate or inhibit the pursuit of public health goals?

None of the three preceding chapters, although they do contribute well to the advertising debate, frame questions concerning the role of advertising *as part of* a larger system that has as one of its goals the minimisation of alcohol-related problems.

van Iwaarden's chapter is a good concise review of the impact of advertising and provides some excellent insights concerning the problems that advertising researchers face. A critical issue here is how advertising effects can be sorted out from the larger *marketing* mix that is used. This is an important issue that could usefully be developed further. McGuinness also addresses this issue.

van Iwaarden also notes three other problems the researcher must face: (i) assessing the psychological influence on the consumer; (ii) separating out message, channel and time effects, and; (iii) the reciprocal relationship between consumption and advertising.

The author poses four possible limitations that might be placed on advertising and suggests two considerations that policy-makers must acknowledge when considering such measures. Possible limitations are: (i) limit ads to present levels of exposure and restrict content; (ii) tax ads; (iii) sponsor health campaigns to counter existing ads, and; (iv) limit the number of ads or ban them outright. Each possibility is developed in a short, to-the-point discussion with more extensive consideration given to the final possibility which incorporates several of the other alternatives. In deciding to embark on any of these policy alternatives the question of whether the consumption of alcoholic beverages would be moderated and whether unanticipated, untoward consequences might occur should, according to the author, be addressed.

van Iwaarden concludes, 'on scientific grounds and with the present state of knowledge, no definite policy recommendations regarding radio and television advertising of alcoholic beverages are warranted. As always with these kinds of issues, the final decision will have to be a political one.' This conclusion is reasonable, as is his earlier statement that any government decision to control purchase of a product associated with public health consequences is an ethical decision. But how do we go beyond still another generation of advertising studies that ignore this very issue, and make it explicit that science doesn't decide but only informs. Waiting for more studies only detracts attention from the difficult question of whether it is contradictory to be very concerned about alcohol problems yet allow relatively (in practice) unregulated access for such ads.

McGuinness, in Chapter 16, estimates separate demand for beer, wine and distilled spirits in the United Kingdom over a 23-year period. Advertising is one of five major variables included in the demand equation. In regard to advertising the author raises the possibility that advertising may influence consumer tastes but notes that the evidence does not support this notion. He then raises a critical issue concerning the possibility that econometric methods may not be appropriate to the task because they usually consider marginal change and control policy may require drastic change. This is an issue that Room returns to in Chapter 19.

Perhaps the most important contribution of this short chapter is that it raises the question of how advertising is defined. Is point of purchase included in the definition? Should it be? If so, how is exposure to these ads measured? This issue is important because McGuinness reports that increased access through increased outlets *plus* an increase in point of purchase marketing may be causally related to increased consumption. Previously it was assumed (in the work cited by McGuinness) that the causal relationship was in the other direction — increased consumption preceded additional outlets. This points to wisdom, long known but seldom discussed in both the physical and social sciences: the way a problem is defined is primarily based on one's perspective or on the methods available to study the problem. Various perspectives are not necessarily right or wrong but

Alcohol Advertising Reassessed 247

only different. Second, causality can be mutual in that it can be interactive and move in both directions at the same time. McGuinness's point, that econometric methods may not be appropriate in this problem area, should be seriously noted.

Strickland, in Chapter 14, provides a preliminary report on the baseline segment of a longitudinal study to assess the impact of alcoholic beverage advertising on alcohol-related problems. Using a population of seventh, ninth and eleventh graders in a US metropolitan community, the study looks at the relationship between televised advertising, consumption and alcohol abuse. Additional information was gained from family members by use of mail surveys. The study also represents a test of social learning theory, the orientation most often invoked when concern about advertising, and media in general, is voiced.

The chapter offers a good review of advertising studies and social learning theory. In general the independent and dependent variables are well specified. As in most studies of this kind there are several methodological issues that need to be raised. First, the 65 per cent completion rate with attrition through parental refusal and absenteeism is potentially quite serious — especially if those refusing or who are absent are not randomly distributed, which they probably are not. Also, because this is a longitudinal study, the attrition rate from the original sample can be expected to increase over time. This could seriously reduce the total N and introduce a large unknown bias of non-response. Second, advertising measures used assume that watching a programme on television equates with watching commercials. Third, the design does not account for attraction to programmes with a high frequency of alcohol advertisements. Fourth, the study does not consider other forms of advertising of alcoholic beverages such as radio, billboards or point of purchase messages. This is important because, as the Strickland study indicates, television exposure for older teens is low and there is a strong correlation between television viewing and age. Also, radio tends to be the channel most relevant to this older teen population. Fifth, the results of the study are based only on self-reported behaviours. Apparently these were not cross-validated by data collected by other means.

The study finds little or no association between advertisements, alcohol consumption and problematic outcomes. A small, but statistically significant advertising effect is found on consumption, but this effect is exceeded by an interpersonal influence effect that is two to three times as great.

This study is to be commended on several points. First, it looks at problem outcomes as a dependent variable. Second, it tests out a well-defined theoretical framework in addressing the advertising issue. Third, it begins to look at advertising as it extends to a larger context — the peer group.

Although the emphasis of these three chapters is not on the larger public health context in which advertising should be considered, they do begin to fill gaps in the advertising puzzle. van Iwaarden suggests that alcoholic beverage advertising restrictions, if used, need to be part of a broader set of alcohol control policy measures. McGuinness suggests that point of purchase advertisements, coupled with increased access, may be important in the early drinking career stage. Strickland, coming from a relevant theoretical framework, illuminates the importance of peer influence on alcoholic beverage consumption of teenagers. The real issue that we need to address, however, is what kinds of studies are needed to answer the important questions concerning advertising of alcoholic beverages. But first we need to decide what these important questions are.

18 THE STRUCTURE AND ROLE OF THE BRITISH ALCOHOLIC DRINKS INDUSTRY

C.W. Thurman

The Market

The Role of the Consumer

Over 40 million people consume alcoholic drinks in the United Kingdom and many millions more enjoy these beverages in Europe and the rest of the world. Since demand for alcoholic drinks has been present for centuries, it is worth noting, as the Americans discovered earlier this century, how resistant this demand is to policies such as Prohibition. Equally, it is all too easy to talk about alcoholic drinks as a whole and to fail to recognise that people drink different beverages at different times for different reasons.

The drinks market is far from static, and over the past decade there have been some major changes in taste. Thus in 1971 lager accounted for 10 per cent of all beer sales in the UK but the figure now is over 30 per cent; while over the same period the relative share held by draught mild (beer) has fallen from 18 per cent to 11 per cent. The main growth in table wines has centred on white wine; and as the relative share held by vermouth has increased, so that held by port has decreased. Finally, there have also been changes in the mix of spirits, with vodka increasing its market share and gin declining.

The Place of Consumption

Historically beer has been the most popular alcoholic drink in the UK and this has normally been consumed at the pub or club. Hence the importance of draught beer, which in 1979 accounted for 78 per cent of all UK beer sales, compared to 29 per cent in West Germany, 21 per cent in France and 41 per cent in Australia. However, as well as selling beer, public houses have always supplied a full range of alcoholic drinks. While there are variations from region to region, sales of whisky and gin have always been important. The approximate volume of each type of drink consumed away from home is given in Table 18.1.

The public house holds an important place in British drinking and social habits. It is in the licensee's own interest to discourage excessive drinking for it could lead eventually to police intervention

Table 18.1: Beer, Wines and Spirits: Background Data, 1979

Topic	Beer	Wines	Spirits	All drinks
Number of drinkers in GB % of all adults				
Men	87.1	74.1	77.9	96.2
Women	47.4	80.9	73.1	92.7
All	66.4	77.6	75.4	94.4
Main varieties of drink With % share of UK market in 1979	Draught mild 11.4	Red table wine 18.1	Whisky 50.3	
	Draught bitter and stout 44.8	White table wine 32.2	Gin 15.4	
		Port 1.7	Vodka 12.8	—
	All lager 29.3	Sherry 11.1	Rum 9.2	
		Vermouth 14.3	Brandy 7.3	
Approximate share of drink consumed in pub and club and restaurant	90%	30%	50%	—
Volume consumed in 1979	68.24 million hectolitres	454.4 million litres	109.5 million litres at 100% alcohol	—
Volume consumed per drinker	0.7 litres per day = 1¼ pints a day	0.04 litres per day = one glass every third day	0.025 litres of 40% alcohol per day = 1 nip a day	—

Sources: Target Group Index, HM Customs and Excise, Brewers' Society.

and the loss of his licence and livelihood. Further, there are social constraints on excessive consumption for, as Prys Williams and Brake (1980) have pointed out, the authority of the licensee is reinforced by the presence of the customer's close neighbours and workmates.

The Alcholic Drinks Industry

The requirements of the consumers are met by the retailers. In turn the needs of the retailers are met by wholesalers (including importers). Once a demand for alcoholic drinks exists, then these two levels of industrial activity exist; the main effects on the economy arise from the third level of activity – manufacturing.

The following types and numbers of retail premises were licensed to sell alcoholic drinks in 1979 in the UK

75,700	full on-licences (public houses and hotels)
20,500	restricted on-licences (private hotels and restaurants)
32,700	licensed and registered clubs
41,100	off-licences

There are important differences relating to the sale of alcoholic drinks between these types of premises, but a consideration of licensing law is outside the scope of this chapter.

There are about 12,500 independent wholesalers and importers licensed to handle alcoholic drinks. Wholesalers and importers vary in size from large companies to small organisations. They are located throughout the country but naturally enough tend to be concentrated in the more densely populated areas.

The manufacturing sector is as follows:

81 brewing companies owning 142 breweries; in addition recently something like 50 very small brewing companies have been established but their total volume is still small.
129 distilleries at work producing whisky, gin, vodka, etc.
230 vineyards, but inevitably their total volume is small relative to imports.
15 manufacturers of made-wine (i.e. made from imported grape must or other fruit), as well as cider and perry producers.

Soft drinks are clearly not alcoholic beverages, but they are closely linked economically to alcoholic drinks in two different ways: (i) they are sold in public houses, clubs, etc. as an alternative to alcoholic drinks; (ii) they are used as mixers; e.g. lemonade with beer to create shandy, or ginger ale with whisky.

Each manufacturing industry has its own specialised plant, production procedures and technological 'know-how'. There is, however, one interesting difference between brewing and distilling. Beer has a relatively short shelf life and so production follows consumption very closely (given a short time lag and some special short-term circumstances). On the other hand scotch whisky has to be matured for at least three years (the legal minimum) and in many cases for considerably longer periods. At the end of 1980 the total whisky stock was over seven times the 1980 production total.

Position in UK Economy

Major Industrial Sector

In 1979, consumers' expenditure on alcoholic drink was nearly £9,000 million and this represented 7.7 per cent of all consumers' expenditure. Currently, the industry employs 3.4 per cent of all people employed in the UK. Brewers and distillers as a group form rather more than 5 per cent of the Stock Exchange's total equity market. Virtually all companies engaged in the alcoholic drinks industries are British owned. With only a few exceptions (e.g. Carlsberg, Seagram) all the major companies are UK controlled.

Capital Expenditure in Production

The production side of the industry is capital intensive. The net output per head for brewing and malting in 1978 was £16,098 or 101 per cent greater than the UK average, while spirit distilling and compounding was £22,869 or 186 per cent above the national average. The drink manufacturers are aware of this and have continued to invest in their production and distribution facilities. Thus in 1978 net capital investment per production employee was £2,371 in brewing and malting and £2,282 in spirit distilling and compounding, compared to a national average of £656.

Consequently, the drink manufacturers have not suffered from the 'disease' facing many other British industries, which is a lack of modern plant. This in turn has helped the UK economy in two ways: (i) UK drinks manufacturers have been able to meet the changing demands of their customers and so the level of imports has remained low

The British Alcoholic Drinks Industry 253

(e.g. lager); (ii) it has given sales and employment to many companies located in a variety of other industries.

About 50 per cent of the cost of a new brewery is connected with the actual buildings and associated services and the rest with specialised equipment. For instance, some of the special plant required in a brewery is shown below:

fermentation vessels	supplied by 15 companies
pipework	supplied by 16 companies
yeast handling	supplied by 8 companies
filtration	supplied by 10 companies
pumps	supplied by 12 companies

Source for number of companies: Allied Brewery Traders Association Directory (ABTA).

Capital Expenditure in Retailing

There are no complete details of new capital investment in retail outlets and the only available data concern brewers. They own 49,000 public houses and for many companies their investment in their licensed estate represents some 60 per cent (and even more) of their capital employed.

It is particularly important that the outlets continue to look attractive and be well maintained. It is perhaps no coincidence that the upturn in the beer market started in the late fifties, shortly after the post-war building restrictions had been eased and brewers were able to modernise and redecorate their public house estate. Since then brewers have invested many hundreds of millions of pounds in these outlets, and in 1980 they spent £266 million in retail activities, most of which was spent on their public house estate. During the three years 1981 to 1983 (inclusive) brewers are expecting to invest £855 million in the retail sector.

The construction of a new public house calls for a mixture of building skills — one part is akin to that of a normal house, while another part is related to running a special kind of business. Once again, investment in public houses affects many other companies, e.g. 7 companies supplying bar fixtures and fittings, 27 companies supplying beer dispensing equipment (source: ABTA).

Purchase of Raw Materials

The main British produced alcoholic drinks are beer and whisky and these are made from malted barley; some 22 per cent of all barley grown in the UK is used for malting. Out of the malt produced 50 per cent is used for brewing and 43 per cent is used for distilling. In addition, there are 5,708 hectares used for the production of hops, the main buyer being the brewing industry. Farmers' income in 1979 was £195 million for malting barley and £17 million for hops. Other raw materials are used in brewing, such as glucose (supplied by 3 companies), brewing sugar (10 companies), and flaked barley and maize grits (3 companies).

Both the brewing and distilling industries produce useful by-products, many of which are used as animal feedstuffs. There are now about 30 plants recovering animal feed materials from Scotch Whisky distilleries and 60 companies buying brewers' grains. The 'spent hops' are sold for fertiliser and excess yeast is sold for tonic and food preparations.

Purchase of Packaging Materials

The drinks industry uses virtually half the number of glass bottles produced in this country and the relative proportion has increased over the past decade (see Table 18.2).

Table 18.2: Usage of Glass Bottles (Millions of Bottles)

Type of bottle	1970	1980
All bottles	6,243	6,406
Wines and spirits	988	1,395
Soft drinks	991	1,314
Beer and cider	323	357
Total number	2,302	3,066
as % of all bottles	36.9	47.9

Source: Glass Manufacturers' Federation.

The other package used for selling beer in small quantities is the can, which may be made of tin plate or aluminium. Draught beers are supplied in casks, kegs or tanks, which are usually made either of stainless steel or of aluminium. Many different companies are involved in this part of the drinks industries' activities:

bottle manufacturers	8 companies
can manufacturers	5 companies
kegs and casks	10 companies
stainless steel tanks	17 companies
plastic crates and cases	4 companies

as well as British Steel and the aluminium producers.

Purchases of other Goods and Services

It is simply not practical to list all the goods and services which are bought by the drinks industries. In the case of brewing, there are over 200 full members of ABTA and their goods or services are classified under 521 different headings. They range from account book manufacturers and acid resisting specialists through to yeast screens and yeast separation plant.

In addition, drinks companies use the services of professional people such as accountants and lawyers and ancillary services such as advertising and market research. The valuation of licensed estate is very important and there are specialist firms of chartered surveyors dealing with such property matters.

Employment: Total Size and Stability

The Brewers' Society believes that the total number of people employed in the alcoholic drinks industry is about 750,000 people. This has to be a best estimate, as the Department of Employment do not produce statistics for each part of the industry, e.g. they publish a figure for brewing and malting but do not publish one for off-licences.

The stability and growth in employment in the alcoholic drinks industry compared to industry as a whole is clearly shown in Table 18.3.

Table 18.3: Employment Statistics, GB (000)

Category	1970	1980	% change
All employees in employment	22,404	22,008*	- 1.8
All manufacturing industry	8,727	6,660	-23.7
All alcoholic drinks	600	750	+25.0

* This figure does not reflect in full the increase in unemployment due to the growth in the labour force.
Sources: Department of Employment; Brewers' Society.

The growth in employment in the alcoholic drinks industry is due to increases at the retail level, with employment in public houses increasing by 62 per cent and clubs 37 per cent over the ten-year period. This change is really only a reflection of the growth in leisure industries as a whole.

Dispersion of Employment

Virtually every community of any size has a public house; larger communities will have several houses and even small villages of only a few hundred people will often have two or three public houses. Sometimes an outlet will be located at a cross-roads away from any population, and is a reminder of the days when such establishments were set up to provide food and accommodation to the traveller. In addition, in the larger villages or towns, there is usually a club serving drinks to its members such as a workingmen's club or British Legion Club or sports club. Thus the industry provides employment throughout the country. In addition, outside of city centres, the peak trading hours are in the evening when part-time staff are both required and readily available.

Breweries are dispersed throughout England and Wales, some in the central belt of Scotland and one in Belfast (see Table 18.4).

Table 18.4: Location of Breweries Analysed by Size of Town, 1980

Size of town	Number of breweries in Conurbations*	Other towns
Over 1 million	2	–
500,000 to 1 million	12	–
250,000 to 500,000	17	7
100,000 to 250,000	14	13
50,000 to 100,000	5	14
25,000 to 50,000	–	22
10,000 to 25,000	–	21
Under 10,000	–	15
Total	50	92

* Defined as towns within the metropolitan counties of England and Wales plus Edinburgh and Glasgow.
Sources: Brewers' Society, OPCS.

Some towns are dependent upon the production of beer, such as Burton-upon-Trent and Tadcaster. However, whether the brewer is located in a large or small town, the company is generally a major employer (see Table 18.5).

The majority of distilleries are in Scotland, although there are some in England and Wales producing gin and vodka. The distilleries are widely scattered across Scotland, with the largest concentration in the North-east Region. They are almost invariably situated in rural areas where there is scarcely any alternative employment; for instance, the 1,500 people living in Dufftown are virtually all wholly dependent on the town's eight distilleries.

Table 18.5. Importance of Brewers as Employers

Type of town	Population	Importance of brewer as employer
County	14,000	Largest employer
County	14,000	2nd largest employer
Commercial and industrial	450,000	3rd largest employer
Industrial, part of conurbation	93,000	3rd largest employer
Industrial	75,000	One of the biggest employers
Industrial	108,000	One of the biggest employers

Source: Brewers' Society.

However, the blending and bottling operations are carried out in plants situated in or near the urban areas of central Scotland. Indeed, in the past few years distillers have undertaken major capital investment programmes in constructing new plants just outside Glasgow and Edinburgh.

Balance of Payments

Taking the position at its simplest, it can be said that every pint of beer produced in this country saves one being imported (given that imports are a simple substitute for home produced goods). The UK is largely self-sufficient, as the following data for the year ending 31 March 1980 show:

1. The UK brewing industry supplied 96.2 per cent of the nation's beer consumption (and two-thirds of the imports came from the Republic of Ireland).
2. The UK distilling industry supplied 80 per cent of the nation's spirits consumption.
3. With only a small production of UK wine of fresh grape, virtually all such wine is imported.
4. Taking made-wine into account, UK manufacturers supplied 12.3 per cent of the nation's wine consumption.
5. The UK cider industry supplied over 99 per cent of the nation's cider consumption.

Further, the drinks manufacturers have been flexible in their response to changes in fashion. Thus when lager became a popular drink, new breweries were built so that it could be produced in the UK: similarly with vodka. Such action has avoided the necessity to increase imports.

There is a positive balance of trade of £449.3 million composed as shown in Table 18.6.

Table 18.6: Imports and Exports of Alcoholic Drinks, 1980, £ million

Drink	Imports	Exports*
Wine of fresh grape	284.5	24.6
Cider	0.6	3.3
Beer	35.6	19.0
(excluding Ireland)	(19.3)	(18.4)
Spirits	110.8	834.0
(of which whisky)	(6.2)	(747.6)
Total	431.6	880.9
(of which EEC)	(324.0)	(208.7)

* Includes re-exports.
Source: HM Customs and Excise.

In addition, there are both invisible earnings and payments and it is believed that the balance is positive. This heading includes income, etc. from overseas subsidiaries and licensing agreements and royalty payments in respect of drinks produced in the UK. Other income is derived from turn-key operations, which utilise the UK's manufacturing expertise.

Taxation

Excise duty is levied on the sale of all alcoholic drinks and it is a very attractive tax to the government for two reasons. First, an increase in the rate of duty usually leads to an increased yield; however, in the current economic climate this is no longer true. Secondly, the cost of collecting it is only 0.9 per cent of the out-turn. This, of course, excludes the costs which arise to the companies, e.g. the finance charge involved as the tax is paid to government by the producer/importer before it is collected from the retailer, or the complications which arise because of the effects of excise requirements upon production. In addition, VAT is also levied on the sales of these drinks. The revenue accruing to the government is shown in Table 18.7.

Clearly, this is an understatement of the total income to government arising from the drinks industry as a whole. As well as VAT and excise duties, drinks companies also pay the same taxes as all other organisations, e.g. income tax on behalf of the employees, corporation tax, national insurance, rates. From a survey the Brewers' Society believes that taxes as a whole account for nearly 50 per cent of the turnover (including VAT) of brewing companies.

Table 18.7: Revenue from Alcoholic Drink in the Fiscal Year 1980, £ million

Drink	Excise duty	VAT	Total
Beer	917	611	1,528
Wine	362	218	580
Spirits	1,152	325	1,477
Cider	12	—*	12
Total	2,443	1,154	3,597
All tax receipts by HM government			54,331
% derived from alcoholic drinks			6.6

* Included in wine.
Sources: Central Statistical Office; HM Customs and Excise; Brewers' Society.

Technology

Compared to the aerospace and electronics industries, the drinks industry is not generally considered as being in the forefront of technology. Nevertheless, with the recent research developments in 'biotechnology' the position might be changing; it is interesting to see that some Brazilians have already set up a large-scale plant producing fuel from alcohol for use in cars and that it is likely to be in commercial operation in 1982.

Both the brewing and distilling industries have undertaken major projects on energy conservation. They have both been very concerned about the effect of water pollution and have successfully installed plant and introduced techniques to overcome such problems.

Both production industries are also well aware of the need to undertake basic research and development. The brewing industry established the Brewing Research Foundation in 1951 and this undertakes basic research into all aspects of beer production. Distillers Company Limited has an establishment in Clackmannanshire and it has made available its findings to the Scotch Whisky Association, and a group of whisky companies have set up the Pentlands Scotch Whisky Research Establishment in Edinburgh.

Conclusions

The drinks industry is like any other major industry — it is fully integrated into the commercial and economic structures of the country and its impact is felt accordingly. Many economic consequences arise from the production sector of the industry:

1. The home industry supplies the following percentages of the nation's consumption:

Beer	96%
Spirits	80%
Wine	12%
Cider	over 99%

2. The industry produces a visible balance of £449 million in favour of the UK.
3. There are significant, but unquantified, invisible earnings.
4. Employment has been consistent, even though unemployment in the UK as a whole has risen.
5. Many breweries and distilleries are dispersed throughout the country, often being the main, or one of the main, employers in the community.
6. Net capital investment per production employee has been considerable; considerably more than manufacturing industry as a whole.
7. This capital investment creates a demand for a whole range of products which are supplied by many different manufacturers.
8. In addition, there is a continuing demand for items such as barley, bottles, cans, etc.

Other economic influences are due to wholesaling, importing and retailing, namely:

1. There are many thousands of small businesses.
2. Retailers, particularly, are located in virtually every community in the country; thereby providing widespread employment.
3. The number employed in retailing has grown significantly during the past decade.
4. The nature of pub and club retailing with periods of peak consumption gives rise to part-time employment.
5. Capital investment in pubs continues to be high.
6. There is a continuing demand for specialist and general goods, e.g. cellar service equipment, glasses, carpets.
7. The government is a substantial beneficiary, receiving in the fiscal year 1980 over £3,500 million, or over 6 per cent of its total revenue.

Acknowledgement

I would like to thank the many different people in different companies and organisations who have provided specific data. In addition, my thanks to those people who have commented most helpfully on earlier drafts.

19 PATERNALISM, RATIONALITY AND THE SPECIAL STATUS OF ALCOHOL

Robin Room

The alcohol studies field may be visualised as a great marketplace or flea market, where people from the different tribes of social and health sciences gather to display their wares, to barter, exchange and profit. Some people are regulars at this market, with permanent stalls; others are day trippers who set up their stalls for a day and then depart.

The conference upon which this book is based was the pretext for a new tribe to visit the market. This tribe was not previously altogether unknown. Esa Österberg and Brendan Walsh had been trading here for some time already and the product of other exhibitors, such as Robert Leu, Philip Cook and Tony McGuinness, was also familiar. In the past, however, members of this tribe have normally been encountered one at a time, so that many of their customs remained hidden. It is the interaction between the economists themselves which has enlarged the understanding of other social and health scientists almost as much as the trading which has now begun in real earnest between the different specialists. It is to be hoped that the new tribe will in future become regular visitors to the marketplace and that they will be attracted to it in substantial numbers.

As emphasised by Esa Österberg's chapter, there was a time two or three generations ago, when economists were one of the dominant groups in alcohol studies. Cost accounting schemes can be found in the American temperance literature as early as 1845, and economic studies played an important role in debates over temperance issues in North America and Britain, just as they did in Nordic countries. When the blue-ribbon US Committee of 50 to Investigate the Liquor Problem published its reports at the turn of the twentieth century, they were organised under three headings: Physiological Aspects of the Liquor Problem; Legislative Aspects of the Liquor Problem; and Economic Aspects of the Liquor Problem. Sociological and epidemiological works primarily crept into the discussion under this last rubric of 'Economic Aspects'. Whatever its failings, the temperance movement was certainly interested in the large issues of concern to economists, namely with the organisation and pursuit of a just society. It is no accident that those at the alcohol studies marketplace are turning to economists again as

Paternalism, Rationality and Special Status of Alcohol 263

such 'macro' level issues of policy and social justice arise in a very different era and framework. For many of the current issues of alcohol studies, the contribution of economists is crucial.

Conversely, in terms of what they may gain from involvement in this particular trading post, one may consider the common experience of another tribe, the sociologists. At a recent conference, Troy Duster (Duster, in press) stated that alcohol is to society as dye or stain is to microscopy. That is, alcohol is so ubiquitous in industrial societies and is relevant to so many public and private issues and contexts, that it is a wonderful tool for outlining and illuminating the structure of our societies. What alcohol does is to bring out the essential contrasts between the different ways in which society functions.

The economists have been particularly helpful in explaining and illuminating the assumptions which other disciplines have brought to bear upon alcohol studies. Of course, their own assumptions differ from those of other orientations, particularly the public health perspective, and some of these conflicts will have important implications for future consideration. While one may share many of the assumptions that economists in general make, as outlined for example in Leu's chapter, this may simply reflect that many people share with economists a historical, cultural and class position, so that their radically individualistic, utilitarian and consumption-oriented presumptions can be regarded as those of the children of the eighteenth-century Enlightenment. Although there is a good deal of paternalism in public health thought, it might be seen as equally paternalistic to impose those Enlightenment presumptions in calculations on behalf of those in Western and other cultures who do not wish to conduct their lives totally in the role of informed consumer.

Some particular assumptions are worthy of note, since they recur and interact particularly with the special nature of alcohol issues. One is the issue of rationality, on which economists appear both to yield too much and yet too little. Several times in the preceding chapters, economists have made an exception for the problem drinker in relation to this assumption of rationality. In doing so, economists pay deference to the fundamental idea, invented by the temperance movement and carried forward by the modern 'alcoholism movement' that at least some of the heavier drinkers have lost control of their drinking behaviour — and, in the temperance and alcoholism movement formulations, of the rest of their life as well — as a result of their drinking. It is an idea which has been fitted into the conventional nosologies of psychiatric thought, the current preferred label being 'the alcohol dependence syndrome'. On the other hand, alcoholism is *not* an idea or condition that the British and American law courts have generally accepted as an exception to their general assumption of rationality on the part of citizens and criminals.

The economists' assumption of rationality presumes that consumers will behave so as to maximise their overall pleasure in terms of their own personal calculus. Looking at it in these terms, the dependent heavy drinker seems empirically to behave in accordance with rationality. He or she places a high value on drinking, but it is not infinite. In experimental situations involving 'happy hours', the habitual heavy drinker proves responsive to price. Finnish data suggest that even Skid Row alcoholics respond in their drinking behaviour to price and availability fluctuations. The demonstration in Cook's chapter of the linkage of price and cirrhosis mortality provides aggregate-level evidence that economic considerations affect long-term heavy drinkers who are close to dying from cirrhosis. From this point of view, the alcohol addict does not look very different from the ski buff or motorcycle racer who have been presented as examples of consumers whose personal calculi discount risks more than is commonplace.

While one may argue that perhaps the alcohol addict does not need to be treated differently from the rest of humanity with regard to the assumption of rationality, it may be that the economic assumptions surrounding rationality are in any case fundamentally flawed. The 'knowledge-attitude-behaviour' model which dominated health education for many years has been under sustained attack and, indeed, is being abandoned in that field. The paradigm that information leads to preference change which leads to consumer behaviour was just as fundamental and congenial to that field as it is to economics. The difference is that health educators, who had to test their assumptions in their daily work, found that they turned out not to match empirical reality.

What one needs instead is a set of assumptions which reflect that the individual preferences and behaviours one observes at any moment are not simply the result of a constantly updated Benthamite calculus carried out by the individual in isolation. The preferences and behaviours reflect the existing structuring of the market and, more generally, a wide range of cultural and historical influences. In modern society, most commodities are subject to habit formation in a technical sense, which is indeed a legitimate object of collective concern. To cry that this is 'paternalism' is to ignore the non-Benthamite functioning

Paternalism, Rationality and Special Status of Alcohol 265

of preferences and purchases and to lend *de facto* support to existing conditions in the system's structuring of consumer behaviour. With respect to alcohol in particular, one needs to examine and draw upon collective historical experiences. Historically, at least in the many European and Anglophone countries and colonies affected by the temperance movement, alcohol has been handled as a special commodity — what the economists involved in the International Study of Alcohol Control Experiences (Mäkelä *et al.*, 1981; Single *et al.*, 1981) (or ISACE) called a 'demerit good', or Mark Moore and Philip Cook, in the context of the National Academy of Sciences panel (Moore and Gerstein, 1981), referred to as a 'hazardous commodity'. What emerged from the seven case studies of ISACE was that, uniformly in the post-war era, there was a movement towards normalisation of alcohol in the marketplace. Many of the societal signals and provisions reflecting alcohol's standing as a demerit good were eroded. With the decline of other organised interest, traditionally focused through temperance organisations, the interests of those who produced and distributed alcohol became more and more dominant.

In this era, alcohol consumption rose nearly everywhere. What was found also was that not only the sequelae of long-term heavy drinking, such as cirrhosis, but also social and casualty problems empirically tended to rise as consumption rose. The attempts to substitute new, less disruptive drinking patterns for old ones, notably in Finland, resulted mostly in the addition of new behaviours to the old ones.

Perhaps in a lagged reaction to this, societies like those studied in ISACE seem to have experienced a point of inflection sometime in the 1970s. Partly, of course, reflecting economic difficulties, consumption stabilised or fell, at least temporarily. In a number of countries and a number of ways, small symbolic steps have been taken towards redifferentiating alcohol from the general market, re-emphasising a special status for it as a demerit commodity. In a literal expression of this, Switzerland and Ireland have provided that there should be a barrier between alcohol and other goods in supermarkets. Nordic countries have experimented with various restrictions of availability, and an initiative petition is currently circulating in Sweden to restore a version of the 'motbok' rationing system. A majority of the US States which lowered the legal drinking age in the early 1970s have partially raised it again. A recent nationwide poll in the USA showed a majority in favour of raising federal alcohol and tobacco taxes, in part to help prevent alcohol problems as well as to boost federal finances. The production of this book must be seen as an indirect result of analogous shifts in the climate of opinion in the United Kingdom.

This history seems to be relevant to economists in two ways. One is that they should recognise its import in their assumptions and calculations. It is as paternalistic for economists to ignore clear societal statements about alcohol's status as a special commodity as it is for consumer preferences to be ignored. Whatever one may think personally about the wisdom of the provision, a society which does not allow children into pubs with their parents is not a society which is treating alcohol like any other commodity.

The second way in which the ISACE work is of relevance is that economists are very much needed in the enterprise of studying and understanding what is going on in this history and its manifestations in the present day. The economists involved in ISACE made valuable contributions but ISACE only scratched the surface of issues in one period to which the tools and paradigm of economics are relevant.

In this regard, it is to be hoped that economists will expand their horizons to study big changes as well as the marginal effects which Tony McGuinness and others have stated were their stock in trade. Big changes in both directions with respect to the entrenchment of psychoactive-drug use in a population are commonplace in history. Concepts like 'latent demand' or the frustration of demand are totally inadequate to characterise or understand the very substantial drop in alcohol consumption in the US in the 1830s, the current explosion of consumption in Papua New Guinea, or the quadrupling of wine consumption in France in the mid-nineteenth century. Economic factors are certainly important in all these instances, and supply manipulation factors play a paramount role in some other big changes, such as the decline in British consumption at the time of the First World War and the decimation of Danish spirits consumption in 1917. But in many of these historical instances, as in the recent events in Poland, major autonomous shifts in sentiments in the population must be taken into account. If there is any ambition to do more than manage the surface ripples on the sea of alcohol-related problems, economists and others must be ambitious enough to study big changes and how they happen.

20 ALCOHOL AND HEALTH ECONOMICS: THE POLICY PERSPECTIVE

David Taylor

The American sociologist David Mechanic recently described much of the thinking which underlies activity in the area of health education as 'vacuous assumption based on inadequate information' (Mechanic, 1980). The same could also be said of some of the work published in the fields of 'alcoholology' and health economics, but not of the chapters in this volume.

They clearly indicate the strengths and the limitations of the knowledge bases and conceptual approaches of both 'disciplines' in a manner which should facilitate a realistic appraisal of the future possibilities for collaboration between researchers with interests in either alcohol or health economics.

The goal of this brief chapter is to draw out and integrate some of the implications of the preceding parts of the book, paying special attention to the policy choices confronting governmental and industry decision-makers. It is divided into four subsections. First, some comments specifically relating to the role of health economics and key criticisms which may be levelled at it. Second, a short discussion of alcohol-containing products in the market place, and of what is known of the balance between their beneficial and harmful properties. Third, a look at the harm control policies available. And fourth, an examination of what future research priorities might sensibly be set, of how research might be organised and of how it may influence policy formation.

The Economic Evaluation of Health — an Amoral Exercise?

To some ill-informed commentators economics seems to be little more than a branch of accountancy, in which the cash costs of given events in society are calculated and 'buying policies' consequently recommended on the basis of what options look more or less expensive. Not surprisingly, those with such a simplistic notion of economics often object to its application to areas like health care. What about, they ask, factors not normally measured in cash terms, like suffering and lost life? Surely they should enter into the cost and benefit 'balance sheet'? The answer is, of course, that they do. Techniques such as those involved in sophisticated cost-benefit analysis attempt to gauge *all* the populations preferences and implicit evaluations, including those in areas where money transactions are not normally involved. Money values are simply used as a generic, common expressor of value to allow broad comparisons and choices between alternative programmes to be made.

Provided that a population's values in a given context can be clearly established, and that the inter-relationships within and consequences of any given set of human transactions can be understood accurately, the skills of economists can be employed to identify the most efficient allocation of resources possible. There can be no serious doubt that the economic tools described in this volume by contributors such as Cook, Schifrin, Gerstein, Schweitzer and Leu are potentially powerful aids to decision-making.

However, there are some balancing or cautionary points to be noted when the role of economics in the 'real world' is considered. First, the ideal situation described above, in which values are known and sufficiently homogeneous to permit meaningful aggregation and in which other necessary data are fully available, rarely exists in practice. Indeed, it is often precisely because of uncertainties in such areas that economists are called in to assist policy formation. This means that their true role is often to identify those aspects of a social question where more empirical data or fresh theoretical explanations are needed and to assist in the process of personal and collective value formation.

By making explicit the implicit evaluations underlying policies, economists serve to question established assumptions and, it is hoped, can help to promote workable consensus. Even so, they cannot usually replace political process and compromise as the final arbiter of policy formation. This is specially so when, in plural communities, different sections of the people have deeply held, yet conflicting, beliefs. To suppose that mathematical manipulation of economic data can in such circumstances somehow magically avoid or make fully 'rational' choices between conflicting value systems would obviously be absurd.

A related cautionary point is that naive or exploitative clients of economists may fail to understand or make clear that sophisticated economic calculations are not in any sense absolute or 'value free'. They usually reflect the valuations of the society within which they are formed. Thus economic analyses of interactions within Britain's National Health Service tend to assume that, for instance, human life

Alcohol and Health Economics 269

and distress is of equal importance in all individuals. Yet in a health system where private funding is dominant, evaluations of such phenomena may be weighted by individual sufferers' abilities to pay.

Partially quoted 'conclusions' from economic studies, used in such a way as to ignore and/or obscure the cautions of their authors, may at best be misleading and at worst be seen as cynical propaganda for particular interest groups. Economists working in the health or any other sector should surely be responsible for preventing their findings from being used in a corrupt manner.

A third and final point in this subsection is that the model of people used by economists, which suggest we are rational, independent decision-makers with rational, independent tastes, can be questioned. Generally speaking, of course, most individuals would probably think of *themselves* in the above way and would reject the idea that others might be better judges of their own well-being than they are. But even so there may still be a number of complex areas where people openly recognise that they cannot decide between the options confronting them rationally. In some of these they may be able to employ an agent to do so. Frequently expediency necessitates the expression of explicit and/or implicit judgements and preferences, even though the rational person may well recognise that his or her choices are not a product of reasoned and/or informed thought.

Misinformation stemming from factors like inaccurate or otherwise misleading advertising and enforced substitution of demand as a result of governmental or (often linked) supplier side decisions not to make alternative forms of consumption available are both additional examples of factors which might be alleged to lead to a 'false demand consciousness'. Conventional analyses, even if based on the most comprehensive psychological observations, may fail to reveal the limitations which such phenomena impose on their credibility, just as they may fail to be able accurately to identify the effects of radical rather than marginal shifts in patterns of demand or supply in any given economic relationship.

Alcohol in the British Market Place

The significance of alcohol-containing products to the British economy can be assessed from a number of rather different standpoints. Those in industry and the commercial/fiscal arms of government may wish to stress their role as exports (there is a £450-million positive balance of trade in alcoholic beverages for Britain each year), as job providers (750,000 people are employed in alcohol production, distribution and retail) and as vehicles for tax collection (approaching £4,000 million of tax revenue annually is currently gained via the alcohol-containing products sold in Britain).

By contrast those concerned primarily with health care and accident prevention may wish to concentrate attention more on the morbidity and mortality associated with alcohol use — with the latter alone perhaps running at up to 10,000 deaths a year in the UK. The lost production costs imposed alone are significant, but difficult to estimate precisely, especially in an economy which combines relatively high levels of unemployment with relatively high transfer payments to the sick or longer-term disabled. And the suffering and other subjective costs involved to the affected minority are of course high.

Against the latter commentators such as Thurman (Chapter 18), who quite rightly are anxious to put the 'industry case' as fully and objectively as possible, many point to the fact that the majority of alcohol consumers experience net subjective benefit. Balancing empirically these two areas, which some economists might regard as 'intangible', is clearly a difficult task which will never be resolved to everyone's satisfaction.

The economist is thus left with a general picture of alcohol-containing products as being generally beneficial to the community if consumed 'in moderation' but as items which at the margin of individual consumption above a certain not precisely defined level impose progressively higher personal and external costs. International data on phenomena like liver disease (see Davies, Chapter 9) suggest that for communities as a whole increases in alcoholic product usage above certain levels also result in exponentially rising marginal costs of consumption (and quite probably exponentially falling benefits), although any assumption of a fixed relation between mean consumption and harm would be unwarranted. In the past an uncritical use of the work of Ledermann (1956) despite its obvious social scientific and mathematical flaws, perhaps led to an overconcentration on the use of community mean consumption as a proxy 'harm warning' indicator and drew attention away from the need to examine detailed drinking distribution patterns (Duffy and Cohen, 1978).

The implication of the above paragraph is that there are optimal individual and community levels of alcohol product consumption, the latter at any one time being a function of both overall usage and the behaviour (variable) of particular 'at risk' groups. It could well be argued that government policy should be to aim at optimal usage levels at both micro and macro levels. Responsible industry might also aim at welfare optimising sales levels, rather than a traditional, crude volume maximising approach. This is now widely becoming seen as correct policy in the albeit much more regulated and safety conscious world of the pharmaceutical industry, and there seems little reason not to extend such thinking to key areas of social drug-taking like drinking.

From this, one conclusion might be that the main priority should be to gather more precise data on the use of alcohol in the population in relatively narrowly defined age/sex/class/culture groups, and from this to go on to research how specific sectors of the market can be 'helped' towards optimal consumption. This would require much extensive, time-consuming and methodologically difficult research. For policy-makers faced with the question 'what do we do now in the face of many conflicting pressures from commercial, union, religious, medical, political and intra-governmental groups?' a call for a long-term commitment to research may seem to be a typically evasive, academic response, desirable though sufficient data for a definitive cost-benefit analysis of alcohol harm control programmes would be.

The next section of this chapter therefore outlines three 'ideal type' policy option 'sets' which might theoretically be taken up by government today, given that the 'no action till further research is done' alternative may not be viable. They are suggested primarily for the purpose of stimulating debate and awareness of the underlying nature of the choices to be made. In practice it must be realised that any integrated approach to social policy across various departments of government and influential private sectors (including organised labour) would be very difficult to achieve.

Harm Control — the Policy Options for Britain

The three 'packages' of harm control strategies presented below are based on three alternative views of the nature of the alcohol market in the UK. The first is that consumers are the best judges of their own welfare and that government has no right or reason to intervene in such a way as to limit arbitrarily the consumption of any product. Rather it should make sure the market works as well as possible in terms of, say, information distribution and product price being an accurate signal of *all* the costs of consumption, and leave the people then to decide how their well-being can best be assured. The indications are that this 'freedom' model might well lead to increased overall drinking levels, providing the economy resumes growth, simply because real incomes and alcohol consumption are usually positively linked.

The second approach is based on the view that although consumer sovereignty is in most respects a desirable principle which in practice usually ensures a reasonably efficient allocation of resources via the market, alcohol is in some ways a special case. People may find it very difficult to judge fully the costs and risks of its use, and history indicates that a free market characteristically tends to promote levels of consumption which are harmful to many people. A 'moderate interventionist' model for harm control might be to say that, on the basis of international (and past British) figures such as those described by Davies, we are now drinking 'enough'. Policy here would probably be to control overall consumption to about its current level, whilst aiming to minimise specific types of harm wherever possible.

The third view is one which could be termed 'paternalistic'. Clinicians and others confronted with the appalling damage caused by the misuse of alcohol, not just in terms of accidents and physical ill health but with regard also to personality destruction and social decay, may feel strongly that most people have neither the experience nor the insight to judge its full costs. Also the populace has little concept of the choices that an alcohol-free world would offer, and according to some it needs clear guidance from society's leaders on the use of this dangerous, addictive but currently widely accepted drug.

Proponents of the 'paternalistic' model may want to see mean alcohol consumption in Britain at least halved from the 1980 level, as well as every effort made to control the various types of specific harm. In the long term they may aim to weaken the political position of the alcohol industry and to shift the populations' attitudes, so that regular drinking is no longer seen as generally acceptable.

The policy approaches which might be put forward by advocates of these various views differ significantly. 'Freedom' arguments are aimed at market improvement. Education of the public to be able to comprehend and respond to risk data is central. Advertising likely to mislead rational consumers would be seen as a major target for reform, as McGuinness has argued.

Those tending more to the 'reasonable prejudice' model, however, have less trust in the processes of free but informed consumer choice. They may well want to see rather more emphasis on price control of consumption, albeit adjusted to prevent disbenefits to poorer families becoming 'excessive'. The return of revenues gained from alcohol to the latter by increased family income supplements (payable to the probably less drink-prone women) or subsidies to essential goods might be suitable strategies. Both Cook's and Walsh's contributions to this volume suggest that loading spirit taxes might be another way of limiting excessive drinking whilst sparing poor consumers from too much economic burden.

Moderate interventionists would also want to see cost-effective initiatives made in 'rescue' services for alcoholics, both in the health sector and elsewhere. And vigorous harm control interventions in areas like road accidents would also be attractive. A 'curfew' speed limit at peak drink times is one option. Increases in breath-testing with those found with *any* alcohol whilst driving being reported to insurance companies which hopefully would raise their premiums is another. (If linked accurately to the external costs associated with even moderate drinking and driving this last would also appeal to 'freedom' theorists who wish to see clear 'market signals' associated with alcohol usage.)

Yet they might not be too concerned with advertising. In as much as they may believe it increases costs and is aimed at inhibiting unchecked competition rather than shifting overall demand, advertising is not a target for members of this centre group, who are not primarily concerned with grass-roots consumer rationality. Instead, they may wish to increase the cost of advertising by a special tax, so probably making the market structure develop a rather more oligopical form and generating funds which might be used for health education 'counter propaganda' aimed essentially at satisfying the vocal political opponents of advertising. This somewhat cynical view of advertising and the role of health education is in a sense supported by Soviet experience, where demand for alcohol does not seem to have been a function of Western-style alcoholic beverage promotion.

By contrast, those in the paternalistic school may want to repress advertising altogether. This is not essentially because they are concerned with any immediate effect it may have on demand for alcohol-containing products, or because they wish to ensure freedom of access to accurate information. It would be unreasonable for those not believing in most people's capacity for rational choice to be so motivated. Rather, 'paternalists' wish to change the emotive attitudes of new cohorts of the population to drinking, to make it less acceptable. The long-term impact of advertising is difficult to measure, but it may well help to make drink an acceptable feature of daily life. Hence it might be thought undesirable.

At the same time this last model demands a generally rather draconian approach to the control of alcohol consumption. Steep rises in taxation, the elimination of 'perks' such as duty free drink for international travellers, harsher penalties for drink-related law breakers and perhaps also compulsory 'treatment' for those at risk of alcohol problems, along the lines of some Scandinavian initiatives, might all be seen as worthwhile moves.

With regard to the alcohol industry, adherents of this school would logically wish to weaken its political position. The use of 'health education' as a form of attacking propaganda would be one direct, if crude, approach. But analysis of the situation suggests more subtle approaches are also available. For instance, the industry could in the long term be encouraged by capital investment grant schemes to eliminate labour and so decrease the voting power of its workforce. It would then be more vulnerable to subsequent threats of 'profit squeezes' and reductions in state funding.

Simultaneously the retail sector might be encouraged to focus progressively on the food rather than the alcohol side of its business. Encouragement of independent cafe-style eating houses could, in an environment with high and rising alcohol prices, theoretically be used to weaken the hold of 'clubs and pubs' over British social life and the vertical grip of the brewer/distiller chains on the retail level. Once again the result might be an eventual reduction in the political power of the industry.

Conclusion – the Research Issues

The range of 'policy ideologies' outlined above suggests a number of areas for potentially profitable economic analysis. One might be closer investigation of family budget decisions relating to alcohol, the factors governing them and the ways in which the impact of alcohol spending on 'at risk' groups like the children of poor, high users might best be moderated. Another might be further examination of the impact of advertising on the alcohol market. Does it increase costs and decrease volume sales but offer relative protection to those sellers able to afford it, or does it in some circumstances encourage price competition and/or. increase overall consumer demand? What are its long-term effects, if any? In a given context, how does it affect the balance of various types of beverage consumed, and what are the real policy issues involved in its control?

A third possibility for research is an international examination of the economics of alcohol control. Multinational companies may sometimes operate in a manner aimed at encouraging governments to focus on sectional national interest in areas like employment or export/import balance maintenance. As a result policy-makers can develop a sort of 'tunnel vision'. Might economists be able to illuminate the range of issues at stake if the role of alcoholic beverages throughout the Western world is examined, and global policies for harm limitation at least discussed, if not acted upon?

Fourth, the value of alcohol 'rescue' services in the health and social care areas could be subjected to more economic scrutiny, and the cost-effectiveness/benefit of various types of intervention programme analysed. It is probably in this last area that the most immediate priorities for research lie. Employment-based 'early warning' services; community psychiatric resource centres; the work of general practitioners; 'detoxification' centres; health education programmes; all are examples of areas of potential interest to economists and alcohol researchers. The costs and benefits of sophisticated treatments for liver cirrhosis will also become of increasing interest, especially as transplantation becomes more viable. If nothing else the latter may have a dramatic impact on some existing alcohol harm figures (for instance, the 500,000-750,000 problem drinkers in English estimates), which are in fact speculative projections based on little more than the 2,000 or so liver cirrhosis deaths that occur annually.

Even when research priorities have been identified, however, there still remain important questions as to how work should be organised and funded. It would be beyond the scope of this chapter to conduct an exhaustive discussion of the issues relating to 'discipline' versus 'domain' oriented research or the problems which seem to have beset certain aspects of Department of Health and Social Security and Social Science Research Council funded research in the health and social service sphere. But one concluding point may be worth making, if only to stimulate debate.

The strength of the disciplinary loyalties and incentives operating in academia may be seen as a significant obstacle to interdisciplinary research in universities. In Britain the state provides a number of alternative environments for social scientists interested in policy, but they tend to be subject to their own disadvantages and to require individuals to spread their expertise over a rather wide range of areas. Also the opportunities for actually influencing events are limited.

A possibly desirable supplement, therefore, might be policy analysis conducted within the industrial sector, funded by those agencies specifically concerned with the manufacture and sales of the relevant products. This is a different proposition to that of setting up schemes such as the new Alcohol Education and Research Council, which will finance external (presumably mainly academic) workers. A strong 'in-house' staff employed in scientific social policy research, operating (either at corporate planning or trade association level) autonomously from 'bottom line' management, might both access information denied to other researchers and build up genuine expertise whilst retaining close links with key decision-makers in industry. Given that in the final analysis few people wish to destroy the alcohol trade but rather to maximise its useful output, increased competence in welfare policy formation could well prove to be a valuable and integral aid to companies wishing both to be privately owned and publicly acceptable.

Yet in reality such thinking is probably very foreign to traditional British management. Fears that in-house research would be seen as biased would probably make many industrialists in the alcohol and other trades reject the direct approach. In so doing they open themselves to the charge that they are funding research by 'the back door'. And they may also blind themselves to the fact that what is needed in such areas is clear argument based on good science, not merely a respectable front.

REFERENCES

Aaron, H.J. (1978) *Politics and the Professors: The Great Society in Perspective* (Brookings, Washington D.C.)

Ackoff, R.L. and Emshoff, J.R. (1975a) 'Advertising Research at Anheuser-Bush Inc. (1963-1968), I', *Sloan Management Review*, vol. 16, no. 2, pp. 1-15

Ackoff, R.L. and Emshoff, J.R. (1975b) 'Advertising Research at Anheuser-Bush, Inc. (1968-1974), II', *Sloan Management Review*, vol. 16, no. 3, pp. 1-15

Adrian, M. (1978) *Statistical Supplement to the Annual Report 1977-78* (Addiction Research Foundation, Toronto)

Akers, R.L. (1977) *Deviant Behavior: A Social Learning Approach*, second edn (Wadsworth, Belmont)

Akers, R.L., Krohn, D., Lanza-Kaduce, L. and Radosevich, M. (1979) 'Social Learning and Deviant Behaviour: A Specific Test of the General Theory', *American Sociological Review*, vol. 44, pp. 636-55

Atkin, C. and Block, M. (1981) *Content and Effects of Alcohol Advertising, Report 1: Overview and Summary of Project* (Michigan State University)

Atkinson, A.B. (1974) 'Smoking and the Economics of Government Intervention', in Perlman, M. (ed.), *The Economics of Health and Medical Care* (Macmillan, London and New York)

Atkinson, A.B. and Meade, T.W. (1974) 'Methods and Preliminary Findings in Assessing the Economic and Health Services Consequences of Smoking, with Particular Reference to Lung Cancer', *Journal of the Royal Statistical Society*, Series A, vol. 137, pp. 297-312

Atkinson, A.B. and Skegg, J.L. (1973) 'Anti-smoking Publicity and the Demand for Tobacco in the United Kingdom', *The Manchester School of Economic and Social Studies*, vol. 41, September, pp. 265-82

Atkinson, A.B. and Townsend, J.L. (1977) 'Economic Aspects of Reduced Smoking', *Lancet*, pp. 492-5

Bacon, S. (1979) 'Progress Report: Continuation of Longitudinal Study of Drinkers in College in 1950', to *Scientific Advisory Council, Distilled Spirits Council of the United States. Inc.* March

Bailey, M.B., Haberman, P.W. and Alksne, H. (1965) 'The Epidemiology of Alcoholism in an Urban Residential Area', *Quarterly Journal of Studies on Alcohol*, vol 26

Bales, R.F. (1946) 'Cultural Differences – Rates of Alcoholism', *Quarterly Journal of Studies on Alcohol*, vol. 6, pp. 480-99

Bandura, A. (1977) *Social Learning Theory* (Prentice-Hall, Englewood Cliffs)

Barnes, J.G. and Bourgeois, J.C. (1977) 'Factors which Influence Per Capita Consumption of Beverage Alcohol', *Report Submitted to the Department of Health and Welfare* (Canada)

Barsby, S.L. and Marshall, G.L. (1977) 'Short-term Consumption Effect of Lower Minimum Alcohol-purchasing Age', *Journal of Studies on Alcohol*, vol. 38, pp. 1665-79

278 References

Barzel, T. (1976) 'An Alternative Approach to the Analysis of Taxation', *Journal of Political Economy*, vol. 84, no. 6, pp. 1177-97
Bass, F.M. (1969) 'A Simultaneous Equation Regression Study of Advertising and Sales of Cigarettes', *Journal of Marketing Research*, vol. 6, August, pp. 291-300
Baumol, W.J. and Oates, W.E. (1971) 'The Use of Standards and Prices for Protection of the Environment', *Swedish Journal of Economics*, vol. 73, p. 42
Baumol, W.J. and Oates, W.E. (1975) *The Theory of Environmental Policy* (Prentice-Hall, Englewood Cliffs)
Baumol, W.J. and Oates, W.E. (1979) *Economics, Environmental Policy and the Quality of Life* (Prentice-Hall, Englewood Cliffs)
Baye, M.R. (1981) 'Optimal Adjustments to Changes in the Price of Advertising', *The Journal of Industrial Economics*, vol. 30, no. 1, pp. 95-103
Beauchamp, D.E. (1980) *Beyond Alcoholism: Alcohol and Public Health Policy* (Temple University Press, Philadelphia)
Berry, R.E. Jr. (1976) 'Estimating the Economic Costs of Alcohol Abuse', *New England Journal of Medicine*, vol. 295, pp. 620-1
Berry, R.E. Jr. and Boland, J.P. (1977) *The Economic Cost of Alcohol Abuse* (Free Press, New York)
Berry, R.E. Jr., Boland, J.P., Smart, C. and Kanak, J. (1977) *The Economic Costs of Alcohol Abuse and Alcoholism — 1975* (National Institute on Alcohol Abuse and Alcoholism, Rockville, Maryland)
Betaenkning afgiven af den af indenrigsministeriat under 16. juli 1914 nedsatte 2 aedruelighedskomission (1927), 11 afsnit, Om forbud mod tilvirkning inførsel og salg af staerke drikke (København)
Blane, H.T. (1974) 'Education and Mass Persuasion as Preventive Strategies', in Room, R. and Sheffield, S. (eds.), *The Prevention of Alcohol Problems: Report of a Conference*, Office of Alcoholism, Health and Welfare Agency, pp. 255-88 (Berkeley, California), (+ discussion on his paper, 289-305)
Blaug, M. (1980) *The Methodology of Economics: or How Economists Explain* (Cambridge University Press, Cambridge and London)
Blizzard, J. (1976) *Commercial Media and Consumer Behaviour in Australia* (Television Society of Australia, Sydney)
Borden, N. (1942) *The Economic Effects of Advertising* (Irwin, Chicago)
Borg, A. (1970) *Alkolen i samfunnsøkonomien — ressurser som destrueres pa grunn av alkoholkonsum* (Industrikonsult A.S. Oslo)
Bourgeois, J.C. and Barnes, J.G. (1979) 'Does Advertising Increase Alcohol Consumption?', *Journal of Advertising Research*, vol. 19, no. 4, pp. 19-29
Breed, W. and Defoe, J. (1979) 'Themes in Magazine Alcohol Advertisements: A Critique', *Journal of Drug Issues*, Autumn, pp. 511-22
Brenner, B. (1959) 'Estimating the Prevalence of Alcoholism: Toward a Modification of the Jellinek Formula', *Quarterly Journal of Studies on Alcohol*, vol. 20, p. 255
Brenner, M.H. (1973) *Mental Illness and the Economy* (Harvard University Press, Cambridge, Mass.)
Brock, F.H. (1916) 'Den nationalekonomiska betydelsen av allmänt rsudrycksförbud.' Nykterhetskommitten X, Bilagor till utredningen rörande allmänt rusdrycksförbud 1 (Stockholm)
Brown, M.M. (1978) *Alcohol Taxation and Alcohol Control Policies* (Brewers

Association of Canada)
Browning, E.K. and Browning, J.M. (1979) *Public Finance and the Price System* (Macmillan, New York and London)
Bruun, K. (1972) *Alkoholi: käyttö, vaikutukset ja kontrolli* (Helsinki)
Bruun, K., Edwards, G., Lumio, M., Makela, K., Pan, L., Popham, R.E., Room, R., Schmidt, W., Skog, O.J., Sulkenen, P. and Österberg, E. (1975) *Alcohol Control Policies in Public Health Perspective* (Finnish Foundation for Alcohol Studies, Helsinki)
Bunce, R. (1982) 'From California Grapes to California Wine: The Transformation of an Industry, 1963-1979', *Contemporary Drug Problems* (in press)
Bureau voor Budgetten Controle (1968-1980) *Overzichten Reclamebestedingen (Surveys of Advertising Expenditures)* (Bureau voor Budgetten Controle, Amsterdam)
Cahalan, D., Cisin, I. and Crossley, H.M. (1969) *American Drinking Practices: A National Study of Drinking Behaviour and Attitudes*, Monographs of the Rutgers Center of Alcohol Studies, no. 6 (New Brunswick, N.J.)
Cahalan, D. and Room, R. (1974) *Problem Drinking Among American Men*, Monographs of the Rutgers Center of Alcohol Studies, no. 7 (New Brunswick, N.J.)
Celentano, D. (1976) 'An Evaluation of Alcoholism Prevalence Estimators', paper presented at annual meetings of the Society for Epidemiological Research (Toronto)
Central Statistical Office (1977) *Household Budget Survey, Annual Urban Inquiry. Results for 1977* (Dublin)
Central Statistical Office (1980) 'The Change in Revenue from an Indirect Tax Change', *Economic Trends*, March, pp. 97-107
Chafetz, M.E. (1965) *Liquor: Servant of Man* (Little Brown, Boston)
Chafetz, M.E. (1976) *Why Drinking Can be Good for You* (Stein and Day, Briarcliff Manor)
Chafetz, M.E., Blane, H.T. and Hill, M.J. (1971) 'Children of Alcoholics', *Quarterly Journal of Studies on Alcohol*, vol. 32, pp. 687-98
Cisin, I.H. and Crossley, H.M. (1969), *American Drinking Practices: A National Survey of Behavior and Attitudes*, Monograph no. 6 (Rutgers Center of Alcohol Studies, New Brunswick)
Cochrane, A.L. (1972) *Efficiency and Effectiveness: Random Reflections on Health Care* (Nuffield Provincial Hospitals Trust)
Colon, I. (1981) 'Alcohol Availability and Cirrhosis Mortality Rates by Gender and Race', *American Journal of Public Health*, vol. 71, pp. 1325-8
Comanor, W.S. and Wilson, T.A. (1974) *Advertising and Market Power* (Harvard University Press, Cambridge, Mass.)
Comité OMS d'experts de la pharmacodépendence (1975) 'Alcoolisme, le danger s'accroit' (Alcoholism, the risk increases), *Chronique OMS*, vol. 29, pp. 115-24
Comstock, G. (1976) *Television and Alcohol Consumption and Abuse* (Rand Corporation, Santa Monica)
Cook, P.J. (1981) 'The Effect of Liquor Taxes on Drinking, Cirrhosis and Auto Fatalities', in Moore, M.H. and Gerstein, D. (eds.), *Alcohol and Public Policy: Beyond the Shadow of Prohibition* (National Academy of Sciences, Washington, D.C.)

280 References

Cook, P.J. and Tauchen, G. (1981) 'The Effect of Liquor Taxes on Alcoholism' (Duke University, unpublished)

Dahlgren, T. (1924) 'Alkoholens nationalekonimiska och statsfinansiella verkningar', In *Handbok i alkoholfrågan* pp. 171-210 (Stockholm)

Dahlgren, T. (1928) 'Ekonomiska samhällsskador genom alkohol-konsumtionen', in *Handledning för lärare vid nykterhetsundervisningen* (Stockholm)

Dahlgren, T. (1930) 'Alcohol och nationalekonomi', *Tirfing*, vol. 24, no. 3, pp. 65-78

Davies, P.T. (1979) 'Some Comparative Observations on Alcohol Consumption, Alcohol-related Problems and Alcohol Control Policies in the United Kingdom and Other Countries of Europe', *British Journal on Alcohol and Alcoholism*, vol. 14, no. 4, pp. 208-32

Davies, P.T. and Walsh, D. (1979) *The Medico-Social Aspects of Alcohol-Related Problems in the Countries of Europe*, Report to the Commission of European Communities, Brussels

Day, N. (1977) *Alcohol and Mortality* (National Institute on Alcohol Abuse and Alcoholism, Rockville, Maryland)

De Lint, J. (1976) 'Review of Bruun *et al.*, Alcohol Control Policies in Public Health Perspective', *Journal of Studies on Alcohol*, vol. 27, p. 1498

De Lint, J. and Schmidt, W. (1968) 'The Distribution of Alcohol Consumption in Ontario', *Quarterly Journal of Studies on Alcohol*, vol. 29

De Lint, J. and Schmidt, W. (1971) 'Consumption Averages and Alcoholism Prevalence: a Brief Review of Epidemiological Investigation', *British Journal of Addiction*, vol. 66, p. 97

Duffy, M. (1981) 'The Demand for Alcoholic Beverages in the U.K.: a Note', mimeo

Duffy, J.C. and Cohen, G.R. (1978) 'Total Alcohol Consumption and Excessive Drinking', *British Journal of Addiction*, vol. 73, pp. 259-64

Duster, T. (in press) *Alcohol and Disinhibition: Report of a Symposium* (February 1981, Berkeley, California, NIAAA Monograph)

Easton, D. (1957) 'An Approach to the Analysis of Political Systems', *World Politics*, vol. 9, pp. 383-400

Edwards, G. (1973) 'A Community as Case Study: Alcoholism Treatment in Antiquity and Utopia', in Chafetz, M. (ed.), *Proceedings of the Second Annual Alcoholism Conference of the National Institute of Alcohol Abuse and Alcoholism* (Government Printing Office, Washington D.C.), pp. 116-36

Ekholm, A. (1972) 'The Lognormal Distribution of Blood Alcohol Concentrations in Drivers', *Quarterly Journal of Studies on Alcohol*, vol. 33, pp. 508-12

Ewan, S. (1976) *Captains of Consciousness* (McGraw-Hill, New York)

Fekjaer, H.O. (1980) 'Alkohol – Nyere data om virkninger, bruk og holdninger', *Tidsskrift om edruskapsspørsmål*, vol. 1

Fisher, I. (1927) *Prohibition at its Worst* (New York)

Frey, R.L. and Leu, R.W. (1981) 'Demographie und inzidenz der öffentlichen ausgaven im Gesundheitswesen' (Demography and incidence of public expenditures in the health sector), *Schweizerische Zeitschrift für Volkswirtschaft und Statistik*, vol. 117, pp. 319-36

Furst, C.J., Beckman, L.J. and Nakamura, C.Y. (1981) 'Validity of Synthetic Estimates of Problem-drinking Prevalence', *American Journal of Public*

Health, vol. 71, pp. 1016-20
Gahn, H. (1928) 'Till frågen on alkoholens vinst-och förlustkonto', *Tirfing*, vol. 22, nos. 3-5, pp. 33-80
Galbraith, J.K. (1958) *The Affluent Society* (Houghton Mifflin, Boston)
Gastineau, C.B., Darby, W.F. and Turner, T.B. (eds.) (1979), *Fermented Food Beverages in Nutrition* (Academic, New York)
Gay, K. (1979) 'Benefit Analysis of Beverage Alcohol: Ontario 1975' (Lake Erie Regional Office of the Addiction Research Foundation, London, Ontario), mimeo
Geary, P.T. (1973) 'The Demand for Petrol and Tobacco in Ireland: A Comment', *Economic and Social Review*, vol. 4, no. 2, pp. 201-7
Gerstein, D.R. (1981) 'Alcohol Use and Consequences' in Moore, M.H. and Gerstein, D.R. (eds.), *Alcohol and Public Policy: Beyond the Shadow of Prohibition* (National Academy Press, Washington), pp. 182-224
Giesbrecht, N. (1977) 'The Extent and Costs of Alcohol Problems with Special Reference to the Recent Situation in Ontario' Addiction Research Foundation Substudy, No. 864
Gillespie, R.W. (1978) 'Heroin Addiction, Crime and Economic Cost: a Critical Analysis', *Journal of Criminal Justice*, vol. 6, pp. 305-13
Goodstadt, M., Smart, R.G. and Gillies, M. (1978) 'Public Attitudes toward Increasing the Price of Alcoholic Beverages', *Journal of Studies on Alcohol*, vol. 39, no. 9, pp. 1630-2
Gould, M. (1981) 'Systems Analysis, Macrosociology and the Generalised Media of Action', in Loubser, J., Effrat, A., Baum, B. and Lidz, V.M. (eds.), *Explorations in General Theory in the Social Sciences*, vol. 2 (Free Press, New York), pp. 470-506
Gravelle, H., Hutchinson, G. and Sterne, J. (1981) 'Mortality and Unemployment: a Cautionary Note', *Lancet*, vol. 8248, Sept. 26, 675-9
Green, J. and Sheskinski, E. (1976) 'Direct versus Indirect Remedies for Externalities', *Journal of Political Economy*, vol. 84, no. 4, pp. 797-808
Greenblatt, M. and Schuckitt, M.A. (1976) *Alcoholism Problems in Women and Children* (Grune and Stratton, New York)
Gronau, R. (1973) 'The Measurement of Output of the Nonmarket Sector: the Evaluation of Housewives' Time', in Moss, M. (ed.), *The Measurement of Economic and Social Performance* (National Bureau of Economic Research, New York)
Guildstream Research Services (1973) *The Brewing Industry — an Annual Review of the Industry and its Prospects* (London)
Gusfield, J. (1976) 'The Prevention of Drinking Problems', in Filstead, W. *et al.* (eds.), *Alcohol and Alcohol Problems: New Thinking and New Directions* (Ballinger, Cambridge, Mass.), p. 275
Halevy, E. (1955) *The Growth of Philosophic Radicalism*, translated by Morris, M. (Beacon, Boston)
Halla, K. (1977) *Alkoholihaittojen kustannukset vuonna 1974*, Sosiaalinja terveysministeriön julkaisuja 1
Halla, K. (1978) 'Alkoholihaitoista aiheutuvat julkistaloudelliset kustannukset', in Manninen, J. (ed.), *Alkoholihaitat ja -vauriot* (Oy Alko Ab, Helsinki), pp. 94-100
Hamilton, J.L. (1972) 'The Demand for Cigarettes: Advertising, the Health Scare

282 References

and the Cigarette Advertising Ban', *Review of Economics and Statistics*, vol. 56, November, pp. 401-11

'Handboken i alkoholfrågan' (1924) *Tirfing*, vol. 18, nos. 5-6, pp. 65-81

'Handboken i alkoholfrågan, Nya uttalanden' (1925) *Tirfing*, vol. 19, no. 3, pp. 40-5

'Handboken i alkoholfrågan Två diskussionsinslägg' (1926) *Tirfing*, vol. 20, nos. 5-6, pp. 90-3

Harris, J.E. (1980) 'Taxing Tar and Nicotine', *American Economic Review*, vol. 70, pp. 300-22

Harwood, H.J. and Cruze, A.M. (1980) *Outline of Methodology for Estimating Costs to Society of Alcohol and Drug Abuse and Mental Illness* (Research Triangle Institute)

Health and Welfare Canada (1981) *Special Report on Alcohol Statistics* (Minister of Supply and Services Cat. no. 439-12, Ottawa)

Heise, D.R. and Bohrnstedt, G.W. (1970) 'Validity, Invalidity and Reliability' in *Sociological Methodology 1970* (Jossey-Bass, San Francisco)

HM Treasury (1980) 'The Change in Revenue from an Indirect Tax Change', *Economic Trends*, pp. 97-107

Hodgson, T.A. and Meiners, M.R. (1979) *Guidelines for Cost of Illness Studies in the Public Health Service* (from the Public Health Service Task Force on Cost of Illness Studies, 31 May)

Hogarty, F.T. and Elzinga, K.G. (1972) 'The Demand for Beer', *Review of Economics and Statistics*, vol. 5, pp. 195-8

Holmes, K.E. (1976) 'The Demand for Beverage Alcohol in Ontario, 1953 to 1973, and a Cost-benefit Comparison for 1971', Addiction Research Foundation Substudy, no. 815 (Toronto)

Holtermann, S. and Burchell, A. (1981) *The Costs of Alcohol Misuse*, Government Economic Service Working Paper no. 37 (DHSS, London)

Holtmann, A.G. (1972) 'Estimating the Demand for Public Health Services: the Alcoholism Case', *Public Finance*, vol. 19, pp. 351-60

Horverak, Ø. (1976) 'Alkoholen i samfunnsøkonomien og alkoholforskningen. Alkoholforskningen og samfunnet', Forskningskonferensen 28-30.4.76

Houthakker, H.S. and Taylor, L.D. (1970) *Consumer Demand in the United States 1929-70, Analysis and Projections*, 2nd edn (Harvard University Press, Cambridge, Mass.)

Huitfeldt, B. and Jorner, U. (1972) 'The Demand for Alcoholic Beverages in Sweden' (Swedish Government Official Reports, Stockholm)

Indstilling til Lov om salg og skjænking av brændevin, øl, vin fruktvin og mjød (1915), Utarbeidet av Alkoholkommissionens flertal Kristiania

Institute of Medicine (1980) *Alcoholism, Alcohol Abuse and Alcohol-related Problems: Opportunities for Research* (National Academy of Sciences, Washington, D.C.)

Intriligator, M.D. (1978) *Econometric Models, Techniques and Applications* (Prentice-Hall and North Holland, Englewood Cliffs and Amsterdam)

Iwaarden, M.J. van (1981) 'Drinkt de Kijker Meer? Alcohol en Reclame (Does TV Advertising Raise Alcohol Consumption?)', *NCR Handelsblad*, April, vol. 4, p. 7

Jaffe, J.H. (1980) 'Drug Addiction and Drug Abuse', in Gilman, A.G., Goodman, L.S. and Gilman, A. (eds.), *The Pharmacological Basis of Therapeutics*, 6th

edn (Macmillan, New York)
Jellinek, E.M. (1947) 'Recent Trends in Alcoholism and in Alcohol Consumption', *Quarterly Journal of Studies on Alcohol*, vol. 8, pp. 1-42
Jellinek, E.M. (1959) 'Estimating the Prevalence of Alcoholism: Modified Values in the Jellinek Formula and an Alternative Approach', *Quarterly Journal of Studies on Alcohol*, vol. 20, pp. 261-9
Jellinek, E.M. (1960) *The Disease Concept of Alcoholism* (Hillhouse, New Jersey)
Jellinek, E.M. and Keller, M. (1952) 'Rates of Alcoholism in the United States of America, 1940-1948', *Quarterly Journal of Studies on Alcohol*, vol. 23, pp. 49-59
Johnson, J.A. (1972) *Taxation of Alcoholic Beverages in Canada: An Economic Evaluation* (Brewers Association of Canada, Ottawa)
Johnson, J.A. and Oksanen, E.H. (1974) 'Socio-economic Determinants of the Consumption of Alcoholic Beverages', *Applied Economics*, vol. 6, pp. 293-301
Johnson, J.A. and Oksanen, E.H. (1977) 'Estimation of Demand for Alcoholic Beverages in Canada from Pooled Time Series and Cross-sections', *Review of Economics and Statistics*, vol. 59, pp. 113-18
Johnson, P., Armor, D.J., Polich, S. and Stambul, H. (1977) *U.S. Adult Drinking Practices: Time Trends, Social Correlates and Sex Roles* (Rand Corporation, Santa Monica, California)
Johnston, J. (1980) 'Advertising and the Aggregate Demand for Cigarettes. A Comment', *European Economic Review*, vol. 14, no. 1, pp. 117-25
Jones, S. and Nobes, C. (1978) *The Economics of Taxation* (Philip Allen, Oxford), Table 11D
Kasurinen, V. (1980) 'Alkoholin käyttöön liittyvät haittakustannukset vuonna 1978', *Alkoholipolitiikka*, vol. 45, no. 5, pp. 187-94
Katzper, M., Ryback, R. and Hertzman, M. (1978) 'Alcohol Beverage Advertisement and Consumption', *Journal of Drug Issues*, vol. 8, no. 4, pp. 339-53
Keller, M. and Efron, V. (1955) 'The Prevalence of Alcoholism', *Quarterly Journal of Studies on Alcohol*, vol. 16, pp. 619-44
Kennedy, K.A., Ebrill, L. and Walsh, B.M. (1973) 'The Demand for Beer and Spirits in Ireland', *Proceedings of the Royal Irish Academy*, vol. 73, Section C, no. 13
Khennet, H. (1929) 'Till Frågan om alkoholens vinst- och förlustkonto', *Tirfing*, vol. 23, nos. 1-2, pp. 20-6
Khennet, H. (1931) 'Alkohol och nationalekonomi. Ett nytt inlägg i diskussionen', *Tirfing*, vol. 25, no. 2, pp. 53-8
Kinder, B.N. (1975) 'Attitudes towards Alcohol and Drug Abuse II: Experimental Data, Mass Media Research and Methodological Considerations', *International Journal of the Addictions*, vol. 10, pp. 1035-54
Kolari, P. (1978) *Assunnottomien alkoholistien yhteiskunnalle aiheuttamat kustannukset* (Espoo)
Kolari, P. (1980) *Assunnottomien alkoholistien hoidon ja kuntoutuksen kustannukset* (Espoo)
Komiteanlausunto valtioneuvostolle alkoholikomitealta, no. 8/1926 (Helsinki)
Komiteanmietintö 1978: 33, Alkoholikomitean mietintö (Helsinki)
Köpniwsky, S. (1979) 'Thoughts on the Social Cost of Alcohol Consumption: its Objectives and Methodological Improvement', *Toxicomanies*, vol. 12, pp. 285-291

284 References

Köpniwsky, S. (1981) 'Synpunktre på frågan om beräkning av alkoholkostnader', in *Alkohol och ekonomi*, NU B 1980: 21 (Stockholm)

Kosonen, P., Österberg, E. and Partanen, J. (1980) 'Calculating Alcohol Costs: the Logic and the Problem' (Finnish Foundation for Alcohol Studies, Helsinki), unpublished paper

Krugman, H.E. (1971) 'The Impact of Television Advertising: Learning without Involvement', in Schramm, W. and Roberts, D.F. (eds.), *The Process and Effects of Mass Communication* (Illinois University Press, Urbana), pp. 485-94

Kuusi, P. (1952) *Väkijuomakysymys* (Helsinki)

Labys, W.C. (1976) 'An International Comparison of Price and Income Elasticities for Wine Consumption', *Australian Journal of Agricultural Economics*, vol. 20, pp. 33-6

Lambin, J.J. (1975) *Advertising, Competition and Market Conduct in Oligopoly over Time: An Econometric Investigation in Western European Countries* (North Holland Publishing Company, Amsterdam)

Lau, H. (1975) 'Cost of Alcoholic Beverages as a Determinant of Alcohol Consumption', in Gibbins, R.J., Israel, Y., Kalant, H., Popham, R.E., Schmidt, W. and Smart, R.G. (eds.), *Research Advances in Alcohol and Drug Problems*, vol. 2 (John Wiley and Sons, New York), pp. 211-45

Lau, J. (1978) 'Improved Estimates of the Current Prevalence of Alcohol Abuse and Alcoholism' (Creative Socio Medics Corporation, Washington, D.C.) mimeo

Ledermann, S. (1956) *Alcool, Alcoolism, Alcoolisation I*, Institut Nationale d.Etudes Demographique, Travaux et Documents, Cahier No. 29 (Press Universitaires de France, Paris)

Ledermann, S. (1964) *Alcool, Alcoolism, Alcoolisation, II*, Institut Nationale d'Etudes Demographique, Travaux et Documents, Cahier No. 41 (Press Universitaires de France, Paris)

Leeflang, P.S.H. and Reuijl, J.C. (1980) *Advertising and Industry Sales: an Empirical Study of the German Cigarette Industry*, I/II, Universiteit van Groningen, Economische Faculteit (Instituut voor Economisch Onderzoek, Groningen)

Lelbach, Werner K. (1974) 'Organic Pathology related to Volume and Pattern of Alcohol Use', in Gibbins, R.J. et al. (eds.), *Research Advances in Alcohol and Drug Problems*, vol. 1 (John Wiley and Sons, New York)

Lemert, E. (1962) 'Alcohol, Values and Social Control', in Pittman, D.J. and Snyder, C.R. (eds.), *Society, Culture and Drinking Patterns* (John Wiley and Sons, New York), pp. 553-71

Leu, R.E. (1978) 'Cost-benefit Analysis of Alcoholism Treatment Programmes', *Wirtshaft und Recht*, vol. 30, pp. 367-99

Leu, R.E. (1982a) *Smoking and Health: An Economic Analysis* (Schulthess, Zurich)

Leu, R.E. (1982b) 'Smoking and Health Care Costs: Plus or Minus?', Discussion paper no. 65 (Institut fur Sozialwissenschaften der Universitat, Basel)

Leu, R.E. and Lutz, P. (1977) *Economic Aspects of Alcohol Consumption in Switzerland* (Schulthess, Zurich)

Leventhal, H. (1964) 'An Analysis of the Influence of Alcoholic Beverage Advertising on Drinking Customs' in McCarthy, R. (ed.), *Alcohol Education for Classroom and Community* (McGraw-Hill, New York)

Lidman, R.M. (1976a) 'Economic Issues in Alcohol Control', Social Research Group, report no. 7 (University of California, Berkeley)
Lidman, R.M. (1976b) 'Measuring Spirits' Price Elasticity in Canada and California: New Findings', *Surveyor*, vol. 12, pp. 9-13
Ligthart, J. (1981) 'Reclame in recessie' (Advertising in a recession), *Intermediair*, vol. 17, no. 29, pp. 1-5
Luce, B.R. and Schweitzer, S.O. (1978) 'Smoking and Alcohol Abuse: a Comparison of their Economic Consequences', *The New England Journal of Medicine*, pp. 569-71
Luft, H. (1975) 'The Impact of Poor Health on Earnings', *Review of Economics and Statistics*, LVII, vol. 1, February
Luft, H. (1978) *Poverty and Health* (Ballinger, Cambridge, Mass.)
Lundquist, G.A.R. (1972) 'Clinical and Socio-cultural Aspects of Alcoholism' in Kisker, K.P. et al., *Psychiatrie der Gegenwart, Forschung und Praxis*, Klinische Psychiatrie II (Berlin), pp. 363-88
Lynn, R. (1981) 'Public Control of Alcohol Consumption by Pricing, Advertising and Legal Deterrence: Experience from Britain and Ireland', in Tongue, E.J. (ed.), *Papers Presented at the 27th International Institute on the Prevention and Treatment of Alcoholism, Vienna, June 15-20* (Anton Proksch Institut/International Council on Alcohol and Addictions, Vienna/Lausanne), p. 459
MacAndrew, R.B. (1981) 'What the MAC Scale tells us about Men Alcoholics: An Interpretive Review', *Journal of Studies on Alcohol*, vol. 42, pp. 604-25
McCarthy, C. (1977) 'Estimates of a System of Demand Equation using Alternative Commodity Classification of Irish Data, 1953-1974', *The Economic and Social Review*, vol. 8, no. 3, pp. 201-11
McGuinness, T. (1980) 'An Econometric Analysis of Total Demand for Alcoholic Beverages in the U.K., 1956-75', *The Journal of Industrial Economics*, September, pp. 85-109
McKeown, T. (1976) *The Modern Rise of Population* (Edward Arnold, London)
McKeown, T. (1977) *The Role of Medicine*, 2nd edn (Blackwells, London)
McLure, Jr. C.E. and Thirsk, W.R. (1978) 'The Inequity of Taxing Iniquity: a Plea for Reduced Sumptuary Taxes in Developing Countries', *Economic Development and Cultural Change*, vol. 26, no. 3, pp. 487-503
Mäkelä, K. (1969) 'Alkoholinkulutuksen mittaaminen' (Measuring Alcohol Consumption), *Alkoholipoliittisen tutkimuslaitoksen tutkimusseloste*, vol. 36, March
Mäkelä, K. and Österberg, E. (1979) 'Notes on Analysing Economic Costs of Alcohol Use', *The Drinking and Drug Practices Surveyor*, no. 14
Mäkelä, K. et al. (1981) *Alcohol, Society and the State: Vol. 1 A Comparative Study of Alcohol Control* (ARF, Toronto)
Malmquist, S. (1948) *A Statistical Analysis of the Demand for Liquor in Sweden* (University of Uppsala, Sweden)
Manis, J. and Lunt, C.L. (1957) 'The Community Survey as a Measure of the Prevalence of Alcoholism', *Quarterly Journal of Studies on Alcoholism*, vol. 18, pp. 212-16
Marshman, J. (chair) (1978) *The Treatment of Alcoholics: An Ontario Perspective*, Report of the Task Force on Treatment Services for Alcoholics (Addiction Research Foundation, Toronto)

Maurel, H. (1974) 'Alcohol in the E.E.C. Production and Marketing Structures of Alcohol in the E.E.C. Countries', *European News Agency* (Brussels)
Mayer, T. (1980) 'Economics as Hard Science: Realistic Goal or Wishful Thinking', *Economic Inquiry*
Maynard, A. and Kennan, P. (1981a) 'The Economics of Addiction: a Survey of the Literature', Report for the Social Science Research Council (University of York), mimeo
Maynard, A. and Kennan, P. (1981b) 'The Economics of Alcohol Abuse', *British Journal of Addiction*, vol. 76, pp. 339-45
Mechanic, D. (1980) *Future Issues in Health Care* (Free Press, New York)
Milavsky, R., Pekowsky, B. and Stipp, H. (1975) 'T.V. Drug Advertising and Proprietary and Illicit Drug Use among Teenage Boys', *Public Opinion Quarterly*, vol. 39, pp. 457-81
Miller, G. and Agnew, G. (1974) 'The Ledermann Model of Alcohol Consumption', *Quarterly Journal of Studies on Alcohol*, vol. 35, p. 877
Mishan, E.J. (1971) *Cost-Benefit Analysis* (Allen and Unwin, London)
Mishan, E.J. (1981) *Introduction to Normative Economics* (OUP, New York)
Moore, M. and Gerstein, D.R. (eds.) (1981) *Alcohol and Public Policy: Beyond the Shadow of Prohibition* (National Academy Press, Washington, D.C.)
Mosher, J. (1980) 'Alcoholic Beverages as Tax Deductible Business Expenses: An Issue of Public Health Policy and Prevention Strategy', Alcohol Research Group Report F136 (Berkeley, California)
Mosher, J. (1982a) 'Federal Tax Law and Public Health Policy: The Case of Alcohol-Related Tax Expenditures', *Journal of Public Health Policy* (in press)
Mosher, J. (1982b) 'Alcoholic Beverages as Tax Deductible Expenses: An Issue of Public Health Policy and Prevention Strategy', *Journal of Health Politics, Policy and Law* (in press)
Mosher, J.F. and Wallack, L.M. (1981) 'Government Regulation of Alcohol Advertising: Protecting Industry Profits versus Promoting the Public Health', *Journal of Public Health Policy*, vol. 2, no. 4, pp. 333-53
Mulford, H.A. and Miller, D.E. (1959 and 1960) 'Drinking in Iowa: the Extent of Drinking and Selected Sociocultural categories', *Quarterly Journal of Studies on Alcohol*, vol. 20 and vol. 21
Myrdal, G. (1930) 'Alkoholens vinst- och förlustkonto', *Tirfing*, vol. 24, no. 4, pp. 106-9
National Academy of Science Panel on Alternative Policies Affecting the Prevention of Alcohol Abuse and Alcoholism (1981) Report: *Alcohol and Public Policy* (National Academy Press, Washington, D.C.)
National Center for Health Statistics (1975) *Vital Statistics of the United States 1982*, vol. 2 (Government Printing Office, Washington, D.C.)
National Institute on Alcohol Abuse and Alcoholism (1978a), *Third Special Report to the U.S. Congress on Alcohol and Health* (Government Printing Office, Washington, D.C.)
National Institute on Alcohol Abuse and Alcoholism (1978b) *Third Special Report to the U.S. Congress on Alcohol and Health, Technical Support Document* (Government Printing Office, Washington, D.C.)
National Research Council (1980) *Energy Taxation: An Analysis of Selected Taxes* (National Academy of Sciences, Washington, D.C.)
Nederlands Economisch Instituut (1966) *Reclame en het verbruik van*

Alcoholhoudende Dranken (Advertising and Consumption of Alcoholic Beverages) (Nederlands Economisch Instituut, Rotterdam)
Niskanen, W.A. (1962) *Taxation and the Demand for Alcoholic Beverages* (Rand Corporation, Santa Monica, California)
Nordiska nämnden för alkoholforskning, P.M. (1979) 'Angående forskning om alkoholens samhällsekonomiska konsekvenser'
Norman, D. (1975) 'Structural Change and Performance in the U.S. Brewing Industry', PhD dissertation (University of California, Los Angeles)
Nyberg, A. (1967) 'Consumption and Prices of Alcoholic Beverages: A Study of the Demand for Alcoholic Beverages in Finland 1949-1965, and of the Price Decisions of the State Alcohol Monopoly' (Finnish Foundation for Alcohol Studies, Helsinki)
Ogborne, A.C. and Smart, R.G. (1980) 'Will Restrictions on Alcohol Advertising Reduce Alcohol Consumption?, *British Journal of Addiction*, vol. 75, no. 3, pp. 293-6
Ohlin, B. (1930) 'Nationalekonomiska synpunkter på alkoholfrågan', *Tirfing*, vol. 24, no. 4, pp. 97-105
Ohlin, B. (1930) 'Nationalekonomiska synpunkter på alkoholfrågan', *Tirfing*, vol. 24, no. 4, pp. 97-105
Ohlin, B. (1939) 'Nationalekonomiska synpunkter på alkoholfrågan', *Blå Boken*, 16:e årg (Stockholm)
Olesen, P. (1976) 'Det offentliges omkostninger ved alkoholmisbruget', *Fredriksbeg efteråret*
Olesen, P. (1977) 'En økonomisk vurderind af alcoholmisbruket', *Agitatoren*, 10/77
Ornstein, S.I. (1980) 'Control of Alcohol Consumption through Price Increases', *Journal of Studies on Alcohol*, vol. 41, pp. 807-18
Ornstein, S.I. and Hanssens, D.M. (1981) 'Alcohol Control Laws, Consumer Welfare and the Demand for Distilled Spirits and Beer', Working paper No. 102 (University of California, Los Angeles), March
Österberg, E. (1976)*Alkoholipoliittinen päätöksenteko ja kustannushyötyanalyysi poliittisen päätöksenteon apuvälineenä*, Alkoholipoliittisen tutkimuslaitoksen tutkimusseloste no. 92 (Helsinki)
Österberg, E. (1978) 'Vadkostar alkoholen folkhushallet?', *Alkoholpolitik*, vol. 41, pp. 45-56
Österberg, E. (1981a) 'Kritiska synpunkter på beräkning av alkoholkostnader', in *Alkohol och ekonomi*, NU B 1980: 21 (Stockholm)
Österberg, E. (1981b) *What does Alcohol Cost the Economy?* Reports from the Social Research Institute of Alcohol Studies no. 153 (Helsinki)
Palda, K. (1964) *The Measurement of Cumulative Advertising Effects* (Prentice-Hall, Englewood Cliffs)
Parker, D. and Harman, M. (1978) 'The Distribution of Consumption Model of Prevention of Alcohol Problems', *Journal of Studies on Alcohol*, vol. 39, pp. 377-99
Parsons, T. (1969) 'Part IV: Theory and the Polity', *Politics and Social Structure* (Free Press, New York), pp. 311-22
Pernanen, K. (1972) 'Discrepancy of Sales Statistics and Survey Estimates of Alcoholism', Addiction Research Foundation Substudy no. 486
Pigou, A.C. (1960) *The Economics of Welfare* (Macmillan, London)

Pittman, D.J. (1980a) *Primary Prevention of Alcohol Abuse and Alcoholism: An Evaluation of the Control of Consumption Policy*, Social Science Institute (Washington University, St Louis, Mo.)

Pittman, D.J. (1980b) 'Health Warning Labels Divide the Field', *Alcoholism: The National Magazine*, Nov./Dec., pp. 39-40

Pittman, D.J. and Lambert, M.D. (1978) *Alcohol, Alcoholism and Advertising: A Preliminary Investigation of Asserted Associations*, Social Science Institute (Washington University, St Louis, Mo.)

Pittman, D.J. and Lambert, M.D. (1979) 'The Effect of Advertising and Other Media on Alcohol Abuse', in *Papers Presented at the 25th International Institute on the Prevention and Treatment of Alcoholism, Tours, June 18-22* (International Council on Alcohol and Addictions, Lausanne), pp. 312-24

Plaut, T.F.A. (1967) *Alcohol Problems: A Report to the Nation by the Cooperative Commission on the Study of Alcoholism* (Oxford University Press, New York)

Polich, J.M., Armor, D.J. and Braiker, H.B. (1980) *The Course of Alcoholism: Four Years After Treatment* (Rand Corporation, Santa Monica, California)

Popham, R.E. (1970) 'Indirect Methods of Alcoholism Prevalence Estimation: A Critical Evaluation', in Popham, R.E. (ed.), *Alcohol and Alcoholism* (University of Toronto Press, Toronto)

Popham, R., Schmidt, E. and de Lint, J. (1976) 'The Effects of Legal Restraint on Drinking' in Kissin, B. and Bergleiter, H. (eds.), *The Biology of Alcoholism*, vol. 4 (Plenum, New York)

Popham, R., Schmidt, E. and de Lint, J. (1978) 'Government Measures to Prevent Hazardous Drinking', in Ewing, J. and Rouse, B., *Drinking* (Nelson Hall, Chicago)

Popham, R.E. and Schmidt, W. (1981) 'Words and Deeds: the Validity of Self-report Data on Alcohol Consumption', *Journal of Studies on Alcohol*, vol. 42, pp. 355-8

Pratschke, J.L. (1969) *Income-Expenditure Relations in Ireland 1956-1966*, The Economic and Social Research Institute, paper 50 (Dublin)

Prest, A.R. (1949) 'Some Experiments in Demand Analysis', *Review of Economics and Statistics*, vol. 21, pp. 33-49

Produktschap voor Gedistilleerde Dranken (1981) *How Many Alcoholic Beverages are being Consumed throughout the World?* (Produktschap voor Gedistilleerde Dranken, Schiedam)

Prys Williams, G. and Brake, G. (1980) *Drink in Great Britain 1900-1979* (Edsall, London)

Public Affairs Consultants (1977) *Advertising in a Mixed Economy from a Consumers' and Producers' Point of View* (Public Affairs Consultants, Amsterdam)

Purontaus, J. (1970) *Kustannus-hyötyanalyysi ja Suomen alkoholipolitiikka* (Pro gradu -työ, Helsingin yliopisto)

Reed, D.S. (1981) 'Reducing Drinking/Driving Costs', in Moore, M.H. and Gerstein, D.R. (eds.), *Alcohol and Public Policy: Beyond the Shadow of Prohibition* (National Academy Press, Washington, D.C.)

Rein, M. (1976) *Social Science and Public Policy* (Penguin Books, New York)

Robertson, T.S., Rossiter, J.R. and Gleason, T.C. (1979) *Televised Medicine Advertising and Children* (Praeger Publishers, New York)

Room, R. (1971) 'Survey vs. Sales Data for the U.S.', *Drinking and Drug Practices Surveyor*, vol. 3, pp. 15-16

Room, R. (1977) 'Measurement and Distribution of Drinking Patterns and Problems in General Populations' in Edwards, G., Gross, M.M., Keller, M., Mosher, J. and Room, R. (eds.), *Alcohol-related Disabilities* (WHO, Geneva)

Room, R. (1981) 'A Farewell to Alcoholism? A Commentary on the W.H.O. Expert Committee Report', *British Journal of Addiction*, vol. 76, pp. 116-23

Rygg, N. (1914) 'Undersökelser angaaende drikfældigheten og dens sociale følger i Norge', Social- og Industridepartementet, Bilag 3, Alkoholkommissionens indstilling (Kristiania)

Sager, T. (1974) *Økonomisk vurdering av bot eller fengsel som promilledom* (Transportøkonomisk institutt, Oslo)

Salaspuro, A. (1978) *Alkoholiin liittynyt terveyspalvelukäyttö Suomessa vuonna 1972*, Alkohplitutkimussäätiön julkaisuja n: o 29 (Forssa)

Schmalensee, R. (1972) *The Economics of Advertising* (North Holland, Amsterdam)

Schmidt, W. (1977) 'The Epidemiology of Cirrhosis of the Liver: a Statistical Analysis of Mortality Data with Special Reference to Canada', in Fisher, M.M. and Rankin, J.G. (eds.), *Alcohol and the Liver* (Plenum Press, New York)

Schmidt, W. and de Lint, J. (1970) 'Estimating the Prevalence of Alcoholism from Alcohol Consumption and Mortality Data', *Quarterly Journal of Studies on Alcohol*, vol. 31, no. 4

Schmidt, W. and Popham, R. (1978) 'The Single Distribution Theory of Alcohol Consumption', *Journal of Studies on Alcohol*, vol. 39, p. 402.

Schmidt, W. and Popham, R.E. (1980a) 'Liver Cirrhosis Mortality as an Indicator of the Prevalence of Heavy Alcohol Use: A Brief Comment on Skog', *British Journal of Addiction*, vol. 75, pp. 361-6

Schmidt, W. and Popham, R.E. (1980b) 'Sex Differences in Mortality: A Comparison of Male and Female Alcoholics', in Kalant, O.J. (ed.), *Research Advances in Alcohol and Drug Problems*, vol. 5 (Plenum, New York), pp. 365-84

Schmidt, W. and Popham, R.E. (1981) 'Alcohol Consumption and Ischemic Heart Disease: Some Evidence from Population Studies' (Addiction Research Foundation, Toronto)

Schramm, C.J. (1977) 'Measuring the Return on Program Costs: Evaluation of a Multi-employer Alcoholism Treatment Program', *American Journal of Public Health*, vol. 67, pp. 50-1

Scitovsky, T. (1951) *Welfare and Competition* (Richard D. Irwin, Chicago)

Seeley, J.R. (1959a) 'Estimating the Prevalence of Alcoholism: A Critical Analysis of the Jellinek Formula', *Quarterly Journal of Studies on Alcohol*, vol. 20, p. 255

Seeley, J.R. (1959b) 'The WHO Definition of Alcoholism', *Quarterly Journal of Studies on Alcohol*, vol. 20, p. 352

Seeley, J.R. (1960) 'Death by Liver Cirrhosis and the Price of Beverage Alcohol', *Canadian Medical Association Journal*, vol. 83, pp. 1361-6

Shadwell, A. (1923) *Drink in 1914-1922, A Lesson in Control* (Longmans, London)

Shafer, R.P. (1973) *Drug Use in America: Problem in Perspective*, Second Report of the National Commission on Marijuana and Drug Abuse (GPO, Washington)

Shepard, D.S. and Zeckhauser, R.J. (1980) 'Long-term Effects of Interventions to Improve Survival in Mixed Populations', *Journal of Chronic Diseases*, vol. 33, pp. 413-33
Simon, J.L. (1966) 'The Price Elasticity of Liquor in the U.S. and a Simple Method of Determination', *Econometrics*, vol. 43, no. 1, pp. 193-205
Simon, J.L. (1967) 'The Effect of the Competitive Structure upon Expenditures for Advertising', *Quarterly Journal of Economics*, vol. 81, November, pp. 610-27
Simon, J.L. (1969) 'The Effect of Advertising on Liquor Brand Sales', *Journal of Marketing Research*, vol. 6, August, pp. 301-13
Singh, G. (1979) 'Comment on "The Single Distribution Theory of Alcohol Consumption"', *Journal of Studies on Alcohol*, vol. 40, pp. 522-4
Single, E. (1979) 'Estimating the Number of Alcoholics in Ontario: A Replication and Extension of an Earlier Study', *Journal of Studies on Alcohol*, vol. 40, no. 11, November, pp. 1046-52
Single, E. and Giesbrecht, N. (1978) 'Regional Variations in Levels of Alcohol Consumption in Ontario 1973', Addiction Research Foundation Substudy no. 943 (Toronto)
Single, E., Giesbrecht, N. and Eakins, B. (1981) 'The Alcohol Policy Debate in Ontario in the Post-war Era', in Single, E., Morgan, P. and de Lint, J. (eds.), *Alcohol, Society and the State 2: The Social History of Control in Seven Countries* (Addiction Research Foundation, Toronto)
Skog, O.-J. (1980a) 'Liver Cirrhosis Epidemiology: Some Methodological Problems', *British Journal of Addiction*, vol. 75, pp. 227-43
Skog, O.-J. (1980b) *Social Interaction and the Distribution of Alcohol Consumption* (National Institute for Alcohol Research, Oslo)
Smart, R. (1977) 'The Relationship of Availability of Alcoholic Beverages to per capita Consumption and Alcoholism Rates', *Journal of Studies on Alcohol*, vol. 38, pp. 891-6
Smart, R.G. and Cutler, R.E. (1976) 'The Alcohol Advertising Ban in British Columbia; Problems and Effects on Beverage Consumption', *British Journal of Addiction*, vol. 71, no. 1, pp. 13-21
Smith, R.T. (1976) 'The Legal and Illegal Markets for Taxed Goods: Pure Theory and an Application to State Government Taxation of Distilled Spirits', *Journal of Law and Economics*, vol. 19, pp. 393-432
Sommarin, E. (1925) 'Några nationalekonomiska synpunkter på alkoholfrågan', *Tirfing*, vol. 19, no. 809, pp. 113-22
Sommarin, E. (1930) 'Till Frågan on alkoholens vinst- och förlustkonto', *Tirfing*, vol. 24, no. 6, pp. 175-83
Statens Offentliga Utredningar 1974: 90 Alkoholpolitik, Del. 1, Bakgrund (Betänkande avgivet av alkoholpolitiska utredningen, Stockholm)
Stigler, G.J. and Becker, C.S. (1977) 'De Gustibus non est Disputandum', *American Economic Review*, vol. 67, no. 2, pp. 76-90
Stone, R. (1945) 'The Analysis of Market Demand', *Journal of the Royal Statistical Society*, vol. 108, 286-382
Stone, R. (1951) *The Role of Measurement in Economics* (Cambridge University Press, Cambridge)
Strauss, R. and Bacon, S. (1953) *Drinking in College* (Yale University Press, New Haven)

Strickland, D.E. (1981) 'The Advertising Regulation Issue: Some Empirical Evidence Concerning Advertising Exposure and Teenage Consumption Patterns', paper presented at the Conference, 'Control Strategies for Alcohol Abuse Prevention, National State and Local Designs for the '80s' (Charleston, South Carolina), September

Strickland, D.E. (1982) 'A Critique and Re-analysis of "Social Learning and Deviant Behavior: A Specific Test of a General Theory" ', *American Sociological Review*, vol. 47, February, pp. 162-7

Strickland, D.E. and Wilson, J.B. (1980) 'Social Learning Theory, Alcohol Consumption and Modes of Interpersonal Influence: A Specification and Empirical Test', Paper presented at the annual meeting of the National Council on Alcoholism (Seattle)

Sulkunen, P. (1976) 'Drinking Patterns and the Level of Alcohol Consumption: an International Overview', in Gibbins, R.J., Israel, Y., Kalant, H., Popham, R.E., Schmidt, W. and Smart, R.G. (eds.), *Research Advances in Alcohol and Drug Problems*, vol. 3 (John Wiley & Sons, New York)

Sulkunen, P. (1978) *Developments in the Availability of Alcoholic Beverages in the E.E.C. Countries*, Report from the Social Research Institute of Alcohol Studies, no. 121 (Helsinki)

Sumner, M.T. (1971) 'Demand for Tobacco in the United Kingdom', *The Manchester School of Economic and Social Studies*, vol. 39, March, pp. 23-36

Suviranta, A. (1978) 'Alkoholi valtion sosiaalibudjetissa', Suomen 76. yleinen raittiuskokous Helsingissä 25-26.11.78 *Luennot ja alustukset*, pp. 31-40

Swint, J.M. and Nelson, W.B. (1977) 'The Application of Economic Analysis to Evaluation of Alcoholism Rehabilitation Programs', *Inquiry*, vol. 14, pp. 63-72

Treml, V.G. (1975) 'Alcohol in the USSR: a Fiscal Dilemma', *Soviet Studies*, vol. 27, pp. 161-77

US Department of Health, Education and Welfare, Public Health Service (1972) *Alcohol and Health*, First Special Report to the US Congress (GPO, Washington)

US Department of Health, Education and Welfare, Public Health Service (1974) *Alcohol and Health*, Second Special Report to the US Congress (GPO, Washington)

US Department of Health, Education and Welfare, NIAAA (1978) *Third Special Report to the U.S. Congress on Alcohol and Health*, reprint copy

US Department of Health, Education and Welfare, Public Health Service (1979) *Smoking and Health. A Report to the Surgeon General*, DHEW Publication no. (PHS) 79-50066 (GPO, Washington)

US Sub-Committee to Investigate Juvenile Delinquency (1955) *Juvenile Delinquency (Television Programs)* (Government Printing Office, Washington, DC)

US Sub-Committee on Commerce (1971) *The Relationship Between Drug Abuse and Advertising* (Government Printing Office, Washington, DC)

US Sub-Committee on Alcoholism and Narcotics (1976) *Media Images of Alcohol: The Effects of Advertising and Other Media on Alcohol Abuse* (Government Printing Office, Washington, DC)

Virolainen, J. (1976) 'Meeting the Financial Burdens of False Dependencies', ICPA Congress (Acapulco)

Wales, T.J. (1963) 'Distilled Spirits and Interstate Consumption Effects', *American Economic Review*, vol. 58, pp. 853-63

Walsh, B.M. (1979) 'Alcohol Consumption, Alcohol Abuse and the Scope for Control Policies in the Irish Context' (unpublished report) (The Economic and Social Research Institute, Dublin)

Walsh, B.M. (1980) *Drinking in Ireland*, the Economic and Social Research Institute, Broadsheet no. 20

Walsh, B.M. (1981) 'The Demand for Alcohol in the UK; a Comment', mimeo

Walsh, B.M. (1982) 'The Demand for Alcohol in the U.K., a Comment', *Journal of Industrial Economics* (in press)

Walsh, B.M. and Walsh, D. (1970) 'Economic Aspects of Alcohol Consumption in the Republic of Ireland', *The Economic and Social Review*, vol. 2, no. 1, pp. 115-38

Walsh, B.M. and Walsh, D. (1973) 'Validity of Indices of Alcoholism', *British Journal of Preventive and Social Medicine*, vol. 27, no. 1, February

Warburton, C. (1932) *The Economic Results of Prohibition* (Columbia, New York)

Warner, K.E. (1977) 'The Effects of the Anti-smoking Campaign on Cigarette Consumption', *American Journal of Public Health*, vol. 67, no. 7, pp. 645-50

Warner, R.S. and Cartwright, B.C. (1976) 'The Medium is not the Message', in Loubser, J., Effrat, A., Baum, R. and Lidz, V.M. (eds.), *Explorations in General Theory in the Social Sciences*, vol. 2, (Free Press, New York), pp. 639-60

Waterson, M.J. (1981) *Advertising and Alcohol Abuse* (The Advertising Association, London)

Weissbach, T.A. and Vogler, R.E. (1977) 'Implications of a Social Learning Approach to the Prevention and Treatment of Alcohol Abuse', *Contemporary Drug Problems*, vol. 6, pp. 553-68

Wieser, S. (1973) *Drink Patterns in Germany. A Medico-Sociological Study* (Nicolai, Herford)

Williamson, J. (1978) *Decoding Advertisements* (Marion Boyars, London)

Wüthrich, P. (1976) 'Measuring Alcohol Consumption in Switzerland', *Sozial- und Präventivmedizin*, vol. 21, pp. 7-12

Zeckhauser, J.R. and Shepard, D.S. (1980) *The Choice of Health Policies with Heterogeneous Populations*, Working Paper no. 612 (National Bureau of Economic Research, Cambridge, Ma.)

Zwart, W. de (1981) *Alcohol Consumption and Alcohol-related Problems* (Stichting voor Wetenschappelijk Onderzoek van Alcohol- en Druggebruik (SWOAD), Amsterdam)

NOTES ON CONTRIBUTORS

Dr Philip J. Cook, Institute of Policy Sciences and Public Affairs, Duke University, North Carolina, USA

Dr Phil Davies, MRC Medical Sociology Unit, Institute of Medical Sociology, Aberdeen

Dr Dean R. Gerstein, Assembly of Behavioural and Social Sciences, National Research Council, Washington, D.C.

Mr Marcus Grant, Alcohol Education Centre, London

Professor Michael D. Intriligator, Department of Economics, University of California, USA

Mr Theo van Iwaarden, SWOAD, Amsterdam, Holland

Dr Robert E. Leu, Institute for Social Sciences, University of Basel, Switzerland

Mr Tony McGuinness, Department of Economics, Sheffield University

Dr Alan Maynard, Department of Economics and Related Studies, University of York

Dr James F. Mosher, School of Public Health, Alcohol Research Group, Institute of Epidemiology and Behavioural Medicine, University of California, USA

Dr Esa Österberg, Social Research Institute of Alcohol Studies, The State Alcohol Monopoly, Helsinki, Finland

Professor David J. Pittman, Department of Sociology, Washington University, St Louis, Missouri, USA

Dr Martin A. Plant, Alcohol Research Group, University Department of Psychiatry, Edinburgh

Dr Robin Room, Alcohol Research Group, Institute of Epidemiology and Behavioural Medicine, University of California, USA

Mr Hossein Salehi, Department of Economics, University of California, Los Angeles, USA

Professor Leonard G. Schifrin, Department of Economics, College of William and Mary, Williamsburg, Virginia, USA

Professor Stuart O. Schweitzer, School of Public Health, University of California, USA

Dr Eric W. Single, Social Policy Research Department, Addiction Research Foundation, Toronto, Canada

Professor Donald E. Strickland, Department of Sociology, Social Science Institute, Washington University, St Louis, Missouri, USA

Mr David G. Taylor, Office of Health Economics, London

Mr Christopher Thurman, The Brewers' Society, London

Dr Larry M. Wallack, School of Public Health, Social Research Group, University of California, Berkeley, USA

Professor Brendan M. Walsh, Department of Political Economy, University College, Dublin, Eire

Mr Robert Weedon, Department of Health and Social Security, London

Professor Alan Williams, Institute of Social and Economic Research, University of York

NAME INDEX

Aaron, H.J. 44
Ackoff, R.L. 203, 226, 229, 236
Addiction Research Foundation 99, 100
Adrian, M. 100
Agnew, G. 160, 162, 168
Akers, R.L. 204, 216
Alcohol, Drug Abuse and Mental Health Administration 63
Alcohol Education and Research Council 276
Alksne, H. 103
Allied Brewers' Trade Association (ABTA) 253, 295
Anheuser-Bush, Inc. 226, 227
Armor, D.J. 55, 59, 164
Atkin, C. 244
Atkinson, A.B. 21, 24, 28, 33, 178, 181, 182, 232

Bacon, S. 104, 164, 208
Bailey, M.B. 103
Bales, R.F. 120
Bandura, A. 204
Barnes, J.G. 203, 227, 231
Barsby, S.L. 111
Barzel, T. 186
Bass, F.M. 226
Baumol, W.J. 28
Baye, M.R. 233
Beauchamp, D.E. 169
Becker, C.S. 182
Beckman, L.J. 113
Bentham, Jeremy 44
Berry, R.E. Jr 25, 38, 57, 62-81
Blane, H.T. 16, 235
Blaug, M. 128, 174
Blizzard, J. 229
Block, M. 244
Bohrnstedt, G.W. 209
Boland, J.P. 25, 38, 57, 62-81
Borden, N. 224
Borg, A. 92
Bourgeois, J.C. 203, 227, 231
Braiker, H.B. 55
Brake, G. 251
Breed, W. 244
Brenner, B. 113

Brenner, M.H. 127
Brewers' Association of Canada 98
Brewers' Society 250, 255-7, 259, 285
Brewing Research Foundation 259
Brock, F.H. 82, 83
Brown, M.M. 141, 142, 144, 153, 157
Browning, E.K. 32
Browning, J.M. 32
Bruun, K. 140, 142, 160, 161, 165-7, 223
Bunce, R. 199
Burchell, A. 138
Bureau of Alcohol, Tobacco and Firearms (BATF) 201
Bureau voor Budgetten Controle 230

Cahalan, D. 69, 103, 164, 208
Carling-O'Keefe 97, 98
Cartwright, B.C. 47
Celentano, D. 103, 105
Central Statistical Office 134, 183, 259
Chafetz, M.E. 16, 28
Cisin, I.H. 103, 164, 208
Cochrane, A.L. 138
Cohen, J.R. 163, 164, 166, 168, 270
Colon, I. 126
Comite OMS d'experts de la pharmacodependence 21
Comonor, W.S. 110, 226
Comstock, G. 203
Cook, P.J. 40, 61, 109, 111, 192-6, 265
Crossley, H.M. 103, 164, 208
Cruze, A.M. 64
Cutler, R.E. 203, 204, 233-6

Dahlgren, T. 83, 84, 85
Darby, W.F. 50
Davies, P.T. 146, 147
Day, N. 54, 55
Defoe, J. 244
De Lint, J. 28, 103, 140, 160,

295

296 Name Index

163, 165
Department of Employment 255
Department of Health, Education and Welfare 21, 32, 67
Department of Health and Social Security 275
Distillers Company Limited 259
Duffy, M. 238, 239, 241
Duster, T. 263
Dutch Economic Foundation 266

Eakins, B. 97, 265
Easton, D. 47
Ebrill, L. 151, 181
Edwards, G. 103, 140, 142, 161, 165-7, 223
Efron, V. 103, 104
Ekholm, A. 163
Elzinga, K.G. 110
Emshoff, J.R. 203, 226, 229, 236
Ewan, S. 244

Fekjaer, H.O. 91, 92
Finnish State Alcohol Monopoly 92
Fisher, I. 87, 89, 90
Frey, R.L. 21
Furst, C.J. 113

Gahn, H. 84, 85
Galbraith, J.K. 225
Gastineau, C.B. 50
Gay, K. 98, 100-2, 105
Geary, P.T. 184
Gerstein, D.R. 54, 140, 190, 191, 265
Giesbrecht, N. 97, 99, 100, 103, 265
Gillies, M. 235
Glass Manufacturers' Federation 254
Gleason, T.C. 207
Goodstadt, M. 235
Gould, M. 47
Gravelle, H. 133, 135
Green, J. 181
Greenblatt, M. 67
Groneu, R. 68
Guildstream Research Services 145
Gusfield, J. 159, 190

Haberman, P.W. 103
Halevy, E. 44
Halla, K. 91, 92
Hamilton, J.L. 227, 228, 232
Hanssens, D.M. 108, 111, 192
Hardwood, H.J. 64
Harman, M. 104, 161, 164, 167
Harris, J.E. 178, 187
Haute Comite d'Etude et d'Information sur l'Alcoolisme 153
Health and Welfare Canada 100
Heise, D.R. 209
Hertzman, M. 229
Hill, M.J. 16
Hiram Walker 98
HM Customs and Excise 250, 258, 259
HM Treasury 34, 36
Hodgson, T.A. 64
Hogarty F.T. 110
Holmes, K.E. 98-100, 104, 105
Holtermann, S. 38, 138
Holtmann, A.G. 31
Horverak, O. 90
Houthakker, H.S. 181
Huitfeldt, B. 110
Hutchinson, G. 133, 135

Institute of Medicine 62, 63
Intriligator, M.D. 119
Iwaarden, M.N. van 229, 231

Jaffe, J.H. 51
Jellinek, E.M. 32, 103, 104, 113, 218
Johnson, J.A. 98, 102, 110, 192
Johnson, P. 59, 164
Johnston, J. 228
Jones, S. 184
Jorner, U. 110

Kanak, J. 57, 62-81
Kasurinen, V. 92, 93
Katzper, M. 229
Keller, M. 103, 104
Kennan, P. 134, 136-8
Kennedy 151, 181
Keynes, J.M. 128
Khennet, H. 83, 84, 85
Kinder, B.N. 203
Kolari, P. 92
Komiteanlausunto valtioneuvostolle

Name Index 297

alkoholikomitealta 82
Komiteanmietinto 1978 91
Kopniwsky, S. 90, 95
Kosonen, P. 90, 95, 101
Krohn, D. 204, 216
Krugman, H.E. 225, 229
Kuusi, P. 89

Labatt's 97, 98
Labys, W.C. 111
Lambert, M.D. 171, 203, 227
Lambin, J.J. 226, 227
Lancaster, K. 41
Lanza-Kaduce, L. 204, 216
Lau, H. 110
Ledermann, S. 28, 103-5, 159-65, 270
Leeflang, P.S.H. 227
Lelbach, W.K. 193
Lemert, E. 159
Leu, R.E. 18, 21, 25, 26, 28, 30, 31
Leventhal, H. 215
Lidman, R.M. 111
Ligthart, J. 228
Luce, B.R. 25, 107
Luft, H. 65, 66
Lumio, M. 140, 142, 161, 165-7, 223
Lundquist, G.A.R. 17
Lunt, C.L. 103
Lutz, P. 25, 26, 28, 30
Lynn, R. 234

MacAndrew, R.B. 53
McCarthy, C. 151
McGuinness, T. 228, 238, 241, 242
McKeown, T. 138
McLure, C.E. Jr 232
Mäkelä, K. 90, 95, 105, 140, 142, 161, 165-7, 223, 265
Malmquist, S. 111
Manis, J. 103
Marshall, G.L. 111
Marshman, J. 100
Maurel, H. 144
Mayer, T. 129
Maynard, A. 134, 136-8
Meade, T.W. 24
Mechanic, D. 267
Meiners, M.R. 64
Milavsky, R. 207
Miller Brewing Company 227

Miller, D.E. 103, 208
Miller, G. 160, 162, 168
Mishan, E.J. 17, 179, 189
Molson's 97
Moore, M. 61, 140, 190, 191, 265
Mosher, J.F. 198, 199
Mulford, H.A. 103, 208
Myrdal, G. 85, 86

Nakamura, C.Y. 113
National Academy of Science 61, 62, 203, 265
National Advisory Council on Alcoholism 169
National Center for Health Statistics 55
National Distillers 98
National Health Service, UK 268
National Highway Traffic Safety Administration 72, 73
National Institute of Health 63
National Institute on Alcohol Abuse and Alcoholism 54, 55, 58, 60, 115, 169
National Research Council 45
National Safety Council 72
Nederlands Economisch Instituut 226
Nelson, W.B. 31
Niskanen, W.A. 110
Nobes, C. 184
Noble, E. 169
Nordiska nämnden för alkoholforskning PM 90
Norman, D. 110
Nyberg, A. 110

Oates, W.E. 28
Office of Populations, Census and Surveys 256
Ogborne, A.C. 204, 231, 234
Ohlin, B. 85-90
Oksanen, E.H. 110, 192
Olesen, P. 91
Ornstein, S.I. 34, 36, 108, 111, 192
Österberg, E. 90, 95, 101, 102, 140, 142, 161, 165-7, 223

Palda, K. 226
Pan, L. 140, 142, 161, 165-7, 223
Parker, D. 104, 161, 164, 167

Name Index

Parsons, T. 47
Partanen, J. 90, 95, 101
Pekowsky, B. 207
Pentlands Scotch Whisky Research Establishment 259
Pernanen, K. 105
Pigou, A.C. 177
Pittman, D.J. 30, 159, 171, 203, 227
Plaut, T.F.A. 235
Polich, J.M. 55, 59, 283
Popham, R.E. 55, 56, 104, 105, 140, 142, 161, 165-8, 196, 223
Pratschke, J.L. 151, 184
Prest, A.R. 110
Prys Williams, G. 251
Public Affairs Consultants 225
Purontaus, J. 91

Radosevich, M. 204, 216
Rein, M. 245
Reuijl, J.C. 227
Ricardo, D. 44
Robertson, T.S. 207
Room, R. 103-5, 140, 142, 171, 208, 223
Rossiter, J.R. 207
Ryback, R. 229
Rygg, N. 82

Sager, T. 92
Salaspuro, A. 91
Schelling, T. 61
Schifrin, L. 61
Schmalensee, R. 225, 226, 227
Schmidt, W. 28, 55, 56, 61, 103, 105, 140, 142, 160, 161, 163, 165-8, 192, 196, 223
Schramm, C.J. 31
Schuckitt, M.A. 67
Schweitzer, S.O. 25, 107
Scitovsky, T. 178
Scotch Whisky Association 259
Seagrams 98
Seeley, J.R. 32, 104, 113, 192
Shadwell, 49
Shafer, R.P. 32
Shepard, D.S. 32
Sheskinski, E. 181
Simon, J.L. 111; 194, 203, 224, 226, 227-9, 236
Singh, G. 166-8
Single, E. 97, 103, 265

Skegg, J.L. 232
Skog, O-J. 40, 140, 142, 161, 165-7, 193, 223
Smart, C. 57, 62-81
Smart, R. 171
Smart, R.G. 203, 204, 231, 233-6
Smith, R.T. 111
Social Science Research Council 275
Social Security Administration 70, 81
Sommarin, E. 84, 88
Stamboul, H. 59, 164
Sterne, J. 133, 135
Stigler, G.J. 182
Stipp, H. 207
Stone, R. 34, 35, 110
Strauss, R. 104, 164, 208
Strickland, D.F. 171, 203, 204, 216, 220
Sulkunen, P. 50, 140-2, 144, 147, 161, 165-7, 188, 223, 224, 236
Sumner, M.T. 232
Swint, J.M. 31

Tauchen, G. 109, 111, 192, 195, 196
Taylor, L.D. 181
Thirsk, W.R. 232
Townsend, J.L. 21
Treml, V.G. 42
Turner, T.B. 50

US Sub-committee on Alcoholism and Narcotics 205
US Sub-committee on Commerce 222
US Sub-committee to Investigate Juvenile Delinquency 222

Virolainen, J. 91, 92
Vogler, R.E. 204

Wales, T.J. 111
Wallack, L.M. 198, 199
Walsh, B.M. 103, 110, 142, 143, 151, 181, 184, 226, 231, 232, 235, 236, 238, 239, 241
Walsh, D. 103, 110, 146, 151, 153, 154
Warburton, C. 49

Warner, K.E. 232
Warner, R.S. 47
Waterson, M.J. 203
Weissbach, T.A. 204
Wieser, S. 32
Williamson, I. 244

Wilson, J.B. 216, 220
Wilson, T.A. 110, 226
Wüthrich, P. 20

Zeckhauser, J.R. 32
Zwart, W. de 230

SUBJECT INDEX

absenteeism 64, 106
accidents 16, 53, 55, 56, 58, 72, 79, 100, 131, 141, 180, 197
addiction *see* dependence
ad valorem taxes 186, 189
advertising 30, 113-25, 132, 133, 137, 170-2, 174, 201-22, 223-7, 238-42, 243-8, 269, 273
alcohol: education 12, 16, 20, 21, 30, 71-2, 85, 95, 138, 159, 267; effects 20, 21; production 11, 25, 26, 50, 84, 106, 139, 199, 249-61; properties 50; use and misuse 28, 50, 52-60, 140-58
alcoholism *see* alcohol-related problems
alcohol-related problems 18, 31, 56-8, 62-81, 94, 115, 208-22, 270
Australia 229, 249

balance of payments 258
barbiturates 41
behaviour 50-60
Belgium 143, 144, 145-7, 150
blood alcohol concentrations (BAC) 72-4, 141, 162, 163
brewing 97
British Columbia 204, 234
bronchitis 56

Canada 55, 192, 193, 203, 227, 262; *see also* Ontario
cannabis (marihuana) 41
cause and effect 20, 52-4
consumer demand analysis 29-30, 42
control policies 13, 15, 18, 21, 23, 31, 32, 47, 49, 82-96, 108, 139, 140-58, 159-72, 173-89, 190-6, 197-200, 208, 223-7, 239-42, 243-8, 270-6
cost benefit analysis 30-2, 43-5, 49, 80, 82-106, 137-8, 174-5, 268
cost estimation 18-20
costs, external *see* externalities
counterfactual 18-21, 94
crimes 48, 58, 64, 76, 79
cross-sectional analysis 30, 140

defence 48
Denmark 91
dependence 17, 24, 26, 50, 142-7, 149, 178, 181-2, 192, 266
detoxification 275
disease concept of alcoholism 10, 25, 53, 103; *see also* Jellinek
distilling 97-8, 249, 256-8
drink trade: Canada 97-8; UK 249-61; USA 226-8

econometric analysis 29, 30, 34-7, 107-27, 184, 188, 203, 238-42, 243
economic efficiency 14
economic model 23-4
education *see* alcohol education
EEC 140, 141, 142, 143, 144-58, 186
efficiency 23, 26, 27, 30, 31, 66
elasticity 34-7, 133-6, 140-58, 184-8, 197, 228
elasticity of demand: for beers 34-7, 108-25, 130, 238-42; for spirits 34-7, 108-25, 130, 238-42; for wines 34-7, 108-25, 238-42
employee assistance programmes 58
employment in the drink trade 255-7, 270
ethics 44
ethyl alcohol 50
exchange value 51
excise taxes 26, 186, 188, 198
exports 257-8, 269-70
externalities 16, 27-8, 31, 57, 176-81

family 16, 64, 65-6
fetus, effects of alcohol upon 171
Finland 37, 88-92, 237
fires 74-5
fiscal policy 49
fiscal tax 28-9
flat rate 187
France 40, 142, 143, 144, 145-7, 151-3, 157, 165, 249, 266
functional equivalent model 159

government *see* control policies
graduated taxes 187

300

Subject Index 301

health education *see* alcohol education
heart disease 55, 56
Holland *see* Netherlands

income 14, 25, 34-7, 64-8, 86, 89
India 165
Inflation 185-6
information costs 27
insurance approach 27-8
interest-demand calculation 43, 47-9, 60
International Study of Alcohol Control Experiences (ISACE) 265
Ireland 40, 140, 142, 143, 144, 145-7, 151-4, 157, 183-8, 198, 234
Israel 10
Italy 10, 40, 142, 144, 145-7, 150, 151, 157, 165

Koyk distributed log model 40

labour 26, 58, 67
licensing laws 146
liver cirrhosis 30, 40, 53, 56, 104, 131, 141, 145, 157, 180, 192-5, 197, 264, 265
log-normal distribution *see* Ledermann
lung cancer 53
Luxembourg 144, 145-7

macroeconomics 44, 68
Manitoba 204, 234
marginal social costs 39-40
market failures 16-18, 26
microeconomics 44-6, 68
military 69, 78-9
minimum drinking age 114-15, 119-20, 121, 123, 126, 133
modified economic model 24-5
monetary policy (monetarism) 128, 198-9
monopoly 200, 237
morbidity 17, 39, 48
mortality (death, *etc.*) 17, 24, 48, 54-7, 69-71
multinational organisations 97-8, 275

national economy 83, 84, 87
neo-prohibitionism 160
Netherlands 143, 144, 145-7, 148, 230
New Guinea 266
non-exclusion 18
non-market production 67, 68, 73

non-rational behaviour 16
non-rival consumption 18
Norway 10, 90, 165

occupational drinking problems 106
oligopoly 236, 273
Ontario 55, 97-106, 163, 192

Papua, 266
peer pressure 204-22
perfect information 14
Pigou Tax 26-7, 177
pluralism 49
pneumonia 56
Poland 237, 266
poverty 86
prediction 128-9
prevalence of alcohol problems 102-5, 138
prevalence of heavy alcohol use 20
prevention 18, 29-31, 77, 84
production costs 21
productivity 58, 90
programme comparison 43, 45-9, 58, 60
prohibition 82, 83, 86, 87-9, 94, 101, 121, 123, 160, 223, 234, 249
psychotropic drugs 41
public health 48, 56-7, 59
Puerto Rico 199
Punjab 165

quantity-frequency scale 104, 105, 207

rationality 17, 30, 99, 124, 198, 263-4, 268
real price 137, 154, 190
relevant costs 21
religion 50, 113-25, 134
research 30, 38, 62, 80, 266, 274-6
resource allocation 14, 15, 25
respiratory disease 62
risk awareness 17, 24, 26, 39

Saint Louis 205
satisfaction 14, 26
Scandinavia 82-96, 262, 274
secondary costs 85
sex differences 67, 68
Sirageldin estimate 68
smoking 21, 24, 25, 55, 173, 187, 228
social costs 23, 38-40
social structural model 160

Subject Index

Spain 10
sports sponsorship 243
state finance 83, 84, 87
Strauss and Bacon scale 104
suicide 53
sumptuary tax 28
surveys 104, 105, 202-22
Sweden 10, 37, 82, 86-9, 90, 91, 94, 136, 165
systems theory 47

taxation 26-9, 83, 88, 101, 135, 136, 140-58, 171-2, 173-89, 190-6, 197-200, 258-60, 265-6
teenagers 201-21, 237, 247
Temperance Movement 82, 84, 96, 262
temperature 38, 121
time lag 40, 42, 194, 265
time series analysis 184
tobacco *see* smoking
tourism 119, 121, 132
traffic accidents 30
tranquillisers 41
transfer payments 102
treatment of alcohol problems *see* alcohol-related problems

UK 136, 142, 143, 145-7, 149, 183, 184, 186, 228, 234, 238-42, 262, 266, 268, 271, 272, 274-6
under-reporting of alcohol consumption 20, 105
unemployment 48, 71, 77, 88, 108, 115, 120, 121, 126
United States Flood Control Act, 1936 31
urbanisation 120-1, 133
USA 56-9, 61, 62-81, 89, 107-27, 136, 155, 186, 190, 193-5, 196-200, 201-22, 243-8, 249-61, 262
USSR 37
utilitarianism 44, 179, 263-5
utility 26, 41, 51

vaccination model 25
value-added tax (VAT) 26
value judgement 14
vascular disease 62
violence 53
Virgin Islands 199
viticulture *see* wine production

welfare 38-9
West Germany 143, 144, 145-7, 148, 249
wine production 97, 199

Printed in the United States
by Baker & Taylor Publisher Services

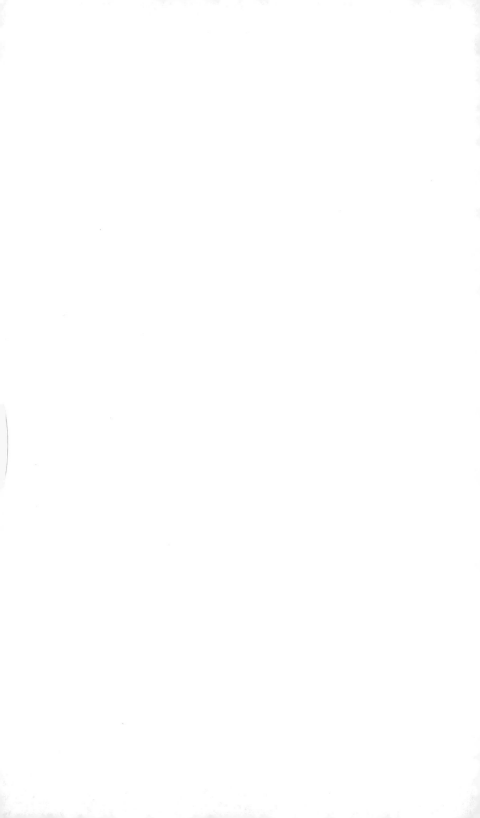